Praise fo[r]

"Gordis's research is extensive and diverse, presenting a broad spectrum of Jewish thought, some of which will likely be new even to readers acquainted with the subject."   —Ari Blaff, *Tablet*

"A deliberative academic work that rises above hackneyed arguments with significant research and a great deal of heart."   —*Kirkus Reviews*

"Gordis is a careful and close reader of history and literature and . . . a gifted storyteller."   —Jeffrey B. Kobrin, *Jerusalem Post*

"Should jump to the top of your books-to-be-read list."
                                              —Aaron Leibel, *Washington Jewish Week*

"*We Stand Divided* is among the best efforts yet to look under the hood at what divides Israeli and American Jews, and to examine unflinchingly our seeming inability to think and speak clearly about those differences."
                                              —Haviv Rettig Gur, *Times of Israel*

"Gordis . . . is not trying to artificially paper over the deep divisions that exist between Israel and its American Jewish cousins. . . . An admirable and critically necessary plea for greater understanding on both sides of the ocean."   —Michael J. Koplow, Israel Policy Forum

"Illuminating study of the rift. . . . [Gordis] imbues the debate with much-needed historical context and philosophical explication."
                                              —Michael M. Rosen, *American Interest*

"With so many people worried about the growing distance between American Jews and Israel, *We Stand Divided* is an extremely important and timely book. Offering a sweeping history of what has been a troubled relationship since the start of the Zionist movement, Daniel Gordis writes with knowledge and clarity about the different conceptions the world's two main Jewish communities have developed about what it means to be a Jew. Realistic but optimistic, he suggests that if both reevaluate their expectations of the other, a shared future as a unified Jewish people remains possible—and is essential for us both."

—Natan Sharansky, former political prisoner in the Soviet Union, former minister of Diaspora Affairs in Israel, and former head of the Jewish Agency for Israel

"Impassioned, brilliant, and riveting, *We Stand Divided* is the essential book for understanding American Jewish–Israel relations. Gordis has made an outstanding contribution to the field."

—Michael B. Oren, former Israeli ambassador to the United States

"Those anguished by the rift between Israelis and American Jews might be surprised to learn it was ever thus. With empathy and deep historical insight, Daniel Gordis traces the roots and development of this disconnect and imagines a future of deepened mutual appreciation aimed at sustaining one unified Jewish people."

—Daniel B. Shapiro, former U.S. ambassador to Israel

"A fascinating and provocative description of the growing gap between American Jews and Israel. This book is a conversation starter—a conversation that is increasingly important. I recommend it highly."

—Deborah E. Lipstadt, author of *Antisemitism: Here and Now*

WE
STAND
DIVIDED

WE
STAND
DIVIDED

THE RIFT BETWEEN
AMERICAN JEWS
AND ISRAEL

DANIEL GORDIS

ecco

An Imprint of HarperCollinsPublishers

HarperCollins books may be purchased for educational, business, or sales promotional use. For information, please email the Special Markets Department at SPsales@harpercollins.com.

Ecco® and HarperCollins® are trademarks of HarperCollins Publishers.

A hardcover edition of this book was published in 2019 by Ecco, an imprint of HarperCollins Publishers.

FIRST ECCO PAPERBACK EDITION PUBLISHED 2020

Designed by Paula Russell Szafranski

Library of Congress Cataloging-in-Publication Data has been applied for.

ISBN 978-0-06-287370-5 (pbk.)

20 21 22 23 24   LSC   10 9 8 7 6 5 4 3 2 1

FOR ELISHEVA

זכרתי לך חסד נעוריך אהבת כלולתיך

לכתנו אחריך אל ארץ אבותינו

I will make them a single nation . . .

Never again shall they be two nations,

And never again shall they be divided into two kingdoms.

Ezekiel 37

CONTENTS

CONTENTS

THE RIFT

INTRODUCTION

"WHY CAN'T WE ALL JUST GET ALONG?"

Sorry Israel," wrote a senior Israeli diplomat, but "U.S. Jewry just isn't that into you."

His formulation hardly put matters subtly, but that was precisely the point. The goal was to awaken Israeli leaders, to alert them to a tectonic shift taking place in the relations between the world's two largest Jewish communities. Even if the political echelons of both countries proclaimed unwavering loyalty to each other, the writer believed, at the communal level, a significant shift was under way. Both communities had long assumed that they shared an unbreakable bond, but any such assumption was overly optimistic. Not only were the bonds not unbreakable, but they had already started to crumble.

The newspaper column was written in 2017 by Alon Pinkas, an Israeli diplomat who had served as consul general of Israel in the United States and who, prior to that, was foreign policy adviser to Israeli prime minister Ehud Barak and chief of staff to several ministers of foreign affairs. Pinkas, in short, was as much of an insider as one could be in the world of Israeli foreign affairs. And he was determined to let his bosses and fellow Israeli citizens know that something dramatic had changed. The world they had assumed would last forever was already largely gone—with potentially dire implications for both communities.

Immediately following that arresting headline, however, came the following interesting subhead: "The love affair lasted just three decades; but intractable conflict and intolerance for liberal Jews are deal-breakers." Contrary to what many people on both sides of the ocean had long believed, Pinkas was saying, not only had the relationship not been "happily ever after," but it had not been "love at first sight" either. American Jews and Israel had had a passionate love affair, true, but it had been much shorter than many people had supposed. The love affair, in fact, had gone on for less than half of Israel's life. The passionate bond between Israel and American Jews had already been nonexistent during long periods of Israel's history, he said, and now another such period was beginning.

Pinkas had an explanation for the rocky relationship. The core problem, he said, lay with Israel's policies and actions. Israel's conflict with the Palestinians had American Jews utterly exasperated. Israel's conflict with the Arab world was almost a century old. First Israel had been at war with neighboring nations, and then, once those wars ended, it became embroiled in a long conflict with the Palestinians. American Jews believed that peace simply had to be possible; after all, America had made peace with Germany, with Japan, with Vietnam—thoughtful leaders could move their countries beyond conflict. Why couldn't Israel do that?

While one of the main causes of the breakup was Israel's relationship with the Palestinians, another was Israel's relationship with Diaspora Jews. Israel's leadership—the rabbinate and numerous politicians—were adopting a dismissive attitude toward non-Orthodox Judaism, resisting its influence in Israel and besmirching its impact in the Diaspora. With some 90 percent of American Jews defining themselves as non-Orthodox, that attitude was also killing the relationship.

Alon Pinkas was right—in some ways. Many American Jews, especially liberals, progressives, and millennials (overlapping categories in many cases), had indeed had enough of the conflict and were beyond offended at what Israeli leadership had to say about their Jewish way of life.

What Pinkas didn't mention, however, was that Israelis were just as exasperated with American Jews. In November 2017, Tzipi Hotovely, Israel's deputy foreign minister, had been invited to speak at Hillel at Princeton University, but was then disinvited after pressure from a little-known progressive organization. Infuriated that Hillel had capitulated, Hotovely unleashed a diatribe about American Jews, explaining why they were so out of touch with Israelis. One factor, she said, was their "not understanding the complexity of the region." She then went on to say essentially that American Jews lived rich, secure, and overly comfortable lives, entirely different from what Israelis experienced. "People that never send their children to fight for their country, most of the Jews don't have children serving as soldiers, going to the Marines, going to Afghanistan, or to Iraq. Most of them are having quite convenient lives. They don't feel how it feels to be attacked by rockets, and I think part of it is to actually experience what Israel is dealing with on a daily basis."

It was hardly mellifluous English, but her point was clear—and American Jews were enraged. Here was Israel's deputy foreign minister essentially telling them that they didn't understand Israel, that they were too coddled to appreciate the challenges that Israelis regularly faced, and that they were essentially spoiled, overprotected, wealthy couch potatoes. Prime Minister Benjamin Netanyahu was forced to chastise Hotovely publicly. Yet when the Reform Movement in America demanded that Netanyahu fire her, he flatly refused. Prime ministers do not fire ministers for such minor missteps; Netanyahu also understood that, ill-chosen though her words may have been, in Israel there was a widespread sense of satisfaction that someone had finally called it like they saw it.

More measured writers and speakers made similar points. Attila Somfalvi, a Romanian-born Israeli journalist for Israel's most popular news website, YNet, addressed American Jews when the subject of the rift arose, asking them: "What have *you* done in recent years to fully understand Israeli society, or to present yourselves to Israel?" Israel was foreign to American Jews because they had not invested any genuine effort in getting to know the real Israel. American Jews were also responsible for the rift.

WHY HAVE AMERICAN JEWS "had it" with Israelis? And why are Israelis no less put out with their American counterparts? What ails the relationship? "Why can't we just get along?" many have begun asking.

The purpose of this book is to trace and then to explain some of the more central causes of the complex, fraught, love-filled, hate-filled relationship that American Jews and Zionists (and then Israelis after 1948) have long had. When did the tensions begin, and why? What led to some periods of calm, even enthusiasm? Why does the relationship between the world's two largest Jewish communities matter? And is there anything that can be done to address the current crisis?

There are, of course, important Jewish communities in many places throughout the world. One reason that this book looks specifically at the relationship between Jews in the United States and Israel, and not at others, is demographic. The American and Israeli Jewish communities total more than 85 percent of the Jewish world and are therefore likely to be the communities that determine the course of Jewish history. But there is a more substantive reason as well. As we will see, the complexity of Israel's relationship with American Jews is due to distinct characteristics of American Judaism not shared by other Diaspora communities. The causes of the rift to which this book will point are not germane to other Diasporas, which have very different (and often less fraught) relationships with Zionism and Israel.

As we look at the story of the unique relationship between American Judaism and the Zionist movement, first in Europe and then in Israel, we will see that for most of the time since Theodor Herzl launched political Zionism at the First Zionist Congress in Basel, Switzerland, in 1897, the relationship between American Jews and Herzl's idea, and then the country it created, has been complex at best and often even openly antagonistic. True, as Pinkas noted, an intense love affair did indeed begin around the time of the 1967 Six-Day War. Yet, as happens with many love affairs, it does not appear to be ending well. Furthermore, as is also the case in human relationships, warning signs of troubles ahead were in evidence from the outset. Tensions between American Jews and mainstream Zionism surfaced in the 1920s, long before there was a Jewish state. There was significant friction between Israel's leaders and American Jewish leaders as Israel was created, long before anyone spoke about Palestinians, decades before American Jews had tired of the conflict, and many years before Israel assumed its dismissive attitude toward American Jewish life. The conflict between the two communities is almost as old as political Zionism itself.

The question at the heart of this book is: why?

I argue that although most observers (like Pinkas, for example) believe that the fraught relationship is due to what Israel *does*, a closer look at the Jewish communities in Israel and the United States suggests that the real reason has to do with what Israel *is*.

We will look at the development of each of these communities, the challenges they had to face in their early decades, the dangers each believed the Jewish people faced, and the unprecedented opportunities they would try to seize. As we look closely, we will see that the two communities have fashioned very different visions of what Jewishness is and ought to be. That, I would suggest, is the real cause of the tension.

No book of this length can explore all the ways in which the two communities are predicated on different visions of Jewishness, so we address only the major disagreements. And of course, neither community is monolithic—members of both the American and Israeli Jewish communities hold a variety of positions and views. Of necessity, I will have to paint some of the issues with a broad brush. I will use terms like "American Jews" or "Israelis" not to suggest that all American Jews or all Israelis hold identical positions on these matters, but to point to the fundamental thrusts of each community's worldview and unique vision for Jewish life.

This book is intentionally brief. It does not discuss all the nuanced subdivisions within each community, and it avoids, at least for the most part, the use of statistical analyses. Statistics on American Jews and Israel invariably raise further questions:

Where did those numbers come from? How accurate are they? Why do other people cite different numbers? What is the margin of error?

Those are all legitimate and inevitable questions, so I mostly steer clear of those studies. My goal is to put the big ideas about the relationship into the public sphere, so that we can all engage in a rethinking of why the relationship between the two communities is fraught, deepen the conversation that many in the Jewish world are having about the rift, and even begin to muse on some possible directions for healing the break.

To begin, therefore, we turn to the rift itself—to a reminder of how dramatically matters have changed in recent decades—and then explore why the conventional wisdom explaining the rift cannot be correct.

A MISTAKEN CONVENTIONAL WISDOM

July 4, 1976, was a Sunday. It was also the bicentennial of the United States, and all of us at the camp where I was working that summer knew that a celebration was in store. The dining hall would be decked in red, white, and blue. There would be fried chicken for dinner and apple pie for dessert. For the older campers and staff, there would be square dancing a bit later.

None of these festivities were intended to be a surprise. So when word spread that the camp director wanted everyone—and he meant *everyone*—to gather on the large lawn in the center of the camp, we were curious. What was going on?

Fairly quickly, everyone assembled. Numbering almost a thousand, between the campers and the staff, we sat and waited. And then, with a bullhorn in hand and a voice cracking with emotion, the camp director, who happened to be Israeli, told us what had just happened in Entebbe, Uganda. An Air France plane en route from Tel Aviv to Paris had been hijacked, after a stopover

in Athens, to Entebbe a week earlier. Determined never to nego-
tiate with terrorists, Israel had just sent one hundred commandos
some 2,500 miles to attack the airport and rescue the hostages.
When the ferocious gun battle ended just a few hours earlier,
the camp director announced, 102 of the 106 hostages had been
rescued. Only four hostages and one Israeli soldier—Yoni Netanyahu, whose brother, Benjamin, would years later become
prime minister—had been killed. The soldiers and the freed hostages were all on their way back to Israel.

We sat, hundreds of us, on that large green hill, stunned and
brimming with pride. The counselors, almost all of them in college, were as moved as the campers. The sentiment was wall-
to-wall. This, once again, was the Israel on which we'd "been
raised." It was an Israel that represented the kind of Jews we all
wanted to be—proud, strong, brave, invincible. I remember that
afternoon and the emotion in the camp director's voice as if it
happened yesterday. Of the bicentennial celebration, I remember
nothing at all.

Thirty-eight years later, in the summer of 2014, Israel's
army was in the news again. This time it was not a commando
force responding to a hijacking, but a full-blown war between
Israel and Hamas in the Gaza Strip. The fighting was bitter, and
the casualties horrifically high on both sides. In the midst of
the conflict, a group of young, mostly post-college-age American Jews founded an organization called If Not Now. As they
told their own story on their website, they created their organization "during the violence of Operation Protective Edge in
2014" and "had three demands: stop the war on Gaza, end the
occupation, and freedom and dignity for all." The fact that there
was also a Hamas-led war on Israel was nowhere mentioned on

their site.* No less instructive, however, was their noting that "we do not take a unified stance . . . on Zionism or the question of statehood." Not only were these young American Jews (who would eventually get so much traction that they would be the subject of a major article in *New York* magazine) unwilling to acknowledge that Israelis were dying and that Hamas was engaged in a war on Israel, but they were even unwilling to state that they endorsed at least the idea of a Jewish state.

Four years later, If Not Now released a thirty-five-page manifesto of sorts, titled "Five Ways the American Jewish Establishment Supports the Occupation." Though the lengthy document assailed Israel's violation of Palestinian rights and the American Jewish establishment's ostensible support of those violations, the report was no less noteworthy for the fact that nowhere did it mention Palestinian violence against Israel, the continued pledge of many Palestinians (including the Hamas government of Gaza) to destroy Israel, any mention of the Jewish right to sovereignty, or even the word "Zionism." These omissions, of course, were not accidental.

The American Jewish world had come a long (and sad) way since November 29, 1947, when Jews huddled around radios listening to the vote in the United Nations General Assembly, breaking out into tears and dance when the resolution to create a Jewish state was passed. Then, Jews had believed that a

---

* This omission made the group's name particularly ironic. "If Not Now" is part of a longer quote of the sage Hillel, who said, "If I am not for myself, who will be for me? But if I am only for myself, who am I? If not now, when?" ("Ethics of the Fathers," 1:14). When If Not Now also failed to demand an end to attacks on Israel, those critical of the group wondered what had happened to the "if I am not for myself" part of Hillel's admonition.

new era of Jewish life was dawning. A mere sixty-five years later, young Americans like those involved in If Not Now could not even bring themselves to say that the creation of a Jewish state was a good thing.

Everything, it seemed, had changed. The Jewish worlds of those two summers, the summer of the bicentennial and the summer of the 2014 war, could not have been more different. It wasn't only that American Jews weren't "that into" Israel, as Alon Pinkas put it. Among some of the young, the hostility to Israel was undisguised and unabashed.

What had happened?

IT HADN'T ALWAYS BEEN that way.

On October 6, 1973, the Baltimore Orioles were scheduled to play the Oakland A's in the first game of the American League playoffs. For die-hard Orioles fans like us Baltimore kids, it was a big day. There was a problem, though: it was also Yom Kippur, and we were going to be in our Orthodox synagogue with our parents all day.

For my brother, such apparent conflicts always seemed more a challenge than an impediment. As we all trudged off to synagogue in our suits and ties, he had a small transistor radio and earphone in his jacket pocket and was planning to listen to the game while strategically stationed in the synagogue bathroom.

Sometime in the midmorning, however, he came running back into the sanctuary to tell us that the radio was reporting the news that Egypt and Syria had attacked Israel. Newscasters were saying that a major war had just erupted. Soon enough, similar rumors were spreading among many of the other congregants as well. What only minutes earlier had been a solemn, serene day of prayer and introspection morphed into controlled bedlam. Dozens of people scurried out of the sanctuary and congregated in the lobby, desperate for any news they could get. Suddenly, my brother, who had planned a day of solitude in the company of only his radio, was the center of attention. "Where's your brother?" one visibly panicked woman pressed me after she heard that he was the one who possessed the coveted radio. "I don't care how he got it or why he has it. Just tell me where he is." That day, in the midst of the horror, the fact that using a radio on Yom Kippur is forbidden to Orthodox Jews did not matter to her at all.

That day was the start of the Yom Kippur War, a devastating war in which Israel lost some 2,700 men, barely managing to claw its way back to the lines from which the war had begun. Although we could not have known it at the time, the war would change the Middle East dramatically. At that moment, all that the hundreds of people in our synagogue knew was that Israel was under attack; in that Orthodox synagogue, worry about Israel trumped Yom Kippur, the most sacred day of the Jewish year.

What made the most lasting impression on me that day, as a young fourteen-year-old just beginning to examine the world critically, was that not once did the rabbi encourage people to come back into the sanctuary. He understood what his flock felt, and he knew better than to try to corral them. Many of them were Holocaust survivors or the children of survivors, and all were horrified that it seemed that the Jews—the Jews in Israel this time—might once again be massacred. What had always moved them about Israel was that it was a symbol of Jewish rebirth. As one observer of American Judaism put it, "Israel stood, symbolically, as a redemption of the Holocaust. Israel made it possible to endure the memory of Auschwitz. Were Israel to be destroyed, then Hitler would be alive again, the final victory would be his."

News of Israel was so precious that day, Yom Kippur notwithstanding, that my brother, for having had the audacity to bring
his contraband radio with him to listen to a ballgame, was for
several hours transformed into the synagogue's most valuable
prayer.

I recall that day and its images as if it were yesterday. I remember the sanctuary being much less full than it usually was,
especially on Yom Kippur, and in the lobby, a swelling group of
pious but desperate American Jews hanging on every word that
came out of the radio. I can still picture the many congregants on
the verge of tears; some were actually weeping. Whenever I recall that day, what comes to mind more than anything is a world
that seems very different from today's, a Jewish world in which
American Jews and their feelings about Israel were simpler, less
fraught, more unified. It was a time when having a Jewish state
was a source of pride, not conflict, for American Jews.

THE WAR DID NOT go well for Israel, at least not at first. The
Israel Defense Forces (IDF), which in 1967 had seemed invincible, now seemed to be crumbling. Israeli aircraft were being
shot out of the skies by the dozens; in the first two days, Israel
lost 10 percent of its air force. Its tank force was being obliterated
as well, and merely twelve hours into the war, the Syrian army
had crossed deep into Israel's territory in the Golan. Some 1,300
Israeli soldiers were killed in the opening days of the war. It was
a disaster.

Israel faced a Syrian incursion in the north and an Egyptian
onslaught from the south. It was not clear how long the country
could hold on. Moshe Dayan, a hero of the Six-Day War, now
feared for the future of the Jewish state. Prime Minister Golda

Meir had to block his appearance on a radio broadcast when she heard that he was going to speak about the possible "destruction of the Third Temple," a reference to the two previous instances (586 BCE and 70 CE) in which Jerusalem had been sacked and Jewish sovereignty ended.

The mood among American Jews turned from shock to grim desperation. A few days later, with the war still raging and Israel's survival by no means guaranteed, my parents took our family to a rally at the Pikesville Armory in the Baltimore suburb where we lived. It seemed that everyone we knew was there. Orthodox Jews, Conservative Jews, and Reform Jews; Jews passionate about Israel and Jews less involved. I still recall the flood of thousands of people, inside the building and out, representing all of the Jewish community. Never in my life had I seen a crowd like that amassed for any cause.

We didn't get a seat inside the armory, so we couldn't hear the speeches. Inside, speaking to a packed house, Dale Anderson, Baltimore County's executive and a (non-Jewish) Democrat, said to a desperately nervous Jewish community, "I am a student of Jewish history and the Zionist cause." Zionism, he continued, was "a great and just cause for every person who appreciates justice and freedom."

When I reread speeches like this one today, they sound surreal. Now, decades later, it is hard to imagine almost any Democratic politician calling either Israel or Zionism "a great and just cause for every person who appreciates justice and freedom." In fact, in 2018, the Pew Research Center reported that "79% of Republicans say they sympathize more with Israel than the Palestinians, compared with just 27% of Democrats." Sympathy is a complicated sentiment, and it is true that having sympathy for the Palestinians does not necessarily mean that one does not support Israel or feel loyal to it. Nonetheless, those statistics are telling. Israel has become what its supporters in America desperately hoped would never happen—it is a "wedge" issue, an issue on which America's parties are sharply divided. Like immigration, tax reform, abortion, or gun control, it has become an issue so deeply ideologically rooted and so divisive that any semblance of the "wall-to-wall" support that was in evidence at the Pikesville Armory in 1973 now seems unimaginable.

Most striking of all, however, is that Israel has become a wedge issue among Jews no less.

NOT THAT LONG AGO, if there was a single issue that could unite Jews of all stripes, it was Israel. Few believed that Israel was perfect, but its creation seemed almost miraculous; given that the most sacred value to Jews in those post-Holocaust years was survival, contributing to its security seemed a sacred obligation. Religious American Jews were fascinated by Israel's traditional sites, by the huge numbers of young men (and with time, young women as well) studying in yeshivot.* Secular Jews were taken with the kibbutzim and their seemingly utopian combination of agriculture and socialism, and with the bronzed and muscular kibbutzniks, no longer bound to the rituals of old.† All Jews, it seemed, still traumatized by what the world had let happen to Jews in the middle of the twentieth century, took pride in Israel's

---

* Yeshivot ("yeshiva" is the singular form) are traditional academies for the study of Jewish texts and law.

† "Secular" is a problematic term for describing non-observant Israelis. In a society like Israel's, the lives of "secular" people are filled with Jewish content. All Israelis speak Hebrew, a language that has Jewish substance built into its very vocabulary. The overwhelming majority attend a Passover

army, the symbol of Jews no longer being as helpless as they had been in the face of pogroms and the Holocaust. To be sure, some American Jews worried about the Arabs living in the areas that Israel had captured in 1967, about what would eventually be called "the occupation."* But for the vast majority, even an awareness that Israel faced a serious moral and demographic challenge in "the territories" did not lessen their passionate attachment to the state and their willingness to stand with Israel in moments of crisis.

Those days are gone. Everywhere one turns, there is a sense of crisis. There are even books on the subject. One argues, like Pinkas, that American Jews are in a "waning love affair" with Israel. Another book argues that "support for Israel among American Jews, though still strong, is not as broad and deep as many, inside and outside the American Jewish community, believe it to be. Nor is it as unconditional and uncritical as it is often depicted in the media." Think tanks have joined the conversation, and in 2017 (the same year Pinkas wrote his column), a leading Israeli research center warned in a study titled "The Future of the Nation State of the Jewish People: Consolidation or Rupture?" that "ties between U.S. Jews and Israel could reach [a] breaking point."

Seder, most fast on Yom Kippur, and many light Sabbath candles and the like. All this is a far cry from the standard meaning of "secular." However, this book uses the term "secular" since that is how both American Jews and Israelis tend to refer to non-Orthodox and non-observant Israelis.

* Nomenclature is an extremely sensitive issue in contemporary discussions of Israel. What some people refer to as the "occupied territories," others call the "liberated territories." Most of the West refers to the "West Bank," while Israelis who believe that this area is rightly Israel's refer to it as "Judea and Samaria." As this book is not about the Israeli-Palestinian conflict and makes no suggestions as to how to solve it, I generally use the language employed by most Western media, as that will be most familiar to readers.

The crisis has been fodder for newspapers as well. Shortly after the publication of that research center report, *Ha'aretz* (Israel's highbrow daily, which generally leans strongly to the left) ran numerous stories on the issue, with headlines such as "Israel's Irreconcilable Differences with U.S. Jews and the Democratic Party May Soon Lead to Final Divorce." Then Thomas Friedman, the Pulitzer Prize–winning *New York Times* columnist, stated in an interview with an Israeli Hebrew paper, *Makor Rishon* (a weekly whose readers are generally right-leaning and religious), "You can't tell American Jews: We want you to come to Israel, but your form of Jewish-religious expression is unacceptable to us." *Ha'aretz*, reporting on that interview, proclaimed what was nothing new to anyone following the widening break: "There's a Crisis Between U.S. Jewry and Israel, Says Jewish-American Journalist Thomas Friedman." Even Western media was fascinated by the storm. What was transpiring was nothing less than the "Fracturing of the Jewish People," said the *Wall Street Journal*. "American Jews and Israeli Jews Are Headed for a Messy Breakup," proclaimed an opinion piece in the *New York Times*.

Jewish community professionals also clearly felt that a crisis was at hand. When the General Assembly of the Jewish Federations of North America, one of American Judaism's largest communal gatherings of the year, met in Israel in 2018, the subject of its annual conference was "We Need to Talk." Covering the event, *Ha'aretz* opined, "The GA's 'We Need to Talk' Slogan Is a Desperate Plea to Save Israel-U.S. Jewish Ties."

True, not everyone was terribly worried about the crisis. Some voices insisted—appearances to the contrary notwithstanding—that American Jews remained resolutely at Israel's side. Still others acknowledged that the chasm was widening, but unlike Pinkas, they did not think Israel ought to be that worried. Yet another view was held by Elliott Abrams, who had served in senior posts on the White House's National Security Council under Presidents Ronald Reagan and George W. Bush. At a conference in Israel in 2018, he went out of his way to tell Israelis that it would be a mistake to exaggerate levels of American Jewish commitment to Israel. "Israelis are from Mars and American Jews are from Venus," he said. When asked whether Israel ought to consider the opinions of world Jewry on a host of different policy matters, Abrams assumed a dismissive attitude toward the Jewish community of his own country. "Your first obligation to world Jewry is to survive," he said to the assembled Israelis, essentially telling them to ignore what he seemed to characterize as American Jewish bellyaching.

While many American Jews were exasperated with Israel, right-of-center American Jews were exasperated with other American Jews. The split between American Jews and Israel was causing a split even *within* the American Jewish community. When the *New Republic* published a series of articles on American Jews and Israel in 2018, it titled the series "A Diaspora Divided."

Divisions have arisen everywhere. Among most observers, the prevailing wisdom is that relations between (non-Orthodox) American Jews and Israel are at an all-time nadir. After decades of cooperation and support, goes the argument, American Jews are asking themselves whether they can continue to support Israel as they have in the past. Many observers believe that there is a real possibility of a dramatic rupture between the two communities. Some say that the rupture has already taken place, and that the best we can hope for is that American Jews and Israel will learn to live together respectfully, even while acknowledging and celebrating "their separate identities."

Of all the issues related to Israel's conduct that distress American Jews, it is the conflict—originally with the Arabs and now with the Palestinians—that looms largest. In the eyes of many American Jews, especially the young, who have no personal memories of the Oslo Accords, Prime Minister Yitzhak Rabin, or subsequent Israeli overtures to the Palestinians, Israel seems first and foremost an occupying power, unwilling to fashion a better, freer life for the Palestinians who live in the areas that Israel captured in the 1967 Six-Day War. For young American Jews, that is untenable. Though the Jewish establishment expects them to make Israel their primary loyalty, they seem more committed to being part of the progressive community than to Israel; to them, commitment to Israel seems at odds with the values of individual dignity, freedom, and human potential at the heart of American liberalism. As Peter Beinart, an intellectual pied piper of American Jewish progressives and millennials, put it pithily in a much-quoted 2010 essay in the *New York Review of Books*, "For several decades, the Jewish establishment has asked American Jews to check their liberalism at Zionism's door, and now, to their horror, they are finding that many young Jews have checked their Zionism instead."

One of the first incidents that led many American Jews to publicly break with Israel took place during Israel's war with Lebanon (now called the First Lebanon War) in 1982. In the late 1970s, southern Lebanon had become the base of a large Palestine Liberation Organization (PLO) terrorist presence that was terrorizing Israelis in Kiryat Shmona and other northern cities with rocket fire and occasional murderous incursions into Israel.

Menachem Begin, Israel's prime minister, fumed that the Jews had not created a Jewish state so that Jewish children would have to sleep in bomb shelters and Jewish families would have to cower in terror of the unknown just as they had in Europe. Israel had been created to change all that, and in failing to make its citizens safe, Israel was failing the very purpose of its creation. Prime Minister Begin was going to make Jewish children safe again.

Finally, in 1982, Begin and his generals sent a massive military force into the area. Nothing about the war went the way that Begin had planned, and Israelis quickly soured on the war, which, they noted, was the first war that Israel had *chosen* to launch. What aroused the fury of many American Jews (as well as Israelis, of course) was a specific incident in the war. During the fighting, the IDF captured and secured an area that contained two Palestinian refugee camps, named Sabra and Shatila. While the IDF was stationed outside the camps, Christian Phalangist fighters entered the camps and murdered between seven hundred and eight hundred Muslim men, women, and children, in revenge for the Muslims having murdered the Christians' leader, Bashir Gemayel.

Israelis had done none of the killing, but there was almost wall-to-wall agreement, both in Israel and abroad, that the IDF and Ariel Sharon, who was commanding the force, could and should have prevented the massacre. As images of hundreds of dead Muslims lying on the roads of Sabra and Shatila flooded the international media, young American Jews were distraught. They felt humiliated and shamed by the country to which they had once pointed with pride. Not only was this the first Israeli war that Israel had started, they said, and not only had Israel invaded a neighboring sovereign country, but much worse, they wanted to know, how did Israel's army look the other way as hundreds of innocent people were massacred? What had happened to the Israel they knew and loved? American Jews took great pride in what they commonly called "Jewish values"; did Israel no longer embody those values?

Many American Jews recall that period as the first time they found their erstwhile pride in the Jewish state slipping away. As Letty Cottin Pogrebin, a founding editor of *Ms.* magazine and a leading American Jewish author and social activist of the period, later recalled, "It was a shameful moment. It was a very difficult time. I think also we lost a lot of young people. . . . You can't behave that way as a nation and expect to spark in young idealistic Jews a passion for Israel, unless you're dealing with fanatics."

Then the issue of Palestinian statehood and Israel's occupation made matters even more complex. In 1987, Palestinians in the West Bank unleashed what is now called the First Intifada (1987–1991) and succeeded in getting the topic of Israel's occupation of the West Bank on the front pages of newspapers around the world. The Palestinian story sounded both sad and compelling, and once again, American Jews found themselves dismayed. Yes, they knew that the PLO continued to insist that it would not cease its attacks until Israel was utterly destroyed, but many American Jews believed that the Palestinians could be moderated. The Palestinians had no country, no citizenship, apparently no brighter future—and it seemed that it was because of *Israel* that the Palestinians had such bleak prospects. That was not the Israel the American Jews had been taught to love.

Since then, peace efforts have come and gone. Israelis have elected both left-leaning and right-leaning governments, but for all intents and purposes, nothing much has changed. Israel still controls the West Bank, sometimes with a heavy military hand and sometimes with a lighter touch. The Palestinians still do not have a state, and progress has stalled. For today's young American Jews, who have no personal recollection of a peace process of any sort, an Israel that does not appear to be pursuing peace, even as it occupies another people, is intolerable. It is, in short, not an Israel they can love or support.

If anything, it is Israel that they must resist.

IF MANY AMERICAN JEWS (like many Israelis) are uncomfortable with Israel's conduct of its conflict with the Palestinians, others, as Alon Pinkas noted, are infuriated by the way Israel treats and speaks about non-Orthodox Jews, who make up the vast majority of the American Jewish community.

Israel has always had an Orthodox chief rabbinate, but in the state's early years the religious community in Israel saw its position as tenuous. In the early stages of Israel's formation, its ultra-Orthodox community was very small. David Ben-Gurion (Israel's first prime minister) agreed to leave matters of state and religion in the hands of the rabbinate because he believed that the ultra-Orthodox would eventually disappear. They were, he was sure, a short-term problem that resulted from their need to flee Europe; they could not and would not survive in Israel.

Ben-Gurion was dead wrong, and today Israel's ultra-Orthodox (Haredi) community has become a powerful political and economic force. In 2017, the number of Haredim in Israel topped one million for the first time, representing 12 percent of the population. With their rise in power, ultra-Orthodox leaders (who include the chief rabbinate) feel increasingly comfortable expressing their views on an array of matters, including those not directly in their purview.

Increasingly, what is a nominally anti-Zionist, anti-intellectual, monolithic, and dismissive chief rabbinate espouses a version of Jewish life that most American Jews find foreign at best, and often abhorrent. It is dismissive of all forms of non-Orthodox Judaism. It ridicules attempts to create more egalitarian roles for women in Jewish ritual life and shows no tolerance for the rights of gays and lesbians. To make matters even worse, Israel's ultra-Orthodox rabbinic leaders have often characterized non-Orthodox Jews in needlessly disparaging ways. Rabbi Shlomo Amar, chief rabbi of Jerusalem and formerly chief rabbi of Israel, remarked that Reform Jews were "worse than Holocaust deniers." Ultra-Orthodox members of the Knesset have accused Reform Jews of "destroying Judaism," while others have called Reform Jews the "Wicked Son" to whom the Passover Haggadah refers.

Beyond the verbiage, the rabbinate's stranglehold on Israeli policy makes Reform and Conservative Jews feel that they are second-class Jews in Israel. Weddings and conversions performed by non-Orthodox rabbis in Israel are not recognized by the state.[*]

---

* While it was David Ben-Gurion who made a deal with the Orthodox rabbinate to continue the status quo that gave them control over all religious matters, he apparently believed that was a political necessity that he would eventually manage to reverse. Even in Israel's early years, when American Jewish leadership objected to the power that Ben-Gurion had given to the Orthodox, Ben-Gurion replied that the matter was entirely academic, since at that point there were no Reform rabbis in Israel. He insisted that "if any Reform rabbi comes to Israel he will enjoy the same rights and privileges as the Orthodox [rabbis]." What Ben-Gurion genuinely thought is not entirely obvious. Given that religious practice mattered very little to him, he might not have cared very much. Yet, though he did believe that the ultra-Orthodox would disappear in a matter of years, he could not possibly have thought that of the more modern Orthodox. How he might wrest control from them, he did not say. It never happened.

(In July 2018, Israeli police, under pressure from ultra-Orthodox authorities, detained a Conservative rabbi for performing a wedding, unleashing a brief but vociferous international uproar.) The central portion of the Western Wall, considered one of Judaism's holiest sites, does not have a section where Reform and Conservative Jews may worship with men and women together, as they do in their home synagogues. Government funding for religious institutions flows readily to Orthodox rabbis of cities and neighborhoods; non-Orthodox institutions have to fight much harder to receive it. For many American Jews, such policies and practices are inimical to a liberal, democratic state and make it much more difficult for them to be passionate supporters of Israel.

As offensive as ultra-Orthodox attitudes are to many American Jews, what makes Israel's comportment utterly intolerable to them is the government's collusion with the rabbinate—or at a minimum, its refusal to stand up to them (which most governments cannot do without losing their majority in the Knesset because of the religious right's political power).* In 2016, after years of pressure from American Jews, Prime Minister Benjamin Netanyahu's government agreed to create a space along part of the Western Wall (the Kotel) where egalitarian prayer could be held; the government promised to create an entrance to that

---

* The Knesset is comprised of 120 seats, which are distributed proportionally according to the percentage of votes received by each party in an election. A political party that receives one-quarter of the vote, for example, wins 30 seats in the Knesset. Given the many competing parties, however, most typically receive much smaller proportions of the vote, and prime ministers therefore have to cobble together coalitions of parties in order to control 61 seats, the minimum number for a majority of the 120. Because parties typically have dissimilar agendas, many coalitions are unhappy and unstable compromises from the outset, and small parties, by threatening to leave a coalition, can hamstring the prime minister. The result is a governmental system whose tumult and instability have plagued Israel since its founding.

area that would be as "central" as the entrance to the "original" space at the Kotel. Yet the following year, despite having given his word, Netanyahu folded and reneged on his promise when Haredi pressure grew. Clearly, the desire to preserve his coalition and stay in power meant far more to him than any promise he might have made to non-Orthodox American Jews, even if they constitute the overwhelming majority of American Jewry.

Netanyahu's change of heart and his refusal to stand by an agreement he had explicitly made infuriated many American Jewish leaders. The Jewish United Fund of Metropolitan Chicago (Chicago's Jewish Federation, one of the largest and most respected in the country) announced that no representative of the Netanyahu government would be welcome in town until the policy changed. Ike Fisher, a leading American Jewish philanthropist, announced with fury that he was done supporting Israel.[*] This controversy, too, eventually blew over, but the incident was one of many that left in its wake the residual feeling of a marriage slowly eroding.

WHILE PINKAS AND OTHERS refer to Israel's relationship with the Palestinians and its conflict with American Jews over matters of religion as the primary causes of the troubled relationship, other Israeli policies have also raised the ire of American Jews. Some had nothing to do with the Arabs *or* with Israel's treatment of other Jews. For instance, Israel's 2018 decision to

---

[*] This, too, was hardly a new phenomenon in the relationship between the two communities. In the early 1950s, angry at Ben-Gurion's disparaging remarks about American Zionists, Rose Halperin, president of Hadassah—perhaps *the* quintessential American Zionist organization—threatened that American Jews would sever relations with Israel.

deport thousands of African asylum-seekers (though that term itself is controversial and only one of a number of possible definitions of their status) smacked to many American Jews of racism.

For all these reasons, as well as others, American Jews are increasingly expressing their ire. In May 2018, low-grade conflict erupted on Israel's Gaza border, and Israeli forces shot several dozen Palestinians they believed were seeking to damage or breach the border fence. *The Forward*, the American Jewish community's hard-left-leaning newspaper, is often unrelentingly critical of Israel.* But that week, *The Forward* outdid even itself and published an opinion piece on the incident with the headline "Israel's Choice to Shoot Palestinians Should Horrify—But Not Surprise Us." At around the same time, Natalie Portman, an Israeli-born American actress, announced that she would not travel to Israel to accept an award she had been given. *The Forward* pithily summarized the state of matters when it announced in a headline that "Natalie Portman Speaks Loudly for Young American Jews with Snub of Israel."

To be sure, there is another powerful and poignant side to this picture. Hundreds of thousands of American Jews are deeply committed to Israel, and they, too, are an important dimension of the picture. At the annual Policy Conference of the American

---

* From the very outset, relations between the American Jewish press and the state of Israel have been periodically contentious. Blaming the American Jewish press for fanning the flames of a crisis between the two countries, Moshe Sharett (who would later serve as Israel's second prime minister) referred to the "combination of stupidity and malice known for short as the JTA [*Jewish Telegraphic Agency*]." Today it is not *JTA* but publications like *The Forward* (which, due to financial woes, ceased its print version in 2019 after 120 years and became digital only) that evoke that ire among the few Israelis who even care enough to follow the American Jewish press. The players have changed over the years, but the reciprocal sentiments have not.

Israel Public Affairs Committee (AIPAC), some eighteen thousand people (most but surely not all of them Jews) gather in Washington, D.C., for what is a passionate, energetic, and inspiring display of commitment to and belief in the State of Israel.* Tens of thousands of American Jews visit Israel each year on delegations from Jewish organizations, congregations, study groups, and more. All of Israel's cities are peppered with signs and plaques indicating the massive amount of money that American Jews raise for Israel and the many institutions that make up Israeli society. Birthright, funded primarily by American Jews, brings nearly forty thousand students to Israel each year—not to look at Israel's divisive political issues, but rather to inspire these young people with the very concept of Jewish sovereignty and Israel's many accomplishments. There is clear evidence that Birthright is having a profoundly positive impact on the attitudes of many American Jews toward Israel.†

Hadassah, the American women's Zionist organization, began its work in Palestine more than a century ago and was a critical force in bringing modern medicine there in the early 1900s; today it continues to support and direct one of Israel's finest hospitals and research centers. Rabbinical students from all streams of American Judaism do some of their training in Israel, while one-year programs continue to attract thousands

---

* AIPAC is the largest and by far the most powerful and effective pro-Israel lobby in the United States. In AIPAC's words, its mission is "to strengthen, protect and promote the U.S.-Israel relationship in ways that enhance the security of the United States and Israel."

† It is thus not surprising that If Not Now occasionally tried accosting Birthright groups at airports before they departed for Israel, hoping to convince them to abandon the group they had pledged to join, since the Israel that Birthright groups are shown is much greater than the sum of its conflicts, an image of Israel much more nuanced than that promulgated by If Not Now.

of American students to Israel for a year of study abroad. The list goes on.

That said, the shift, particularly among young American Jews (those under forty, and especially millennials), is real. Note that *The Forward* article cited earlier made a point of stressing that Natalie Portman was ostensibly speaking for "*young* American Jews" in her decision to not travel to Israel to accept her award.

The changing attitude of "young American Jews" became even more painfully obvious after Israel's first two twenty-first-century conflicts. From 2000 to 2004, Israel was embroiled in the Second Intifada, a conflict that left more than 1,000 Israelis dead and 8,000 wounded. Then, in 2006, the Second Lebanon War ended inconclusively, with 120 IDF soldiers killed and more than 1,200 wounded. Whatever complacency Israelis and Jews across the world might have previously felt was now gone; Israel's ongoing vulnerability to Palestinian terror was clear. That made a study that two American Jewish sociologists conducted the following year all the more striking, particularly for what it showed about the attitudes to Israel among young American Jews. The survey asked American Jews of various ages whether they agreed with the statement that "Israel's destruction would be a personal tragedy."

Not surprisingly, of those age sixty-five and older (many of them the sorts of people who had gathered in my Baltimore synagogue's lobby in 1973), some 80 percent said that yes, for them the destruction of Israel would be a personal tragedy. Among those thirty-five years old or younger, however, the figure was significantly lower—slightly less than half felt this way. And note the wording of the questions: the researchers asked not about Israel's disappearance, or its withering away, but about its "destruction," such as from a cataclysmic event in which tens of thousands of Jews, perhaps many more, would presumably die. Still, only one-half of the younger cohort said that Israel's "destruction" would be a "personal tragedy" for them. In fact, their feelings about Israel may have been even more stark than that number suggests. Owing to the structure of their sample, the authors noted, "one has to presume that the 'real' levels of attachment among those under 35 are lower still."

The passage of time since the Holocaust has clearly affected the relationship between American and Israeli Jews. The extermination of the Jews in the Holocaust (and 90 percent of perhaps the world's most important Jewish community, Polish Jewry, which numbered 3 million before the war but was reduced to 300,000 by the war's end) shook many American Jews to their core. A disproportionate number of them had immigrated just a generation or two earlier from Jewish communities that now no longer existed. Why had they deserved to survive while members of their families who had stayed behind in Europe were incinerated? For many American Jews of the post-Holocaust generation, the cloud of Nazi genocide was perhaps *the* defining issue in their lives. For them, Israel was the very symbol of the Jewish people's rebirth.

For today's younger American Jews, however, Israel is not a symbol of rebirth. How could it be when the Holocaust feels like ancient history? Think about it this way: the beginning of the Holocaust is already about half as long ago as the end of the American Civil War. And how emotional does anyone get when thinking about the Civil War? Unlike their parents, and certainly unlike their grandparents, young American Jews cannot imagine a world without Israel. And because the first days of the Yom Kippur War were also the last time that Israel's survival seemed to be in question, they also cannot imagine that Israel actually faces an existential threat. If they are asked about "Israel" and "vulnerability," they think of Palestinians. They are too young to remember Prime Minister Yitzhak Rabin's dramatic embrace of the Oslo Accords and his (unhappy) handshake with Yasser Arafat, his former (and future) nemesis. They have known nothing other than an Israel that is "the startup-nation": powerful, stable, (seemingly) invulnerable, but also, in their minds, the reason that the Palestinians live such unfortunate lives. One generation has made all the difference.

One generation has made a great deal of difference in Israel as well. Unbeknownst to many American Jews, Israel's social and demographic makeup has been changing in a way that affects American Jews' view of Israel. The story we tell of Israel's founding is almost always a European-centric narrative, because that is where Theodor Herzl, David Ben-Gurion, Ze'ev Jabotinsky, Menachem Begin, Eliezer Ben-Yehuda, Chaim Weizmann, and many others were born and raised.

But the demographic sands in Israel are shifting. In Israel's early decades, European (Ashkenazi) Jews often looked down on Mizrachim, who came largely from North Africa, Yemen, Iraq, and Iran; Israel's mostly Ashkenazi political leaders kept the Mizrachim at the periphery of Israeli society, marginalizing them economically and politically. Fortunately, however, Mizrachim have made great strides in Israeli life over the decades. They now constitute a slight majority of Israeli Jews and are increasingly represented in government, the professions, religious leadership, the arts—almost all sectors of mainstream society. Marriages between Ashkenazi and Mizrachi Jews, once rather rare, are no longer even noteworthy. Not quick to forgive Israel's ostensibly liberal parties for years of discrimination, though, Mizrachim have flocked to Israel's political right, where they both strengthen right-wing parties and—since right-leaning parties want to hold on to the Mizrachi voting bloc—make those parties more determined to reflect a Mizrachi worldview.

And what is that worldview? Mizrachim typically represent a socially, culturally, and politically conservative force in Israel. They have a resilient religious faith that has withstood decades of secular influence. Having been evicted from Arab lands, they are typically less optimistic than their Ashkenazi counterparts about the possibility of resolving the Israeli-Arab conflict and less willing to take what seem to them foolish, hopeless risks for a peace they do not believe can be had. Although the Mizrachim have their own feminist movement and women activists, gender roles among most are more traditional, as are their religious views; even Mizrachi feminists are focused much more on social advancement than on changing women's roles in religion. Mizrachim typically resist the sort of religious change—such as egalitarian gender roles—often advocated by Reform and Conservative Jews in America. Reverence for religious authority is an even greater value among Mizrachim than it is among religious Ashkenazim, and most Mizrachim are content to leave their hallowed, centuries-old religious way of life unchanged.

How does this affect Israel's relationship with American Jews? The demographic rise of Mizrachim and their concomitant greater influence on Israeli society and culture helps shape an Israeli society that strikes many American Jews as distinctly illiberal. American Jews may not fully realize that this increasing mainstreaming of a former underclass is a sign of social progress; what they *do* see is a country that *seems* to be moving further and further away from the progressive discourse common among much of American Jewry.

The rise of Mizrachim is a telling example of the conundrum in which American Jews will increasingly find themselves: as advocates of the social underdog, they should celebrate the progress that Mizrachim have made. Their progressive values, however, are at odds with those of Mizrachim, making it even more difficult to embrace Israel as wholeheartedly as was once possible.

THUS, WE CAN REFRAME Alon Pinkas's claim that "U.S. Jewry just isn't that into" Israel this way: the more illiberal Israel seems, the less attached to it young American Jews feel. As they confront Israel's positions on Palestinians, religious pluralism, and the treatment of the non-Jews and people of color (Jewish and non-Jewish alike) in its midst, these usually progressive Jews, with a substantially less powerful connection to the Holocaust and the creation of the State of Israel, increasingly find Israel unpalatable. As a leading sociologist of the American Jewish community has put it, "Israel is a Red State and American Jews are a blue country." Or to use a biblical metaphor, American Jews wish for a country based on the teaching of the biblical prophet Isaiah—the wolf lying down with the lamb, nation not lifting up sword against nation anymore—while Israel seems to act more like King David—battling the Philistines and wielding power at every turn. Israel and American Jews have adopted almost opposite models of leaders and visions of Jewish life from among those found in Jewish culture.

THE PREVAILING VIEW, THEREFORE, is that the root cause of the rift between American Jews and Israel is what Israel *does*:

if Israel only behaved better, the relationship could be healed. There is only one problem with that explanation: it is wrong.

Why is the conventional wisdom mistaken? Let's return to our marriage metaphor. When a couple quarrels over dishes left in the sink or socks dropped on the floor, the problem is rarely about kitchens or bedroom floors. The issues in the dynamic are generally much deeper, more profound and far-reaching, than the immediate issues that triggered the quarrel. The same is true with Israel and American Jews. That is not to say that Israel's conflict with the Palestinians is not a critically important security, demographic, and moral challenge, the resolution of which may ultimately determine whether Israel can remain both Jewish and democratic. It absolutely is. In particular, millions of Palestinians living under Israeli occupation—even if it is an occupation that Israel did not seek and has tried to end—is terrible for the Palestinians and a threat to Israel's moral and democratic core.

Nor is the suggestion that something deeper than the immediate triggers is at play meant to suggest that the Israeli rabbinate's views of non-Orthodox Jews are not gratuitously offensive and callously dismissive of those with whom they disagree. Or that Israel's handling of an African asylum issue is not key to the kind of country Israel will or should become. All of those are profound issues that everyone who cares about the Jewish state needs to take very seriously.

The proof that these explanations are insufficient lies in the fact that the fraught relations between American Jews and Israel predate *by decades* the conflict with Arabs and then the Palestinians; the tensions arose long before the ugliness of Israel's treatment of non-Orthodox Jews. The real issue that divides the world's two largest Jewish communities, as we have noted, is not what Israel *does*, but what Israel *is*. The essential issue, we will suggest, is that, at their core, America and Israel are exceedingly different: created for different purposes, they believe in and foster very different sorts of societies with very different values and different visions of Judaism.

For decades, American Jews have assumed that the more Israel emulates the United States the more admirable it will be. The more Israel acts in ways that highlight the differences between its values and those of the United States, however, the more difficult it becomes for American Jews to support it.

Yet American Jews misunderstand Israel when they assume that Israel's founders *wanted* or *expected* it to mirror America's core values. And Israeli Jews often wrongly read American Jews' differences as disloyalty, or laziness, without appreciating that American Judaism has a profound, but very different, set of core values. Israel's founders never hoped that Israel would be an imitation of America, and American Jewish leaders recognized from the outset that a Jewish state would threaten some of their deepest commitments. The divisions between American Jews and the Zionist project have always run deep, in large measure because the values and priorities of Zionism are diametrically opposed to many of the values that have made America the extraordinary country it is.

The United States and Israel were created for entirely different purposes, and as a result, they are fundamentally different experiments in how to enable humans to flourish. In the chapters that follow, we will look at several of the key commitments that make Israel and America so different.

To uncover the origins of today's fraught relations between American Jews and Israel, we need to begin with the very origins of Zionism itself.

A RIFT OLDER THAN THE STATE ITSELF

At four o'clock in the afternoon on May 23, 1960, the plenum of Israel's parliament was packed with members of the Knesset, public observers, and just about anyone who could find a seat in the crowded hall. Rumors had circulated that Prime Minister David Ben-Gurion had unprecedented news to relay. As the assembled crowd waited for him to speak, the feeling in the chamber was electric.

Ben-Gurion approached the podium and began:

> I have to inform the Knesset that a short time ago one of the great Nazi war criminals, Adolf Eichmann, the man responsible together with the Nazi leaders for what they called the Final Solution, which is the annihilation of six million European Jews, was discovered by the Israel security services. Adolf Eichmann is already under arrest in Israel and will be placed on trial shortly under the terms of the law for the trial of Nazis and their collaborators.

With that, Ben-Gurion walked away from the podium and departed the chamber.

The hall was silent. Each person in the room struggled with the enormity of the announcement and its implications. Would the State of Israel finally exact even a modicum of justice from one of the architects of the annihilation of European Jewry? Would some measure of retribution finally be found for the millions of defenseless Jews murdered and tortured, gassed and burned or buried alive, and the million Jewish children whose lives had been cut off by the Nazi genocidal machine? Would there be an accounting for the sisters and brothers, parents and spouses, of many of those who sat in the room and of thousands of other Israelis?

Adolf Eichmann had been a Nazi SS-Obersturmbannführer (lieutenant colonel) and one of the architects of the Holocaust, a central figure at the Wannsee Conference from which the idea of a "Final Solution" emerged. At the time of his capture, Eichmann was the highest-ranking Nazi official still alive. He had spent most of his time after the war hiding in Argentina, living under a pseudonym. Yet the Mossad, one of Israel's security agencies, had managed to locate and capture him; it then secreted him out of Argentina and into Israel.

Finally, it seemed, one of the archenemies of the Jewish people was about to pay for his crimes. Because the Jews had a state, their enemies had no refuge. Now those who sought to destroy the Jews would be held accountable.

Spontaneously, those in the hall shattered the silence and shook the chamber with thunderous applause.

While most rank-and-file American Jews shared that sense of deep satisfaction among many American Jewish leaders, the response to Eichmann's capture was not celebration but outrage. Joseph Proskauer, a former president of the American Jewish

Committee (AJC), urged Prime Minister Ben-Gurion not to try Eichmann in Jerusalem but to turn him over to an international tribunal. Proskauer, who had been at the helm of the AJC's anti-Zionist wing and had explicitly objected to the creation of a Jewish state, had said years earlier that he viewed Zionist efforts to establish a Jewish commonwealth in Palestine as nothing less than a "Jewish catastrophe."[*] He might have softened in the interim, but Proskauer was still appalled by Israel's move. To try Eichmann in Jerusalem would be to acknowledge that Israel spoke for and acted in the name of world Jewry, and the AJC had long been on record as taking the position that the small Jewish state was anything but the center of the Jewish world. Nor did Proskauer, a member of a generation of American Jews deeply conscious of how they were seen by "ordinary" Americans, seem comfortable having the spotlight on Jews alone. Eichmann, he reminded Ben-Gurion, had committed "unspeakable crimes against *humanity*, not only against Jews." Proskauer actually clipped a *Washington Post* editorial that insisted, "Although there are a great many Jews in Israel, the Israeli government has no authority . . . to act in the name of some *imaginary Jewish ethnic entity*," and sent it to Ben-Gurion.

Erich Fromm, the German-born Jewish psychoanalyst and philosopher, was also enraged. He wrote (somewhat inexplicably) that by grabbing Eichmann, Israel had committed an "act of lawlessness of exactly the type of which the Nazis themselves . . . have been guilty." Erich Fromm, of course, was hardly a fool, and

---

[*] Though the AJC had significant anti-Zionist and non-Zionist camps in the years prior to Israel's creation, it—like many major Jewish organizations—has undergone a dramatic transformation in the intervening decades. Its website now proclaims: "Around the world . . . AJC advocates for Israel at the highest levels. And when Israel is under assault, whether from the terrorist organizations on her doorstep or the global BDS movement, AJC helps bring the world the truth about Israel."

equating Israel's capture of Eichmann with the actions of the Nazis was an extraordinary accusation. What could have provoked his response?

In contrast to Fromm, Rabbi Elmer Berger, a leader of the vehemently anti-Zionist American Council for Judaism, which had long opposed a Jewish state because it believed that "Jewish nationalism tends to confuse our fellowmen about our place and function in society and diverts our own attention from our historic role to live as a religious community wherever we may dwell," was clear about the reason for his objections to Eichmann being tried by Israel.[*] The Jewish state's trying of Eichmann would essentially define Israel as the center of Jewish gravity, which would in turn disenfranchise American Jews. Berger would eventually call the Eichmann trial "a Zionist declaration of war" against American Jews' claim to equal citizenship.

David Ben-Gurion was appalled and outraged by the reaction of American Jews to what he saw as the enormous accomplishment of Israel's security apparatus. He believed with every fiber of his being that the creation of Israel was the fulfillment of a biblical promise and two thousand years of Jewish aspiration. For him, as for most of his colleagues in the leadership of the Zionist movement and the Jewish state, the course of European history had proven without a shred of doubt that Jews dared not

---

[*] Berger was more than simply opposed to the idea of Zionism. He was a board member of the pro–Arab American Friends of the Middle East and a friend of Fayez Sayegh, a central figure at the Arab Information Center in New York. In that regard, he was in some ways the forerunner of strategies like that of the Jewish Voice for Peace, widely recognized despite its intentionally misleading name as an expressly anti-Israel organization, which partners with the BDS (Boycott, Divest, Sanction) movement to do harm to Israel. The line between principled hesitation regarding the wisdom of the idea of a Jewish state and active work to conspire with its enemies to undermine it has always been exceedingly thin.

live without a country of their own. And to him, it was patently obvious that Israel had every right to try Eichmann. After all, the very point of the Jewish state was that people could not kill Jews with impunity, as they had done as long as the Jews had not had a state. Not only would the Eichmann trial hold Eichmann responsible as an individual, but it would make clear the long reach of Israel's arm. No murderous enemy of the Jewish people would ever be safe again, anywhere.

Ben-Gurion minced no words, arguing that "Israel is the only inheritor of these Jews [murdered in the Holocaust] for two reasons; first, it is the only Jewish state. Second, if these Jews were alive, they would be here because most, if not all of them, wanted to come to live in a Jewish State." Neither of those arguments was terribly convincing, but to Ben-Gurion, the issue was more heart than head. To him, Jews who did not wish to live in a Jewish state, now that it had been reestablished, were an inexplicable aberration; his long-simmering resentment of American Jews—who of course had no intention of moving to Israel—was about to boil over.

When Nahum Goldmann—who had been born in a shtetl called Vishnevo (now in Belarus) but who was by then living in the United States and serving as president of the World Zionist Organization (WZO)—suggested that foreign jurists serve on the court tribunal, Ben-Gurion accused him of having an inferiority complex, since the mere suggestion implied that Goldmann questioned not only Israel's *right* to conduct the trial, but also its *ability* to do so in an impartial manner. So disgusted was Ben-Gurion with American Jewry's response that when Edward Bayne of the American Universities Field Staff suggested that Eichmann not be tried in Jerusalem, Ben-Gurion asked him if he, too, was an American Jew. When Bayne responded that he was not, Ben-Gurion smugly replied, "I thought only an American Jew would question our right to try Eichmann."

A mere twelve years after Israel's creation, the relationship between American Jews and Israel seemed to be at the breaking point. Nor did time heal all wounds. More than half a year after his original announcement of Eichmann's capture, Ben-Gurion's ire had not subsided. In his December 1960 speech to the Twenty-Fifth Zionist Congress he said, as the *New York Times* reported it, "Judaism of the United States . . . is losing all meaning," and "in the free and prosperous countries [Judaism] faces the kiss of death, a slow and imperceptible decline into the abyss of assimilation." Ben-Gurion, not a religious believer in any standard sense of the word, even invoked God in his rhetorical wrath. Jews living outside Israel are "godless" and "violated the precepts of Judaism every day they remained away," he sputtered, later justifying himself by noting that the Talmud states that "whoever dwells outside the land of Israel is considered to have no god."

No one in this vitriolic war of words, of course, had any doubt as to Eichmann's guilt; that Eichmann had been intimately involved in the Nazi genocidal machine that had exterminated one-third of the Jewish people was beyond question. Eichmann himself scarcely denied it. There would be little doubt that Eichmann deserved whatever punishment he might receive. (Israel would convict him in April 1961 and execute him in May 1962.) Why, then, did his capture and trial cause such a massive eruption of enmity between the two communities?

The truth is that it was not the Eichmann trial that caused this eruption. The conflict over Eichmann was merely a reflection of a division that had begun to simmer almost half a century earlier.

The enmity between the two communities was almost as old as the Zionist movement itself. Even today, it is impossible to meaningfully understand the tensions between the two communities without first appreciating how differently European Zionists and American Jews understood what it was that Zionism was seeking to accomplish.

For the Europeans, Zionism was a consciously revolutionary movement. It was a revolution against the condition of Jews as landless residents of foreign countries dependent on the goodwill of their hosts, which had often run out. It was time for the Jews to refuse to be victims-on-call, European Zionists believed, living wherever they might call home until their host country decided to evict or murder its Jews.

Even "mere" eviction, after all, was often a death sentence. When Jews fled whatever country had tired of them, many died along the way; the lucky ones—who could take with them only whatever they could carry or put on an animal—were reduced instantaneously to abject poverty wherever they ended up. Louis IX evicted the Jews from France in 1254. England evicted its Jews in 1290. Spain in 1492. Portugal in 1496. Nuremberg in 1499. Frankfurt in 1614. Other examples, sadly, abound. (Though Zionism's leaders could not know it then, Germany would soon follow, but instead of evicting the Jews, it would exterminate them.) And all the while, complained Zionist leaders with anger and mockery, Diaspora Jews remained passive, weak, fearful, and huddled over ancient sacred texts instead of defending themselves and taking history into their own hands.

That, said many early Zionist thinkers, was what had to change. It would be hard to overstate their revolutionary zeal. Zionists were so desperate to proclaim an end to a passive, weak, victimized Judaism that they even changed their names. Israel's first four prime ministers are cases in point. David Ben-Gurion had been born David Gruen. Moshe Sharett was born Moshe

Shertok; Levi Eshkol was originally Levi Shkolnik. Golda Meir (Israel's first female prime minister) had been Golda Meyerson. Altering their names was a way of saying "no more"—even their families were not their families. It was time for a new Jewish worldview, a new Jewish physique, a new Jewish home, and new Hebrew names. It was time for a "new Jew," a Jewish people reborn, a people who would flock to the shores of their ancestral homeland and reconstitute themselves as a people. No intellectual mind-experiment, European Zionism was a rugged political movement designed to wrest Palestine from the Ottomans (and later the British) and create a state that Jews from around the world would build together, redeeming not only themselves but the Jewish world from which they hailed.

After centuries of exile, European Zionism—whose leaders would come to define the central ethos of Israel when it was created—was also about restoring the Jewish people to the cultural richness that a people have when they live in their ancestral homeland, speak their own language, and chart the course of their own future. If the Jews had been scattered to what the prophet Isaiah and their liturgy called the "four corners of the earth," Zionists hoped to gather them back together once again. If millennia of exile had reduced Hebrew, once spoken and vibrant, to a language reserved for sacred and liturgical texts, Zionism would breathe new life into that ancient tongue. Reconstituted in their ancestral homeland, the Jewish people would produce music, art, literature, and poetry like all other peoples. There would be high culture and popular culture. Jews would live in the cities that their ancestors had known and build new cities uniquely their own, like Tel Aviv, the modern world's first Hebrew-speaking city. Jews restored to the Land of Israel would walk the same paths that had been home to their biblical forebears. Jewish leaders would make policy on war and peace, economics, health care, and immigration. Nothing less than a genuine state, with real successes and ugly failures, would satisfy the revolutionary zeal of European Zionists.

Some early Zionists intuited that their passion would prove uncomfortable for their Diaspora partners, and that a conflict between the two groups was inevitable. In 1920, for example, Berl Katznelson—who was born in Russia but immigrated to Palestine at the age of twenty-two and became an intellectual pillar of the pre-state Jewish community in Palestine and Ben-Gurion's closest friend (Ben-Gurion described him as "the dearest man in my life")—returned from a meeting of the Zionist Congress in London and complained bitterly about the Diaspora's dismissive attitude toward what was being built in Palestine. "Whoever has not had the privilege of being present at Zionist gatherings in the Diaspora cannot begin to imagine the unique joy and unbridled pleasure with which every quip and dismissive comment at the expense of the Land of Israel is embraced in those [self-]important Zionist circles."

The reason for the dismissiveness was evident to Katznelson: what the Jews were building in Palestine was radically different from the most fundamental assumptions of Diaspora Jewish living. "The Yishuv* of the Land of Israel is beginning to take on its own character and nature. And the nature of this community is entirely at odds with the predilections of its 'masters,' of the World Zionist Organization," he wrote. "This young, small community has developed its own spine and distinct characteristics. . . . We are becoming ever more sensitive to

---

* *Yishuv* is Hebrew for "area of settlement." The term "Yishuv" is commonly used for the pre-state Jewish community in Palestine. The Yishuv, with its own government and army, eventually became the State of Israel.

every insult and instance of paternalism [from the Diaspora]. We are developing courage and are losing patience, feeling urgency—in short, we are becoming revolutionary." Katznelson was certain he knew where this would lead: "Because of this, there will yet emerge bitter conflict between [Diaspora] Zionism and the Land of Israel." He was right.

Zionism was never a unified or monolithic movement. Even among the passionate Europeans, deep schisms were more the rule than the exception. There were both religious groups of Zionists and secular, almost virulently antireligious groups. There were Communist Zionists, Socialists, and even those with views that came much closer to what today we would call free market capitalists. There were divisions between "mainstream" Zionists like Herzl—and later Ben-Gurion—and those who were more revolutionary; known as Revisionists, the latter were led originally by Ze'ev Jabotinsky and later by Menachem Begin.

Possibly the deepest and widest split, however, was between Zionists in Europe and Palestine, on the one hand, and American Zionists, on the other. American Jews—even those positively inclined toward Zionism—were living in a setting radically different from that in Europe and could not embrace the statehood-centric version of European Zionism. Even the First Zionist Congress foreshadowed how difficult it was going to be to get American Jews onboard; despite the fact that there were some 937,000 Jews in America, of the approximately 200 delegates to the Congress, only four came from the United States.[*]

American Judaism was becoming anti-Zionist even before

---

[*] Not all four were even official representatives of the American Jewish community. Davis Treitsch (1870–1935), though listed as a participant from New York City, was apparently a German national living in New York who

there was Zionism. In 1885, American Reform rabbis adopted what is now known as the Pittsburgh Platform, the movement's statement of core beliefs and commitments. In it, these rabbis declared, in part, that the Jews were no longer a people but now constituted a religion. "We recognize, in the modern era of universal culture of heart and intellect, the approaching of the realization of Israel's great Messianic hope for the establishment of the kingdom of truth, justice, and peace among all men," they said as they jettisoned Judaism's long-standing particularism and embraced the universalism then much in vogue in philosophic and cultural circles. "We consider ourselves no longer a nation, but a religious community," they said, and since Jews were no longer a national community, they expected "neither a return to Palestine,[*] nor a sacrificial worship under the sons of Aaron, nor the restoration of any of the laws concerning the Jewish state."

A few years later, just a year after Theodor Herzl launched the Zionist movement, Reform leaders applied that sentiment specifically to the United States. "We are unalterably opposed to political Zionism," they said, and they explained why. "The

---

paid his own way to Basel. Rosa Sonneschein (1847–1932), the irrepressible editor of *The American Jewess*, was there in her capacity as a journalist. The other two American participants were Rabbi Dr. Schepsel Schaffer of Baltimore (1862–1933) and Adam Rosenberg (1858–1928) of New York City, who was a leading Zionist of his era.

[*] In what is surely one of the great ironies of Zionist history, that very same argument—that the Jews are a religion, not a nation, and therefore had no need or right to return to Palestine—was also key to the Arab objections to the United Nations plan to divide Palestine into two states, one Jewish and one Arab, in November 1947. The Syrian delegate, for example, argued, "The Jews are not a nation. Every Jew belongs to a certain nationality. None of them in the world is now stateless or without nationality. . . . The followers of a certain religious creed cannot be entitled to national aspirations." Reform Judaism has evolved significantly since the Pittsburgh Platform, and the movement is now unabashedly committed to the State of Israel.

Jews are not a nation, but a religious community. . . . America is our Zion."

How deeply did American Jews internalize the notion that America was their new national home? A fascinating indication is a 1904 stained-glass window of Congregation Sherith Israel in San Francisco, which depicts a classic biblical scene: Moses descending from a mountain holding the Ten Commandments. What is remarkable about this artwork, however, is that it shows Moses descending, not from Mount Sinai, as in the Bible's account, but from Yosemite's El Capitan.

For many American Jews, Sinai had come to California, and revelation had been relocated to the United States.

Across the ocean, Theodor Herzl sensed early on that Judaism in America was going to be a unique challenge for Zionism. As early as 1901, just four years after he launched the movement in Basel, Herzl penned a public letter to American Jews. "Today," he said, "the Zionist movement has spread and received approval all across the world. Everyone recognizes that [Jewish settlement in the Land of Israel] is the only solution to the Jewish question. . . . The numbers of those formerly distant from us who are now attaching themselves to us is growing most successfully."

A few lines later, however, Herzl's tone changed. He was writing more than a century before Deputy Foreign Minister Tzipi Hotovely's outburst at American Jews, but some similar sentiments lay not far beneath the surface. "Unfortunately," he wrote, "that cannot be said of America. America, with its Jewish population growing day by day thanks to Jewish immigration, has not fulfilled its obligation of participating in the Zionist enterprise to an appropriate degree. Friends, brothers, awaken! We need your support, not merely your enthusiasm that emerges from your mass gatherings but then disappears like a whiff of smoke."*

Herzl apparently intuited even then that the American Diaspora was unlike anything the Jews had ever known. He was right: America's invitation to the Jews was unprecedented, and American Jews were understandably deeply reticent to risk that welcome.

America's welcome, Jews understood, was not unconditional. Nothing expresses the conditional nature of this welcome more clearly than a speech that President Woodrow Wilson delivered in 1915 to newly naturalized citizens:

> You cannot dedicate yourself to America unless you become
> in every respect and with every purpose of your will thor-
> ough Americans. You cannot become thorough Americans
> if you think of yourself in groups. America does not consist
> of groups. A man who thinks of himself as belonging to a
> particular national group in America has not yet become an
> American, and the man who goes among you to trade upon
> your nationality is no worthy son to live under the Stars and
> Stripes.

---

* Though unwittingly, Herzl was unleashing what would become a characteristic of Zionist and Israeli relations with the Diaspora over the long
term. Berating American Zionists for not doing enough for the cause indeed
became a mainstay of the movement. Shortly after Israel's creation, with the
country struggling under a tremendous financial burden and Ben-Gurion
deeply worried about the possibility of the Korean War diminishing American aid to Israel, he berated Rose Halperin, president of Hadassah, a woman
who had devoted her entire life to creating and supporting the state. Drip-
ping with condescension, he excoriated her: "We are in a serious position
and we count on you to do your duty. You in America can do a little more
than you do now. . . . I know this has nothing to do with Zionist policy, but
it has something to do with our survival."

Far from the rarefied circles of American politics and Washington's elites, Wilson's viewpoint was the prevailing ethos even of American factories. In the early 1900s, the Ford Motor Company had a position called "Director of Americanization." In 1919, around the same time Wilson gave his speech, Clinton C. DeWitt, who held that position, described a pageant that the company held when its employees completed Americanization school:

> All the men descend from a boat scene representing the vessel on which they came over; down the gangway representing the distance from the port at which they landed to the school, into a pot 15 feet in diameter and 7½ feet high, which represents the Ford English School. Six teachers, three on either side, stir the pot with 10-foot ladles representing nine months of teaching in the school. Into the pot 52 nationalities with their foreign clothes and baggage go and out of the pot after vigorous stirring by the teachers comes one nationality, viz. American.

Wilson was hardly the only president to focus on the need for immigrants to jettison all other national ties. Calvin Coolidge, in an October 1925 speech attacking the Ku Klux Klan, said, "I recognize the full and complete necessity of 100 percent Americanism." In words that for some sounded almost like Lincoln, he continued: "But 100 percent Americanism may be made up of many various elements. If we are to have . . . that union of spirit which is the foundation of real national genius and national progress, we must all realize that there are true Americans who did not happen to be born in our section of the country, who do not attend our place of religious worship, who are not of our racial stock, or who are not proficient in our language." Coolidge was clearly willing to cast a wide net, but his goal, like Wilson's, was "100% Americanism."

What would such Americans have said if they heard that American Jews were seeking entrée into America *and* at the very same time building another homeland in the Middle East?* That was undoubtedly what troubled Jacob Schiff, one of the most prominent members of Jewish high society in America, when he stated unequivocally, "As an American, I cannot for a moment concede that one can be at the same time a true American and an honest adherent of the Zionist movement."

It was in this context, with both its invitation and its expectations, that, in June 1916, Louis Dembitz Brandeis became the first Jew ever appointed to the Supreme Court of the United

---

* The viewpoint espoused by Wilson and Coolidge would persist. More than sixty years after Coolidge's comments, Ronald Reagan reflected the same attitudes in his farewell address, delivered in January 1989. America had changed a great deal in that time, but some of its most foundational ideas were very much intact. "I've spoken of the shining city [on a hill] all my political life," Reagan said. "In my mind it was a tall, proud city built on rocks stronger than oceans, windswept, God-blessed, and teeming with people of all kinds living in harmony and peace." He believed that this city was "still a beacon, a magnet for all who must have freedom, for all the pilgrims from all the lost places who are hurtling through the darkness, toward home."

The language, which verges on the poetic, is a tribute to Reagan, the grandeur of whose vision for America has often been ignored (whatever one thought or thinks of his politics). Yet though Reagan certainly intended no warning in that speech, his description of immigrants as pilgrims "hurtling through the darkness, toward home," did not exactly invite American Jews to comfortably speak of another home. In Reagan's language, America was no mere "welcoming land" or "safe harbor." It was "home." If America was home, however, *only* America could be home.

States. He was born in Kentucky in 1856 to secular Jewish parents who had immigrated to America from Bohemia (today in the Czech Republic). In 1914, he assumed the helm of the Federation of American Zionists, which at that time numbered some 12,000 members. Although an unlikely candidate to head the American Zionist movement, by 1919, under his leadership, the organization had grown to 176,000 members, which constituted a fifteenfold increase. Arguably, Brandeis led more than the American Zionist movement. With the European-based World Zionist Organization essentially paralyzed as a result of the outbreak of World War I, Brandeis was able to fill the movement's power vacuum and become to a degree the titular head of the Zionist movement.

Yet Brandeis understood that a Jew—particularly if he was a justice of the U.S. Supreme Court—had to be very careful not to upend the progress that American Jews were finally making in their drive to be fully accepted in American life. What he did, therefore, was to fashion a uniquely American brand of Zionism that sought to make clear that, in making commitments to Zionism, American Jews were in no way distancing themselves from their new American home. It was critical that they be perceived as no less enthusiastic Americans than any of the other millions of immigrants then painstakingly inching their way into American society.

"We should all support the Zionist movement although you or I do not think of settling in Palestine," Brandeis said. He amplified this message: "Let no American imagine that Zionism is inconsistent with patriotism," for "a man is a better citizen of the U.S. for being also a loyal citizen of his state, and of his city; for being loyal to his family . . . every American Jew who aids in advancing the Jewish settlement in Palestine, though he feels neither he nor his descendants will ever live there, will likewise be a better man and a better American for doing so."

This was a Zionism unlike that of Europe, where Zionists were preoccupied with politics and the messiness of helping Jews establish a sovereign national entity far away from home. To European Zionists, desperate to escape a continent that they believed might soon be aflame, Brandeis's characterization of Zionism sounded like obfuscation and was a strange—even useless—distraction from the goal of saving the lives of millions of Jews who might not survive the anti-Semitism in which Europe was mired. When Brandeis said, "To be better Americans we must become better Jews, and to be better Jews we must become better Zionists," he could only have aroused deep suspicion among European Zionists about whether American Zionism had any value whatsoever. No less ominously, Brandeis's sentiment also helped lay the groundwork for the belief among generations of subsequent American Jews that Israel should be just like America.

From the outset, then, the challenges that European Jews and American Jews had to face—and thus the Zionisms they fashioned—could not have been more different. If European Zionists were animated by a sense of foreboding about the future of European Jewry because of a deep-seated anti-Semitism that invariably raised its ugly, murderous head there, American Jews faced almost the opposite problem. They found themselves in an environment that was willing to welcome them as full Americans—but only as long as they stopped "thinking of themselves in groups." They were welcome "in," but only if they were "all in." The tension between that invitation and the thrust of Zionism—which was predicated on Jews' "otherness," vulnerability, and a state of their own—was as fundamental as it could possibly be.

THEN DEVELOPMENTS IN THE British Empire added fuel to the fire. As Brandeis was creating his ethereal Zionist vision, the British government put its weight behind the creation of a Jewish entity in Palestine. In November 1917, Lord Alfred Balfour (who was then foreign secretary but had previously also served as prime minister) issued what would become known as the Balfour Declaration, which stated that:

> His Majesty's government view with favour the establishment in Palestine of a national home for the Jewish people, and will use their best endeavours to facilitate the achievement of this object, it being clearly understood that nothing shall be done which may prejudice the civil and religious rights of existing non-Jewish communities in Palestine, or the rights and political status enjoyed by Jews in any other country.

There was much that the Balfour Declaration did not say. There were no maps appended to Lord Balfour's brief statement, though many Zionists assumed that it referred to the entire area of the Mandate[*]—what is today Israel, the West Bank, Gaza, and Jordan. The Balfour Declaration did not say that His Majesty's government favored the creation of a Jewish state, though to Zionists, a meaningful "national home" simply *had* to be a state.

Despite everything that it did not say, the Balfour Declaration was a significant step forward. A mere twenty years had elapsed since Theodor Herzl gathered a few hundred delegates

---

[*] The "Mandate," as it is commonly called, was the "British Mandate for Palestine," which was in effect from 1923 to 1945. One of several "mandates" created by the League of Nations, the British Mandate for Palestine followed the Ottomans' defeat in World War I and gave Great Britain control over the region.

in Basel to launch the Zionist movement, and now the creation of a "national home for the Jewish people" was already the official policy of the world's most powerful empire. The dream of a Jewish state was gaining significant traction.

While European Zionists celebrated the Balfour Declaration, across the Atlantic many American Jews found it exceedingly problematic. Because many were willing to pay the "price" that Wilson's invitation to America exacted, they found the move toward an actual state disconcerting. In March 1919, almost a year and a half after the Balfour Declaration, almost three hundred Reform rabbis sought to convince President Wilson not to express support for Balfour's sentiments. Going much further than Brandeis's tepid endorsement of a "Jewish settlement in Palestine rather than an actual state," they rejected even Brandeis's formulation. In a letter to the *New York Times*, they wrote, "We raise our voice in warning and protest against the demand of the Zionists for the reorganization of the Jews as a national unit, to whom, now or in the future, territorial sovereignty in Palestine shall be committed. . . . We reject the Zionist project of a 'national home for the Jewish people in Palestine.'" In a sentiment that foreshadowed Rabbi Elmer Berger's comments during the Eichmann kerfuffle, they said, "We protest against the political segregation of the Jews, and the re-establishment in Palestine of a distinctly Jewish state." Others joined the rabbis in signing the letter; they included a Jewish congressman, a Jewish ambassador, a Jewish professor at Columbia University, the founder of the Jewish Publication Society, and Adolph Simon Ochs, publisher of the *New York Times*.

The European Zionists (and their counterparts in the Yishuv) were making too much headway and were far too preoccupied with their own work to engage in a nuanced conversation about the challenges that American Jews faced. But to whatever extent they *did* think about what Brandeis was advocating, they had no patience for his thought experiment. With Europe growing darker, and with no guarantee that a Jewish state would ever come to be, Brandeis's platform seemed to many of the Europeans a pathetic bastardization of what "real" Zionism was on the road to accomplishing. Chaim Weizmann, who had been instrumental in the battle for the Balfour Declaration and who would eventually become the first president of Israel, called Brandeis's religious worldview "Yankee Doodle Judaism."

The battles between the American and European Zionists grew complex and intense. The Europeans conceived of the World Zionist Organization as the deliberative and legislative forum of the Jewish people and as a body that represented the sovereignty-in-potentia of a united Jewish people. American Jews were understandably disconcerted by the idea of a legislative forum of the Jewish people. They were wholly American; no body of Diaspora Jews could represent them.

To lower the flame of the Zionist movement's political work, the Americans favored replacing part of the WZO with a Jewish Advisory Committee that would focus exclusively on building Jewish life in Palestine. The Europeans, of course, were adamantly opposed to ending the political work of the WZO. The Americans wanted to move the offices of major players from London to Palestine, but the Europeans, intent on maintaining their political work on the Continent, were opposed.

This, inevitably, led to disagreements about budget and funding, all of which came to a head when Weizmann went to America to confront Brandeis in June 1921, at which point he declared, "I do not agree with the philosophy of your Zionism. . . .

We are different, absolutely different. There is no bridge between Washington and Pinsk."

Nothing, Weizmann believed, could bridge the gap in attitudes between Pinsk, near where Weizmann had been raised and educated, and Washington, D.C., where Brandeis served on the Court. As far as he was concerned, those two forms of Zionism had virtually nothing in common.

As far as European Zionists were concerned, Diaspora Judaism was part of the problem. Shortly after he attended the First Zionist Congress in 1897, Ahad Ha'am, one of Zionism's most important thinkers, penned his classic essay, "A Jewish State and the Jewish Problem." Diaspora life, he said, put the Jews in an impossible bind. To survive, they needed to take on the appurtenances of Diaspora life and culture; but doing so was destroying the essence of Judaism. A Jewish state, he believed, would solve that problem: "As Judaism has come to recognize that it can no longer bear the burden of the 'baggage of exile,' which the drive for survival had forced upon it once they left its land but without which its very life would be endangered, Judaism now seeks to return to its historic center, where it might live a life of natural development."

As political Zionism grew in strength, its dismissive attitude toward Diaspora Judaism grew even more explicit and antagonistic. In 1926, Hayim Nahman Bialik, by then the widely acknowledged poet laureate of Zionism and one of its chief men of letters, penned an angry condemnation of the rot that he believed was at the core of Diaspora Zionism and of what he saw as the inconsequential Jewish world it was seeking to protect:

It is up to us to choose between extinction and redemption.

The Remnant of Israel, which has been tried in fire and water and which over the generations has withstood, with pride, manifold trials and tribulations without ever surrendering, will not allow itself to be sacrificed. It must recognize its responsibility to save itself from the rot and destruction of life in exile. . . . Every Jew must certainly recognize that even the little that we are thus far doing in the rebuilding of Jerusalem is a thousand-fold more consequential than everything we are building in the Exile. . . . Our brothers who are on the front lines are sacrificing their flesh and blood . . . while those who remain afar are committing a sin against their people for which there can be no expiation. The time has come for us all to recognize this, to muster all our strength to fulfill the weighty obligation which history has bequeathed to our people.*

Astoundingly, even Bialik's fiery tone pales in comparison to that of Ben Zion Dinur, who would eventually serve as one of Israel's early ministers of education. Though Dinur would moderate his tone when he became an official of the government, his views of the Diaspora—shared to some degree by much of Israel's founding establishment—could not have been clearer or more denigrating:

* Zionism's denigration of "exile," or "Diaspora," is implied even in the symbol of the modern State of Israel, the Menorah. There are many different artistic renditions of the Menorah, but Israel's symbol is based on the image of the Menorah found on Rome's first-century Arch of Titus, which celebrates the Roman conquest of Judea. The arch depicts the Jews being forced into exile, and the Menorah being taken with them. That image of the Menorah became synonymous with exile and humiliation. Choosing that symbol was Israel's way of saying that it was reversing what Titus had done, and in re-establishing Jewish sovereignty, was figuratively restoring the stolen Menorah to Jerusalem.

What is the ideological basis of Zionism? First and foremost, it is denigration of the Exile—to understand Exile and to teach our students about the various characteristics of Exile from Egypt through our own time, to make clear the accommodation and inauthenticity at the heart of Exile, its instability and the rises and declines it invariably brings. . . . Zionism is a revolution against Exile, a declaration of war on it. The first requirement for victory is to know the enemy, [which is] Jewish life in Exile.

At the time they were writing, Bialik and Dinur had in mind primarily European Jews, certainly much more than American Jews. Yet by the end of the Second World War, Hitler had wiped out European Jewry, and only one sizable Diaspora Jewish population remained—the Jews of America. Especially as the Jewish state grew after the war, the two Jewish communities of statistical substance were those of Israel and the United States.[*] The seeds that Bialik and Dinur had planted in the Zionist movement—which color the movement to this very day—were critical in setting the tone for a relationship that has been built on enmity from the very outset. The mistrust and resentment that erupted when David Ben-Gurion announced Eichmann's capture was nothing other than the almost inevitable derivative of what had long been a fundamentally unbridgeable divide.

THERE WERE ALSO, OF course, notable moments of passionate American Jewish endorsement of Zionism. At the famed Biltmore

---

[*] Though there were several million Jews in the Soviet Union, they were trapped behind the Iron Curtain and largely cut off from the rest of the Jewish world.

Conference at New York's Waldorf-Astoria Hotel in 1943, Rabbi Abba Hillel Silver, one of the leading lights of the Reform Movement, delivered a historic speech that played a pivotal role in convincing many American Jews to issue a full-throated call for a Jewish state. Other leaders at the conference, including many Zionists, were still tepid in their support, hesitant for all the reasons we have seen to lend their wholehearted support to the cause. But Rabbi Silver, a towering personality and dominant figure not only in Reform Judaism but in American Judaism writ large, would not abide that hesitation. In a fiery and passionate oration, he reminded the participants of the Nazi atrocities unfolding across the ocean. He challenged them to internalize the lessons of what was transpiring in Europe even as they gathered in luxury in New York:

> The reconstitution of the Jewish people as a nation in its homeland is not a playful political conceit of ours. . . . It is the cry of despair of a people driven to the wall, fighting for its very life. . . . From the infested, typhus-ridden ghetto of Warsaw, from the death-block of Nazi-occupied lands where myriads of our people are awaiting execution by the slow or the quick method, from a hundred concentration camps which befoul the map of Europe . . . comes the cry: "Enough, there must be a final end to all this, a sure and certain end!"
>
> How long is it to last? Are we forever to live a homeless people on the world's crumbs of sympathy? . . . Should not all this be compensated for finally and at long last with the re-establishment of a free Jewish Commonwealth? Is not this historic justice, and is this world today not reaching out so desperately and so pathetically for a new world order of justice? . . . Are we not deserving of it?

Silver understood the delegates' instinctive hesitation, born of the Wilsonian dream for America, but he urged them to look beyond it. "Are we going to take counsel here of fear of what this one or that one might say, of how our actions are likely to be misinterpreted," he asked them, "or are we to take counsel of our inner moral convictions, of our faith, of our history, of our achievements, and go forward in faith?"

Nothing that they had heard before had ever moved the delegates that way, and as one historian notes, "Weeping delegates rose to sing *Hatikvah*,[*] over and over again, and then resoundingly moved to endorse the resolution calling for the establishment of a Jewish commonwealth." The Biltmore Conference would be remembered as a significant milestone in Zionist history.

Yet Silver's Zionist passion was but one facet of a much more complicated picture. American Jews remained fundamentally uncomfortable with Jewish sovereignty. The very same year Abba Hillel Silver delivered his oration, Houston's Reform congregation, Beth Israel synagogue, declared that Zionists could not be members of the congregation. Even in 1943, with the Holocaust raging and the argument for the need for a Jewish state more compelling than ever before, the congregation specifically referred to the Pittsburgh Platform's statement that "we consider ourselves no longer a nation, but a religious community," and agreed that an oath of loyalty to America would be required for membership. It further ruled that those supporting Zionism could not be full members of the congregation or hold office. Beth Israel did not begin accepting Zionists as members again until 1967, almost two decades after Israel's creation.

---

[*] "Hatikvah," "The Hope," was first the anthem of the Zionist movement and is now Israel's national anthem.

Though he was once a larger-than-life figure on the American Jewish scene, Abba Hillel Silver has faded from collective American memory and is all but forgotten now, in large measure owing to his passionate Zionist stance. The same is true of the passionately Zionist Biltmore Conference.

THE CREATION OF THE State of Israel did nothing to settle the feud; if anything, it only intensified the vitriol between the two communities. In Israel's early days, Prime Minister David Ben-Gurion had no compunction about going to the United States, urging American Jews to immigrate to Israel, and speaking of Israel (which was then home to barely 5 percent of the world's Jews) as the new center of the Jewish world. But Jacob Blaustein, who as president of the American Jewish Committee (and unlike Proskauer, a declared non-Zionist rather than anti-Zionist) was to some degree the titular head of American Judaism, would have nothing of it.* He made clear to Ben-Gurion that the leadership of the American Jewish community would not abide Israel overstepping its bounds. In a major 1950 position paper, he responded not only to Ben-Gurion but to the school of thought represented by Bialik, Dinur, and many others:

---

* Blaustein's family story is a fascinating one, and a potent reminder of why his generation had such veneration for the United States and such a fear of undermining their position in their newfound home. Blaustein's father, Louis, had come to the United States from Lithuania as a teenager, and he became a horse-and-buggy peddler in eastern Pennsylvania. The family moved to Baltimore in 1888, where Jacob was born and where Louis sold kerosene, again from a horse and buggy. They ultimately established the American Oil Company, which became one of America's largest oil companies. By the 1950s, they employed some twenty-six thousand people.

American Jews—young and old alike—Zionists and non-Zionists alike—are profoundly attached to this, their country. America welcomed our immigrant parents in their need. Under America's free institutions, they and their children have achieved that freedom and sense of security unknown for long centuries of travail. We have truly become Americans, just as have all other oppressed groups that have ever come to these shores.

We repudiate vigorously the suggestion that American Jews are in exile. The future of American Jewry, of our children and our children's children, is entirely linked with the future of America. We have no alternative; and *we want no alternative.*

Since America was not "exile," Blaustein warned Israel, pleas to American Jews to immigrate to the Jewish state were both misplaced and bound to fail. As for Ben-Gurion's claim that Israel was now *the* center of the Jewish world or *the* spokesman for Jews everywhere, Blaustein was equally direct: "there can be no *single* spokesman for world Jewry no matter who that spokesman might try to be."

Most extraordinary was Blaustein's explanation of why the American Jewish Committee had chosen to endorse the partition of British Mandatory Palestine into two states, one Jewish and one Arab, which the United Nations had weighed—and approved—in November 1947. The decision had nothing to do with realizing an ancient biblical dream or giving a home to a renewed Hebrew and Jewish cultural revival, as Zionist leaders such as Ahad Ha'am had hoped for. Rather, Blaustein said, the AJC had supported the 1947 idea of partitioning Palestine into two states, one Jewish and one Arab, for much more utilitarian reasons. "We had cooperated" in the approval of partition, he said, "in the conviction that [a Jewish state] was the only practicable solution for some hundreds of thousands of the surviving Jews of Europe." American Jews, just beginning to make headway in American society, culture, and business, did not want hundreds of thousands of postwar Jewish displaced persons coming to America's shores. Ben-Gurion saw Israel as a rebirth of Jewish peoplehood, but many of American Judaism's leaders were either entirely opposed to the very idea of a Jewish state or saw the state merely as a utilitarian solution to a demographic problem that they did not want to shoulder.*

There could not have been a wider, deeper ideological chasm between the two communities.

Interestingly, even American Jews who would become stalwart supporters of Israel saw their experience in America as a dramatic exception to the millennia of Jewish history and exilic life. Rose Halperin, president of Hadassah, was an unabashed and passionate Zionist. Yet when it came to Jews being at home in America, even Halperin agreed with Blaustein the "non-Zionist." "We do not accept the concept that we are in exile," she said. "Jews are in exile where they live in fear or in torture, or where they cannot leave their countries and emigrate freely to Israel. . . . Jews in the United States are part of the Diaspora where we live in freedom." Whatever American Judaism might be, it was not an Exile.

---

* Ironically, Blaustein's utilitarian take on Israel's purpose also led him to encourage Ben-Gurion *not* to admit certain Jews to the country. He shared the view of the State Department that "the present rate of immigration may economically break the back of Israel and that some kind of slow-up is indicated." Ben-Gurion replied that such a policy would be entirely unacceptable to the Israeli public, and that Israel's very purpose was to provide "a home to the Jews who need or desire to come," regardless of their health, their economic position, or Israel's seeming ability to absorb them.

Along those same lines, Norman Podhoretz, who would become a leading neoconservative thinker and passionate supporter of Israel, wrote after his first visit to Israel in 1951 that if there were any place that he *would* feel in exile, it would actually be in Israel:

> No doubt the Jewish people had been in exile, but not *this* Jew, not me. *My* true homeland was America, and the Jewish homeland was, so far as I was concerned, a foreign country. . . . I was very happy that it had been established as a sovereign state to which persecuted Jews in need of refuge could flee, as millions of them, and at the cost of their lives, had been unable to do only a short while back. But I could not imagine any such thing ever happening to me, or to the Jews of America in general; and if, God forbid, it ever did and I was forced to settle in Israel, I would almost certainly feel that I was *now* in exile.

When Ben-Gurion—who had always assumed that Jews would flock to the new Jewish state en masse—began to understand that even American Jewish Zionists had no intention of moving to Israel, he came to believe that "there was no practical difference between them and the rest of American Jewry." As far as Ben-Gurion was concerned, when American Jews called themselves Zionists, they rendered the term virtually meaningless.

IF ANYTHING WAS GOING to usher in a honeymoon period between the long-squabbling communities, one would have imagined that it would be the IDF's victory in the Six-Day War. That victory followed the *hamtanah* (the "period of waiting"), the harrowing three weeks of dread in which Israelis dug thousands of graves in anticipation of a looming Egyptian massacre of the young Jewish state. Israel preempted the fighting, however, by destroying Egypt's air force while it was still on the ground, essentially guaranteeing the outcome of the conflict before it even began. By the time the fighting ceased less than a week later, Israel had defeated Egypt, Jordan, and Syria and more than tripled its size. From Egypt, Israel took the Sinai Peninsula and the Gaza Strip. Jordan lost the West Bank, East Jerusalem, and the Old City, including the Temple Mount. Syria's Golan Heights was now in Israeli hands. Not only had disaster been avoided, but Israel seemed secure, invulnerable. Its ragtag army of 1948 had proven itself an exceedingly effective military machine. Its nine-mile-wide narrowest point had been substantially widened. The Arab armies were vanquished, and it seemed that for the first time in two millennia, the Jews could finally exhale.

In Israel, what followed was a period of unbridled euphoria. Israelis flocked by the thousands to the Western Wall, the Old City of Jerusalem, Jericho, and the entire West Bank. Thousands of volunteers, Jews as well as non-Jews, came to Israel to see the miraculous state firsthand and contribute to its flourishing. Russian Jews, who had been imprisoned behind Soviet bars for years already, now wanted to become part of the unfolding story that was Israel and began in earnest their drive to be freed and to be allowed to emigrate from the Soviet Union.

Suddenly, something shifted in American Jewish life as American Jews also joined in the relief and the revelry. In a later reflection on the Six-Day War, Podhoretz noted that "thus did Israel now truly become the religion of American Jews." American Jews contributed millions of dollars to the Jewish state; corporate and individual giving reached an all-time high. Those who had no money to give found other ways to express first their worry and then their jubilation. One man arrived at the New York offices of the Jewish Agency with his two sons and said to the agency representative, "I have no money to give but here are my sons. Please send them over immediately." It was a time of unbridled pride, optimism, and euphoria, for Jews in the Jewish state as well as for Jews in the Diaspora.

The honeymoon stage is well recognized. What is much less commonly acknowledged is that even this astonishing development also had its underbelly for the relationship between American Jews and Israel. In the late 1960s, the central story that occupied the minds and souls of young American Jews was not Israel but Vietnam. It was the era of campus protests, of hippies, of Woodstock, and later, of the killings at Kent State. And what young Americans—American Jews very much among them— were protesting was colonialism and America's use of massive firepower against an indigenous people and defenseless civilians.

Yet Israel had destroyed three Arab armies, and some young American Jews could not help but note that it had used massive force and was now occupying land that had previously been part of Egypt, Jordan, and Syria. What made matters even more painful was that while Israel had soundly defeated its enemies, the United States was *losing* the Vietnam War.

Thus, a new question began to emerge: if what Israel was now engaged in was not colonialism, what was? As one writer noted, "American Jews of the New Left, who had cheered Israel's victory in the 1967 war, suddenly realized that Zionism was no longer seen as the national liberation movement of the Jews, rather as a colonial and oppressive anathema."

It was, to some degree, that accusation of colonialism that spelled the end of the easy alliance between African Americans and Jewish Americans. The relationship would sour over decades, and eventually, in 2018, Black Lives Matter, which was ostensibly committed to civil rights in America, would add a rabidly anti-Israel clause to its platform. But the seeds of that break had been planted half a century earlier. In retrospect, despite the euphoria at the time, the overlap of the Vietnam War and the Six-Day War also contributed to the conflicts that would later emerge more clearly.

The Six-Day War, however, was a relatively late complication in what was already a long-fraught relationship between American Jews and Israel. The tensions, we have seen, had much earlier roots. What we explore next is precisely why that was.

THE CAUSES

A PARTICULARIST PROJECT
IN A UNIVERSALIST WORLD

On July 8, 1776, four days after the Second Continental Congress voted in Philadelphia to approve the Declaration of Independence, Philadelphians were summoned to the yard of the Pennsylvania State House (today Independence Hall) by the public ringing of the city bells. There, at noon, Colonel John Nixon read the Declaration publicly for the first time.

"When in the course of human events," he began, proclaiming Jefferson's now immortal opening words. The phrase is so well known that we no longer pay much attention to how extraordinary it is. What is noteworthy about this phrase is not so much what it says as what it does not say. The Declaration did not open by saying, "When in the course of Christian events. . . ." Nor did it employ any other term that might have limited the applicability of its universal message. The point of the Declaration, like that of the American experiment itself, was that America's founders believed that what they were creating was an ideal for all humanity.

America's founders were Christians. Yet while they invoked the "Creator," the "Supreme Judge," and "Divine Providence" in the Declaration, not once did they use the words "Jesus," "Christian," or "Christ." The Declaration is infused with a theistic faith in a higher power, but there is nothing essentially Christian about it. It is, at its core, an invitation to human beings of all creeds and backgrounds. It is one of the earliest indications of the profound universalism that would characterize American life and culture.

One hundred and seventy-two years later, on a Friday afternoon in May 1948, David Ben-Gurion stood in what was then the Tel Aviv Museum of Art (interestingly also now known as Independence Hall). "The land of Israel," Ben-Gurion declared as he read the opening sentence of Israel's Declaration of Independence, "was the birthplace of the Jewish people." Much of the remainder of the Declaration is a recitation of the Jewish people's history, intertwined with references to its eternal longing to return to the Land of Israel.

When Israel's Declaration of Independence refers to God, in a conscious evocation of Jefferson's phrase "faith in Divine Providence," it uses the phrase "faith in the Rock of Israel," as close an approximation as Hebrew allows to Divine Providence. It is worth noting, however, that while Jefferson's "Divine Providence" is a thoroughly universal evocation of God's name, "Rock of Israel" refers to the idioms ubiquitous in Jewish tradition that many Jews would have understood: the Land of Israel, the People of Israel, and even the God of Israel. Thus, even the name of God that the Declaration chose to employ reflects the Jewishness and deep commitment to the Jewish people above all other peoples. That commitment not only suffuses Israel's Declaration of Independence but, more importantly, is the very purpose of the country. Israel would have citizens of many creeds and ethnicities, but there could be no doubt about its raison d'être. It was a state designed to foster the flourishing of the Jewish people.

America's universalism and Israel's particularism are evident everywhere one looks. Consider national symbols. America's symbol is the bald eagle, a creature of grace and strength not associated with any particular people; the symbol that Israel chose was the Menorah, the seven-branched candelabrum that once stood in the ancient Temple in Jerusalem. With minor changes, almost any nation could sing America's national anthem, "The Star-Spangled Banner." What nation does not think of itself as "the land of the free and the home of the brave"? Yet Israel's anthem, "Hatikvah," is distinctly about the Jewish people and their return to their ancestral homeland. "As long as deep in the heart, the soul of a Jew yearns," it begins, and then goes on to speak of two thousand years of Jewish yearning. Then there are the flags. America's flag is made of stars and stripes, elements found on dozens of national flags; Israel's, with a Jewish star flanked by two blue stripes, is specifically designed to be in conversation with the *tallit*, the traditional Jewish prayer shawl.

Unlike America, Zionism has always been highly particularistic; Zionism, after all, was the national liberation movement of the Jewish people. Therefore, when we imagine that Israel ought to be a smaller, newer version of the United States situated in the Middle East—or more colloquially, as a Hebrew-speaking, falafel-eating version of America—we miss the point of both countries entirely.

THIS TENSION BETWEEN UNIVERSALISM and particularism is nothing new—it is as ancient as the Bible itself. It is a critical dimension of a long-standing difference between the ways that Judaism and other segments of Western civilization have seen the world. The Old Testament (or the Hebrew Bible, as Jews refer to it) and the New Testament (or the Christian Bible, in Jewish nomenclature), as we will now see, have very different conceptions of how human beings ought to think about themselves and their lives—about what our world ought to look like. It may seem strange to discuss the Bible in a book on the rift between American Jews and Israel, but it is there that some of the underlying issues first took root. Unless we understand the fundamental difference in worldviews between Judaism and much of Western civilization, we cannot understand the conflict that has unfolded since.

Let's start with the Hebrew Bible. The first chapters of Genesis all raise questions about the most critical questions that shape human life. The story of creation introduces the concepts of "man, heaven, and the created order." The tale of the Garden of Eden explores questions of temptation, sin, responsibility, and sexuality, and the conflict between Cain and Abel grapples with hatred and murder. The flood deals with the inevitable imperfection of humankind.

Situated among these tales is the famous story of the Tower of Babel. What is the message of *that* chapter? The basic story is well known. Worried that they will be dispersed ("lest we be scattered all over the earth"), human beings decide to build a tower, with its top in the heavens, that will somehow bind them all together. Yet their project angers God. So God confounds their languages, making it impossible for them to communicate, thus bringing the tower's construction to a premature end. Then God "scattered them over the face of the whole earth."

This seemingly strange story is actually our first introduction to the Bible's politics. Interestingly, right before the Tower of Babel story, the story of Noah ends with the floodwaters subsiding and Noah's three sons leaving the ark and spreading out. "From these the maritime *nations* branched out . . . by their lands, each with their language, their claims, and their *nations*." Thus, after God unleashes the flood to destroy a sinful world, a new order emerges: nations spread out and live each in their own land, with their own language, their clan, and their way of life.

But as the Tower of Babel story opens, something has gone awry with that new world order. Suddenly, "everyone on earth had the same language." The people do not wish to spread out. They seem to want to ignore, perhaps even erase, the differences between peoples and nations. So God has to upend their plan, and the Tower of Babel story ends with the world restored to what it had been prior—peoples are dispersed, living in their own lands, with languages and cultures distinctly their own.

Now the Bible can introduce Abram (later Abraham), who immediately comes onstage. It is as if the Bible were saying, "Now that we have illustrated the importance of distinct peoples to our worldview, we are ready to track the particular people who will be at the heart of the rest of *this* story—the Jewish people—and their love for their own land."

The Jews never left the Land of Israel voluntarily, but they were exiled twice, first by the Babylonians in 586 BCE and then by the Romans. For centuries after the Romans sacked Jerusalem in 70 CE and exiled its Jewish population, Jews harbored a hope that one day they would be restored to their ancient ancestral land. There, they imagined, they would live among their own clan, conduct their lives with their own traditions, and speak their own language.[*] That hope, in a nutshell, was the essence of Zionism.

Why does it matter today what the Bible's view of nationalism might have been? The answer is not theological, but cultural. Even deeply secular, often antireligious, early Zionists quoted the Hebrew Bible endlessly. To them, the Bible was essentially a diary of their people documenting their loves and losses, their dreams and dreads. It was a window into their people's very soul. David Ben-Gurion kept a Bible on his desk, knew it inside out, and hosted a regular Bible study group, even when he was busy with matters of state. Classic secular Zionist poets like Shaul Tchernichovsky, Rachel the Poetess, Leah Goldberg, and many others wrote in dialogue with the Bible (as do even modern secular Israeli novelists like Amos Oz and David Grossman) because the "Book of Books" was the wellspring of the visions that animated their life's work. To their minds, the Bible explained the revolution on which they were embarking.

That is why no sooner does Israel's Declaration of Independence open by saying that the Land of Israel is the birthplace of the Jewish people, it then continues: "Here they first attained to statehood, created cultural values of national and universal significance and gave to the world the eternal Book of Books." This new state, Ben-Gurion was essentially saying, was going to be a project in the image of the Hebrew Bible's idea for humanity, and

---

[*] They may have harbored that hope, but hardly any Jews acted on it. Rabbi Yehuda Halevi, in his classic twelfth-century work *The Kuzari*, acknowledges that though Jews prayed daily for their return to Zion, liturgical phrases such as "Who restores His Presence to Zion" were "little more than the chirping of a starling, for we do not think about what they mean" (*Kuzari* 2:24).

it would be, to paraphrase but misquote Lincoln's Gettysburg Address, "of the Jews, by the Jews, and for the Jews."

IF ZIONISM'S DEEPLY ROOTED particularism emerged from the Hebrew Bible, American universalism reflected the worldview of the Christian Bible. The politics of the Christian Bible is radically different from that of the Hebrew Bible. In the Christian Bible, the differences between cultures and human beings that so often lie at the core of the nation-state (and of the conflicts in the Hebrew Bible) are explicitly dismissed, nowhere more clearly than in Paul's Letter to the Galatians. "There is neither Jew nor Greek, slave nor free, male nor female," Paul says there, "for you are all one in Christ Jesus."

To be sure, the Jewish tradition has a distinct universal streak as well, and the Catholic Church would often become very political and particularist in its own way; still, the fundamental Jewish tendency toward particularism is at odds with Christianity's instinctive universalism.[*] Zionism—and then Israel once it was established—saw the Jewish people as the central purpose of the project. America, in contrast, is colored by Christian universalism, a sense that what the founders were building was not about Christians or any one people, but about the world at large.

No one people figured centrally in the story that the United States told about itself. Almost a century after America's founding,

---

[*] There was often, of course, a wide gap between theology and reality. Just as Judaism often failed to live up to its biblical messages, Christianity, too, often failed to internalize its universal worldview. The Crusades and the Inquisition were hardly expressions of universalism, and the often-bitter divisions between Protestants and Catholics, which sometimes led to war, were at variance with Paul's message in Galatians.

as Abraham Lincoln headed to his inauguration and prepared to try to preserve the Union, he reminded his listeners of the universal reach of the American project. The Declaration of Independence, he said, "gave liberty, not alone to the people of this country, but, I hope, *to the world*, for all future time." For the majesty of this vision, Lincoln expressly gave credit to Jefferson, the man "who, in the concrete pressure of a struggle for national independence by a single people, had the coolness, forecast, and capacity to introduce into a merely revolutionary document an abstract truth, *applicable to all men and all times*."

America's applicability to "all men at all times" and Israel's commitment to the flourishing of the Jewish people are starkly opposite foundations for two different countries. That is why for many American Jews, to whom America's universalism seems both natural and the indisputable ideal for the basis of a country, there is something deeply problematic and discomfiting about the very purpose of the State of Israel.

ZIONISM WAS A PARTICULARIST project from its very beginnings. In the nineteenth century, as those biblical seeds of a promised Jewish return to Zion began to sprout, Zionism's great thinkers were never abashed about particularism. One of the first people to articulate Zionism's vision was Moses Hess. Hess was a socialist with universalist tendencies, but toward the end of his life he sensed that European socialism would not liberate the Jew the way that many had hoped or expected. It was time, he thought, to give up the charade:

> As long as the Jew denies his nationality, as long as he lacks the character to acknowledge that he belongs to that unfor-

tunate, persecuted, and maligned people, his false position must become ever more intolerable. What purpose does this deception serve? The nations of Europe have always regarded the existence of the Jews in their midst as an anomaly. We shall always remain strangers among the nations.

The Jews deceive themselves, he said, if they imagine that Europe will welcome them into a large, universal human family. It was time for the Jews to unabashedly embrace their own particular story, their destiny—and their hope for a country.

Hess was a man before his time. When he penned those words in 1862, the Jewish world was not yet ready to hear him; for decades, his idea languished, largely ignored. Theodor Herzl, who later in his life admitted that he had essentially just given new life to an idea that had been proposed before him, had much better luck: his pamphlet *The Jewish State* took the Jewish world by storm when it was first published in February 1896. It was printed, translated, and read more quickly and more widely than any other Jewish work of the modern era. In 1896 alone, it was published in seven languages, beyond the German original: English, Hebrew, Yiddish, Romanian, Bulgarian, Russian, and French.

Students, in particular, were enthused by his proposal; almost overnight, the appearance of *The Jewish State* transformed Herzl from a lone voice into the leader of an international movement. And key to that international movement, which would eventually create the State of Israel, was an explicit rejection of Jefferson's and Lincoln's universalism:

It might further be said that we ought not to create new distinctions between people; we ought not to raise fresh barriers, we should rather make the old disappear. But men who think this way are amiable visionaries; and the idea of a native land will still flourish when the dust of their bones will have vanished tracelessly in the winds. *Universal brotherhood is not even a beautiful dream.*

Max Nordau, a leading European intellectual who ultimately became a leading Zionist thinker, also understood that Zionism was essentially about Jewish peoplehood. "Whoever . . . believes that the Jews are not a nation can indeed not be a Zionist," he wrote, while "he who is convinced to the contrary that the Jews are a people must necessarily become a Zionist." Nordau saw no intermediate possibilities. One was either in or out.

Zionism's early ideologues minced no words. They were relentlessly opposed to the universalism then in vogue in Europe, both because it was not living up to the promises it had made to the Jews and because there was something about it that seemed to them inexorably at odds with the finest of the human condition. George Eliot (Mary Anne Evans's pen name), in her classic novel *Daniel Deronda*, makes the case for Zionism as a road to human flourishing more eloquently than anyone before or after her:

> A human life, I think, should be well rooted in some spot of a native land, where it may get the love of tender kinship for the face of earth, for the labours men go forth to, for the sounds and accents that haunt it, for whatever will give that early home a familiar unmistakable difference amidst the future widening of knowledge: a spot where the definiteness of early memories may be inwrought with affection.

Home could not be just anywhere; it had to be in "some spot of a native land." Only there could human beings live with a sense of "familiar unmistakable difference," and only there would their "early memories . . . inwrought with affection" shape their lives.

"Some spot of a native land" was exactly what the early Zionists sought, and precisely what many Israelis find so moving about life in the Jewish state. Yet that is also what makes Zionism and embrace of Israel so complicated for many Jews today. For America's grandeur, the source of such pride for many American Jews, is predicated on precisely opposite instincts.

THE ROOTS OF AMERICA'S universalism run just as deep. America's signature commitment has long been a beckoning to and acceptance of whoever came to her shores. "Give me your tired, your poor, your huddled masses yearning to breathe free, the wretched refuse of your teeming shore," wrote Emma Lazarus in "The New Colossus." Today her poem sits cast in bronze at the foot of the Statue of Liberty, America's famous beacon of welcome to immigrants from across the earth. "Send these, the homeless, tempest-tost to me, I lift my lamp beside the golden door!" Though Jewish, and later in her tragically short life ever more committed to Jewish causes, Lazarus captured America's imagination with her poem precisely because it did not speak about Jews or Christians, Irish or Germans, or any other group. America's greatness, for many, has been its consciously Galatians-like blindness to those distinctions.

Or consider the Liberty Bell, yet another iconic American symbol. Like the Statue of Liberty, the Liberty Bell is adorned with words of Jewish origin, not from a contemporary Jewish poet but from one of the more universal verses in the Hebrew Bible: "Proclaim liberty throughout all the land to all its inhabitants."

That openness, that rejection of the idea that America would be distinctly Christian, was what made America unique. It was what allowed a nation of immigrants to become the kindest, most welcoming haven the Jews had ever known outside their own land. George Washington had gone out of his way to assure the young republic's Jews that "it is now no more that toleration is spoken of as if it were by the indulgence of one class of people that another enjoyed the exercise of their inherent natural rights." The Jews were in America by right, not because anyone had done them a favor. Taking a page from the biblical prophet Micah, Washington wished that "the children of the stock of Abraham who dwell in this land continue to merit and enjoy the good will of the other inhabitants, while everyone shall sit in safety under his own vine and fig tree and there shall be none to make him afraid." The government of the United States, he said memorably, would "give to bigotry no sanction, to persecution no assistance."

Europe, in contrast, had been and remained obsessed with the *Judenfrage*, or "the Jewish question." Everywhere one turned, it was the Jews with whom Europe was consumed. Karl Marx, born Jewish though he later converted to Lutheranism, wrote an essay titled "Zur Judenfrage" ("On the Jewish Question"). Thomas Mann wrote an essay with almost the same title, "Zur jüdischen Frage." Even Theodor Herzl gave his famed book, *The Jewish State*, a subtitle that read "Modernen Lösung der Judenfrage" ("A Modern Solution to the Jewish Question"). Perhaps most ironically and painfully, the actual German name that the Nazis gave to their plan to eradicate world Jewry was "Endlösung der Judenfrage" ("The Final Solution to the Jewish Question"). In Europe, west or east, democratic or despotic, there was no escaping "the Jewish question." For both Jews and their enemies, the Jewish question was nothing less than an obsession.

Yet "the Jewish question" never came to America. To be sure, America was at times beset by anti-Semitism, but never was the Jewish question a central American obsession. Whatever issue America had with its many minorities, it was rarely preoccupied specifically with the Jews. Its universalism afforded the Jews a welcome never extended to them before, a siren so inviting that for many, embracing what America had to offer was not even a decision—it was the most basic of instincts. American Jews came to see America as the best model of what a liberal Western democracy could be.

America and Israel are fundamentally different enterprises, but that essential fact is hardly ever raised in discussions between and about the two communities. And that failure to surface this core difference obfuscates the real issues that the two communities need to address, thus adding to the toxicity of the discourse between them. American Jews cannot fully understand the desperation for statehood that had European Jews in its grip. And Israelis have never fully appreciated that it was America's unprecedented invitation that led American Jews to reshape Judaism and to tailor Zionism to meet their unique needs.

Fully cognizant of what had made America so hospitable to them, American Jews sought to preserve those values for others. Welcoming the stranger, dignity for all human beings, equality under the law, and respect for dissent and ethnic difference became religious principles for American Jews. That was what attracted so many American Jews to the liberal politics of the Democratic Party and the cutting-edge social issues of their day. Irving Howe, the astute twentieth-century observer of American Judaism and author of the classic *World of Our Fathers*, had this to say about Jewish socialist radicals: "Rebelling against the parochialism of traditional Jewish life, the [American] Jewish radicals improvised a parochialism of their own—but with this difference: they called it 'universalism.'"

Howe was right. For many young American Jews, universalism became the new Judaism. That was true, however, not only of Jewish socialist radicals but to greater or lesser degree of the vast majority of American Jews in the early to mid-twentieth century (and perhaps even beyond).

Now we can understand better the motivations of those Reform rabbis in Pittsburgh who declared that Jews were no longer a nation but a religious community, and who neither expected nor sought a return to Palestine. In large measure, their work was fueled by a passionate embrace of modernity and the theological constraints it shattered; yet they also understood that their revised religious platform would fit well into their new American setting. Their radical rewriting of Judaism would also enable them to take advantage of America's unprecedented welcome.

In light of that, American Jews' reluctance to passionately embrace Zionism now makes much more sense. Herzl, as we saw, was put out with them. But his exasperation, as is often true of Israeli exasperation with American Jews today, stemmed not only from his blinding devotion to his own cause but also, and perhaps no less important, to his being an outsider to America and thus his inability to fully appreciate the radically different challenges faced by American Jews and the unprecedented opportunities they did not wish to squander.

For American-Jews-as-liberals, a nation-state for a particular people, or a certain religion, is a problematic idea. Their discomfort with Israel stems in part from the fact that the idea of a country specifically for the Jews is fundamentally at odds with their universal vision for humanity. Nordau himself understood that a century ago. He had no patience for what he called "the social work Zionism of the Americans helping their poor European cousins." Nordau correctly assessed their discomfort with Zionism but, like many Zionists who followed, was hardly magnanimous in seeking to understand the source of that discomfort.

Even Albert Einstein, once he was living in the United States, made it clear that he opposed the creation of a Jewish state; he believed that Judaism had "transcended" nationalism. Einstein, as close as one could get to Jewish royalty in America, told celebrants at a Passover Seder before World War II, "My awareness of the essential nature of Judaism resists the idea of a Jewish state with borders, an army, and a measure of temporal power." History had changed the Jew, he felt. "I am afraid of the inner damage Judaism will sustain—especially from the development of a narrow nationalism within our ranks. We are no longer the Jews of the Maccabee period."

Since the era of the Maccabees, who had fought in the first and second centuries BCE to end Greek rule and influence in the Land of Israel, Judaism had been "liberated" from the need for a sovereign state. Judaism should no longer be defined by what Einstein called a "narrow nationalism." Interestingly, even Israel's creation changed his view only marginally. "I have never considered the idea of a state a good one, for economic, political and military reasons," he told a friend shortly after David Ben-Gurion declared the state. "But now, there is no going back, and one has to fight it out." It was hardly an inspiring endorsement.

CLASSIC ZIONISTS COULD NOT have disagreed with Einstein more strongly. Many, like Ze'ev Jabotinsky, saw themselves as deeply committed liberals in the tradition of John Locke or Jean-Jacques Rousseau, with no contradiction between their commitment to Western values of democracy and liberalism and their belief in the importance of a Jewish state. These thinkers, like many Israelis today, would be quick to point out that coupling a proud particularism with a universal liberalism is characteristic not only of Zionism but of many other nationalisms as well.

Winston Churchill is a perfect example. Precisely two months to the day before Jabotinsky died in August 1940, Prime Minister Churchill delivered an address to the House of Commons. It has become a classic. Churchill, largely credited with helping to save Western civilization from the Nazis, was unabashed in his love, first and foremost, for the island he called home. He concluded his lengthy remarks to Parliament with these immortal words:

> I have, myself, full confidence that if all do their duty, if nothing is neglected, and if the best arrangements are made, as they are being made, *we shall prove ourselves once again able to defend our Island home,* to ride out the storm of war, and to outlive the menace of tyranny, if necessary for years, if necessary alone.
>
> Even though large tracts of Europe and many old and famous States have fallen or may fall into the grip of the Gestapo and all the odious apparatus of Nazi rule, we shall not flag or fail. We shall go on to the end, we shall fight in France, we shall fight on the seas and oceans, we shall fight with growing confidence and growing strength in the air, *we shall defend our Island,* whatever the cost may be, we shall fight on the beaches, we shall fight on the landing grounds, we shall

fight in the fields and in the streets, we shall fight in the hills; we shall never surrender.

There was, for Churchill, nothing contradictory about fighting to defend freedom for all humanity *and* declaring his eternal allegiance to "our Island." Love of nation did not have to come at the expense of love of the West, just as love of one's family need not come at the expense of devotion to one's society or to humanity at large. Zionists agreed.

THIS DEBATE OVER WHETHER the nation-state (and therefore Zionism, too) is a good idea or a loathsome, dangerous one has been at the heart of critical Jewish conversations for decades. Therefore, it is interesting to note how that disagreement played out in the extensive correspondence between Gershom Scholem and Hannah Arendt, who may no longer be familiar to most Jews but who were the towering intellectual titans of Jewish life in their day. Their intellectual sparring once captivated Jewish intellectual circles and many Jews beyond. Given that much of their vituperative exchange unfolded just as Israel was approaching independence, their passionate disagreements are a powerful window into the history that still colors Judaism's deep divide over Israel.

Scholem, born in Germany in 1897 (the same year as the First Zionist Congress), established himself early as an academic star and later became the world's leading scholar of Jewish mysticism. Under the influence of leading Zionist thinkers, he moved to Palestine in 1923, where he lived until his death in 1982. Soon after his arrival in Palestine, Scholem joined the faculty of Hebrew

University and became part of a movement known as Brit Sha-lom (the Covenant of Peace), a political movement spearheaded largely by Hebrew University faculty members. Brit Shalom worked actively toward Jewish-Arab understanding and, in defiance of mainstream Zionism, advocated not a Jewish state but a binational state to be shared by Jews and Arabs alike.

Hannah Arendt was also born in Germany, in 1906 (nine years after Scholem). She fled the Nazis through a series of European countries, eventually moving to America in 1950, where she lived until she died in 1975. Scholem and Arendt had an extensive correspondence (128 letters) that continued until Scholem responded with outrage to Arendt's book *Eichmann in Jerusalem* (first published in 1963), in which Arendt argued that Eichmann was a cog in a larger machine, not the embodiment of evil. She was also critical of Israel's conduct of the Eichmann trial and even of how some Jewish leaders had acted during the Holocaust. Scholem, incidentally, was hardly the only Jewish leader to express outrage: Arendt became persona non grata in many parts of the Jewish world.

Shortly after the end of World War II, their conversation turned to the question of the Jews' quest to create a state; their vehement disagreement captured the essence of the ideological debate between American and European Zionists, and later, American Jews and Israelis. Even Scholem, whose membership in Brit Shalom placed him on the far left of Palestinian Zionism, found Arendt's dismissive attitude toward Zionism deeply offensive. In a January 1946 letter, he suggested that part of their disagreement about Zionism stemmed from his ready embrace of the idea of a Jewish people. "I am a sectarian and have never been ashamed of expressing in print my conviction that sectarianism can offer us something decisive and positive," he wrote, rejecting in no uncertain terms the universalism so popular in parts of the West. Unlike many Zionists, however, Scholem was hardly infatuated with the idea of the state per se; he cared about the Jewish people, not about a Jewish state. "I couldn't care less about the problem of the state," he continued, "because I do not believe that the renewal of the Jewish people depends on the question of their political or even social structure. If anything, my own political credo is anarchistic."

Scholem, however, hurried to explain his objection to the universalism with which Arendt seemed infatuated (and which would later color much of the worldview of American Jews). He had come to believe, he said, that the Jewish embrace of universalism was naive, even dangerous. He admitted that it had once drawn him, too, but the harsh lessons of Jewish history, he said, had pushed him back into the particularist camp. Jews, he said, adopt universalist, anti-peoplehood positions with an enthusiasm matched by no other people, while ignoring the fact that the rest of the world does not allow them to erase their ethnic differences and will always pursue them, simply because they are Jews.

> I cannot blame the Jews if they ignore so-called progressive theories which no one else in the world has ever practiced. Even though I have a clear notion of the vast differences between partition and a binational state, I would vote with the same heavy heart for either of these two solutions. You make fun of both with truly breathtaking ignorance. The Arabs have never accepted a single solution that includes immigration, whether it be federal, national or binational. . . . I regret to say so, but Zionist politicians are not being complete idiots when they declare that, given the sabotage efforts made by the British administration, there is no chance of reaching

any kind of understanding, however formulated. Certainly, as an old Brit Shalom follower, I myself have once belonged to the opposite camp. But I am not presumptuous enough to think that the politics of Brit Shalom wouldn't have found precisely the same Arab enemies, enemies who are mainly interested not in our morality or political convictions, but in whether or not we are here in Palestine at all.

He may not have cared that much about or for the state, Scholem told Arendt, but history and realism had essentially forced him into an endorsement of Jewish statehood. Even those Jews who had advocated Jewish-Arab cooperation were being rebuffed; Arabs simply did not want Jews in Palestine. If the Jewish people were to survive, they needed to return to their ancestral homeland. And if they were to survive in Palestine, they would need a state to protect them.

It was precisely on that point that Arendt disagreed with Scholem, long before she became a pariah to much of the Jewish world. They disagreed not only about statehood; they disagreed about the value of the survival of "the Jews as a nation" no less. "I can't prevent you from being a nationalist," she answered him, "though I find it hard to understand why you are so proud of the fact. I am also not of the opinion that nationalism is dead. Quite the contrary. What is dead is the nation."

Many years after Arendt wrote her letter to Scholem, Barbara Tuchman, a Pulitzer Prize–winning American essayist, author, and historian, noted that of all the peoples of the world who had existed three thousand years earlier, it was only the Jews who—as a result of the re-creation of a Jewish state—lived in the same place, spoke the same language, and practiced the same religion. If that fact filled Tuchman with admiration, however, nothing about it moved Arendt. The nation-state should be dead, she argued, because peoples did not matter very much anymore. "This principle should be clear to any historian who knows that the nation depends on its sovereignty and on the identity between state, people and territory. That the nation isn't eternal should come to no surprise to anyone."

THE SCHOLEM-ARENDT DEBATE IS an important reminder, given how controversial a Jewish nation-state has become in some American Jewish circles, that even great Jewish intellects who were not infatuated with the idea of a state felt compelled by the realities of history to endorse it. There was a brief period not all that long ago when people like Scholem, the advocate of Hebrew culture, the towering Zionist intellect Ahad Ha'am, the historian Ernst Simon, and others were all deeply committed to the revitalization of the Jewish people, but felt that that could be accomplished without the mechanics of a state. History, however, would prove them all wrong. With time, the Zionist binationalism that Brit Shalom endorsed became, as one observer has called it, "the road not taken."

How many of the people who wish that Zionism was less adamantly state-centered today know that there were Zionist leaders deeply committed to the idea of a binational state even before Israel was created? If they know about Brit Shalom and other groups like them, have they asked themselves why the idea failed and why even many of its members and sympathizers— who included Scholem, Ahad Ha'am, and Judah Magnes (the first chancellor of Hebrew University and later its president)— concluded that it could never work? Many young American Jews, imbued with the idealism that has long been one of America's great qualities, have evinced no interest in what history's painful lessons taught those idealistic Zionist founders.

SCHOLEM AND ARENDT ARE long gone, but their disagreement drags on between American Jews, in the tensions between Israel and American Jewry and in the tensions between western European nations and the Jewish state. In fact, Mark Lilla of Columbia University has argued that today's post-national Europe objects to Israel not (only) because of Israel's policies, but because the Jewish state is the nation-state of one particular people:

> It is not the idea of tolerance that is in crisis in Europe today, it is the idea of the nation-state, and the related concepts of sovereignty and the use of force. . . . Many Western European intellectuals, including those whose toleration and even affection for Jews cannot be questioned, find all this [the founding of the State of Israel] incomprehensible. The reason is not anti-Semitism nor even anti-Zionism in the usual sense. It is that Israel is, and is proud to be, a nation-state—the nation-state of the Jews. And that is profoundly embarrassing to post-national Europe.

American Jews share that embarrassment.

Lilla does not in any way dismiss the concerns of many young American Jews about the nation-state. In fact, he readily acknowledges that commitment to the nation-state has also led to many ills, but he virtually channels Scholem when he insists that open-eyed Jews have no choice but to endorse it: *"The legitimacy of the nation-state should not be confused with the idolatry of the nation-state."* But for many in western Europe today, learning the grim lesson of modern history has also brought with it a forgetting of all the long-standing problems that the nation-state, as a modern form of political life, managed to solve. The Zionist tradition knows what those problems were. It remembers what it was to be stateless, as well as the indignities of tribalism and imperialism. It appreciates the wisdom of borders and the need for collective autonomy to establish self-respect and to demand respect from others. It recognizes that there is a cost, a moral cost, to defending a nation-state and exercising sovereignty, but it also believes that the cost is worth paying, given the alternatives.

Lilla's take on Europe's issue with Israel is actually surprisingly simple. "Frustration with the very existence of Israel and the way it handles its challenges has a more proximate cause in European intellectual life. That cause is the crisis in the European idea of a nation-state."

Israel finds itself in an unenviable predicament, for what Lilla wrote about Europe could just as well have been said about American Jews. The problem between many American Jews and Israel is not only, as we said earlier, what Israel *does*, but no less importantly, what Israel *is*.

THERE IS MUCH MORE at stake here than American Zionism. This long-simmering clash between contemporary universalism and the particularism that lies at the heart of Zionism will shape not only American Jews' relationship with Israel but the very future of American Judaism itself. For what some American Jews are beginning to debate, using Israel as a departure point, is whether the survival of Judaism matters at all.

In May 2018, the Jewish author Michael Chabon addressed the graduating class of Hebrew Union College (the academic center of Reform Judaism). Chabon, a best-selling author and winner of the Pulitzer Prize for fiction, had established himself as a left-leaning voice in the American Jewish community.

When Chabon railed against Israel and the occupation, that was to be expected.* That he believed the Jewish community ought to embrace intermarried couples was also hardly surprising. His suggestion that Jews should actually *try* not to marry other Jews ("an endogamous marriage is a ghetto of two," he said) was a bit edgier. What was most stunning about his speech, however, was his claim—reminiscent of Hannah Arendt's letter almost half a century earlier—that Jewish survival was not an ultimate value:

> What would happen to Judaism if all, or even most, of the world's Jews married out of Judaism? Judaism might disappear from the face of the Earth, forever! I don't believe that's ever going to happen, but let's say that it does. On the day that the last Jewish couple dies, after watching their children marry Hindus, Lutherans, atheists, Sunnis, Buddhists—the fault for that extinction will lie squarely with Judaism itself, and not because Judaism failed to enforce its teachings against intermarriage but because it was necessary ever to have such teachings in the first place. . . . If Judaism should ever pass from the world, it won't be the first time in history—far from it—that a great and ancient religion

---

* It is worth noting that if arguments about particularism, human flourishing, and the nation-state are true for the Jews, then they are true, period. And that means that the same justification could be used for the idea of a Palestinian state. Progress toward a Palestinian state has been stymied for an array of reasons far beyond the purview of this discussion. Committed Zionists, however, and particularly those on the right, ought to acknowledge that many of the arguments that they use to justify a Jewish nation-state can be applied to Israel's neighbors as well.

lost its hold on the moral imaginations of its adherents and its relevance to their lives. Nor will it be the first time that an ethnic minority has been absorbed, one exogamous marriage at a time, into the surrounding population. We will grieve that loss, you and I, if we're still around to witness it. But we probably won't be, and anyway the history of the Jews, like the history of humanity and every individual human who has ever lived, is just one long story of grief, loss and fading away.

David Biale, a highly regarded Jewish historian at the University of California, Davis, said something very similar shortly after the Chabon brouhaha.

Intermarriage also has virtues in its own right. True, the number of once-Jewish partners and their children who no longer identify as Jews almost certainly exceeds the number of those non-Jewish partners and their children who take on a Jewish identity. On the other hand, there is something to be said for the transformation of the Jewish "gene pool" into something more diverse than its Ashkenazi roots. Furthermore, the high rate of intermarriage means that Jews are increasingly part of Gentile families in a way that promotes integration. (That the Clinton and Trump families each have proudly identified Jewish members is something inconceivable to an earlier generation.)

It was through this lens that one could see the enormous differences between communities founded around particularism and those committed to universalism. In Israel, Haredi members of Knesset could bemoan American Jewish assimilation and call it a "Silent Holocaust," while in America, some highly articulate

American Jewish voices (Chabon chief among them, but he was hardly alone) were arguing that Jewish survival did not matter. To be sure, Israel's Haredi community is (for the most part) an extreme example of religious and cultural parochialism, while Chabon's is a radical example of the intellectual ends to which universalism can lead.

Yet views like those of Chabon, which conversations about Israel elicit, will have implications far beyond the rift between American Jews and Israel. A community no longer certain that its survival matters cannot endure. The conversation that is ostensibly about Israel, therefore, may well be a harbinger of something much deeper and darker.

AS THE ISRAELI-ARAB CONFLICT drags on, it becomes increasingly possible that it may not be resolvable. How Israelis and American Jews think about that possible eventuality speaks volumes about not only their views of Israel, but of the importance of Jewish survival, no less.

Israelis, obviously, find the notion that the conflict may not be solvable distressing. They dream of a world in which their children, or their grandchildren, will not have to go to war, but at the same time, with any progress on a peace settlement increasingly distant, it is their sense of purpose that leads the vast majority to stay in Israel and to soldier on. Though peace is nowhere in sight, Israelis rank among the happiest populations on earth. Israel was rated the eleventh happiest country by the World Economic Forum in 2018, while the United States was eighteenth. Israelis are overwhelmingly comfortable with a Law of Return that guarantees Jews, but no one else, an automatic right to citizenship. Infused with a deep sense of purpose, Israeli Jews have more children than almost any other first-world country. And that is not only because of the ultra-Orthodox community. In fact, "since the beginning of the twenty-first century, fertility has actually *declined* by about 10 percent among Haredim, risen slightly (5 percent) among religiously observant women, and risen significantly, by 15–20 percent, among all other sectors of Israeli Jewish society."

More than anything, perhaps, Israelis still believe deeply in peoplehood, and like Scholem and Lilla, they and their society have learned lessons of Jewish history. They largely want peace (though with time, the percentage of those willing to make significant compromise for it is eroding), but the lack of that peace does not fundamentally upend their commitment to Zionism and to Israel.

Across the Atlantic, however, some American Jews, despairing of ever achieving a "two-state solution," are willing to give up on the project. Here's Michael Chabon again, making the claim that a state does not really matter: "I want [my children] to marry into the tribe that sees nations and borders as antiquated canards and ethnicity as a construct prone, like all constructs, to endless reconfiguration." A relatively recent poll of American Jews similarly noted that, of "1,008 American respondents, 71% said that if a two-state solution fails, they favor a bi-national democratic state over a Jewish state which deprives Palestinians of citizenship."

Or consider the following comment by Daniel Levy, one of the founders of J Street, a once marginal and now increasingly mainstream (though left-leaning) American Jewish organization that defines itself as the "political home and voice for pro-Israel, pro-peace Americans." Discussing American foreign policy in the Middle East and contemplating the possibility that there may be no resolution to the conflict there, Levy said, "Look, bottom line: If we're all wrong, if we're all wrong and a collective Jewish presence in the Middle East can only survive by the sword . . . then Israel really ain't a very good idea."[*]

If forced to choose between peace and a Jewish state, perhaps between peace and Jewish survival, Levy said that he would choose peace and give up on the state. Israelis, obviously, would make—indeed, they *have* made—precisely the opposite choice.

It is in light of the universalism-particularism divide and some American Jewish voices questioning whether Israel is a good idea that we can perhaps now understand better why the young progressives at the core of If Not Now refuse to endorse Jewish statehood. To Israelis, that refusal sounds treasonous. But for members of If Not Now, consciously or not, refusal to endorse Jewish statehood is in many ways a natural outgrowth of the universalism that has defined America since Thomas Jefferson, since Abraham Lincoln, ever since America began welcoming to its shores millions of "homeless, tempest-tost" souls desperately seeking a home.

FOR AS LONG AS the Hebrew and Christian Bibles have defined Western civilization, humanity has been engaged in a debate over whether life is better lived through devotion to a particular people, ethnicity, or even clan or, alternatively, to humanity at

---

[*] Levy suggests that Israel is currently living "by the sword," but that assertion is by no means obvious. Israel is, without question, embroiled in a long-standing and painful conflict, but in most years the low-level conflict claims many fewer victims than many other conflicts. The tensions are constant, but death, though tragic when it happens, is much less common, thankfully, than Levy's "living by the sword" image suggests.

large. Both, of course, are worthy commitments, and the Jewish tradition rejects neither. That said, Zionism chose to focus on the former, while American society is dedicated to the latter. *That* is the root of the rift between American Jews and Israel, and it is from there that any future mutual understanding will have to begin.

But that fundamental disagreement is hardly the only cause of the rift between the two communities. Also contributing to it are their radically different takes on whether, and how, Jews ought to become actors in history.

IDEALIZED ZION MEETS THE
MESSINESS OF HISTORY

They are simple black-and-white photos, usually of a Bar Mitzvah or wedding reception, but they stop me in my tracks. Every time.

The person who gives me the photograph is visibly excited, for it's a picture of their own Bar Mitzvah or wedding, or maybe that of their parents. The rabbi at the occasion was my grandfather, who in his day was a leading American rabbinic figure, and now they want me to have the picture. I thank them, of course, and later look at the picture more carefully. Usually, there is the smiling young man or newly married couple, a beautifully adorned social hall, and in some cases people elegantly dressed or fancy food. And then I turn the photo over. More times than I can count, a handwritten caption on the back has read: "Wedding of—, June 1944." Or "Bar Mitzvah of—, May 1943."

Across the Atlantic, at the very moments that those photographs were taken, European Jewry was being exterminated.

In Auschwitz alone (and there were many other extermination camps), some ten thousand people were being gassed and incinerated each day. In August 1944, Auschwitz's killing capacity reached its peak and some twenty-four thousand people were murdered in a single day. And in New York, Jews were having catered affairs?

I have heard similar stories from the children and grandchildren of other rabbis of that period. Now our grandparents are gone. It is too late to ask them what they knew, and how they and their communities pressed on as usual when the Jewish people were being erased.

The horrifying difference between the placid lives depicted in these photographs and what was transpiring in Europe at the very same moment is a stark reminder of how differently history has played out for Jews in the United States and elsewhere. Though many American Jews were understandably anguished during the Holocaust because they had family caught in the fires of Europe, those who had come to America were physically safe. America had granted its Jews a "time-out" from history.

SHOULD JEWS IN MODERNITY return to history or escape it? That is another of the fundamental questions at the heart of the American Jewish–Israel divide. No one captured the sensibilities of many American Jews more pithily than Saul Bellow, one of the all-time giants of American Jewish literature. His novel *Humboldt's Gift*, for which he won the 1976 Pulitzer and Nobel Prizes, tells the story of Von Humboldt Fleisher, the son of a Jewish-Hungarian immigrant father. Humboldt is thrilled to be American and feels very distant from his former European existence. While many things appealed to him about America, its placidity was chief among them. "History," he said, "was a nightmare during which he was trying to get a good night's rest."

Many Jewish immigrants to America came, essentially, to flee a nightmare, to get that good night's sleep. The United States afforded European Jews a safe and placid harbor of which they had once thought they could only wistfully dream. To be sure, thousands of American Jews fought valiantly in World War II. That horrific war, though, was about saving the West; Jews understood that if the West were to lose, human life as they knew it would cease to exist. In less exceptional times, though, America has offered Jews from across the world, many of them from war-torn regions, a respite from a war-ridden history. The thousands of Iranian Jews who fled their native land after the fall of the Shah during the 1979 Islamic Revolution wanted "quiet," a way out of a region in which quiet seemed unattainable. The 750,000 (some say up to 1 million) Israelis who now call America home have chosen to make their lives in a country that has no military draft and where houses are built without bomb shelters. For Jews, America has indeed been a place to escape the nightmare of history, a place to get a good night's rest.

Zionism, to the contrary, had no interest in Jews escaping history. The Jews who made their way to Palestine, who pledged to drain the swamps and build the infrastructure of a still nonexistent country in a hostile region, had no illusions that they were going to get a good night's rest. Their goal was precisely the opposite. What Zionism sought was a Jewish return to history.

Gershom Scholem also reflected on the Jews reentering the messiness of history:

In my view, Zionism is a movement devoid of messianism. . . . Zionism is about the Jewish people's entering history.

The Zionist project is not meant to solve the Jewish question on a metaphysical or metahistorical plane—where there is no solution to the Jewish problem. Rather, Zionism was meant to renew Jewish life inside the realm of history, to take responsibility for what we do and do not do, what we build and what we destroy.

Many Israeli writers have echoed that sentiment. A. B. Yehoshua, one of Israel's greatest novelists and essayists, writes: "We have returned to history . . . and have created a wholly Jewish reality, with defined, sovereign borders. . . . In this reality, everything is Jewish. The territory, the language, the army and the police, the way of life—and most importantly, sovereignty and responsibility."

To live in a Jewish state, Yehoshua argues, is to consciously embrace the complexities and messiness of life in history. Life in a Jewish state, he says, means engaging with questions about "unemployment compensation, conditions in prisons, policy on wages and economic distribution, attitudes to minorities and foreign workers, questions of the legitimacy of the use of torture by security forces to obtain critical information, questions of the morality of war and government policies." That is why the Jews needed a state. A Jewish state would "describe, respond, judge and if possible, direct" the complex, messy, and sometimes morally ambiguous issues that make up human life.

Yehoshua also understands how radically different American Judaism is. On a different occasion, he told young American Jews visiting Israel, "Israelis are the total Jews," mincing no words about which he thought was preferable. "Our values are Jewish values, because we live here. It's not what the rabbis say that defines Jewishness, but what we Israelis do every day—our actions and our values." And then the coup de grâce, which more than made up in clarity whatever it lacked in political correctness: "This is the reason I say to American Jews: you are partial and we are total. . . . If you really want to be Jewish, come here. It's not easy, [it's] full of questions, [and] your nice warm Jewish identity in your community will be over. But this is real and not imaginary."

THAT TENSION BETWEEN "REAL" and "imaginary" haunts the relationship between American Jews and Israel. For many years, American Jews had imagined Jewish life in Palestine as idyllic. As Brandeis University professor Jonathan Sarna, today's preeminent historian of American Judaism, notes, "the Zion that [American Jews] imagined in their minds, dreamed about, and wrote about—was for centuries a mythical Zion, a Zion that reveals more about American Jewish ideals than about the realities of [the land of] Israel." Zion was, in the minds of American Jews, a "projection of America as it ought to be."

In the late eighteenth and early nineteenth centuries, for example, American Jews thought of Zion as a place where desperately poor, scrupulously pious Jews lived lives of study and prayer. Zion was, as they imagined it, "a land . . . where the material life, values and practices of Jews were precisely the reverse of American Jews' own." An 1838 letter seeking American Jewish financial support for Palestine's Jews (long before Zionists began to settle there) addressed American Jews, saying, "You, protected by the liberal constitution of America, living in freedom, opulence and prosperity: turn your eyes to the horrible state of slavery and misery, under which our brethren are weeping in the Holy Land!" Letters like those portrayed an

"America [that] represented modernity's lures and perils, while Israel symbolized tradition and suffering with the promise of redemption."

Later, once the Zionist movement was under way, American Jews grew infatuated with the image of Palestine's Jew as the laborer, the pioneer—as if to disprove the widespread European anti-Semitic accusation that Jews were parasites. Still later, as we have already seen with Louis Brandeis, American Jews imagined the growing Jewish community in Palestine as a miniature America.

Yet there was an underbelly to loving this imagined Zion. American Jews concocted images of Palestine that "developed from—and addressed—the needs of *American* Jewry and were, as a result, increasingly out of touch with reality back in [the land of] Israel." Life on the ground could never measure up to the highly idealized, utopian image that American Jews had of their coreligionists in Palestine. "While American Jews dreamed on about a 'model state' where democracy and social justice reigned," Sarna notes, "the Jews in [the land of] Israel focused, of necessity, on security, resistance, and the need for new settlements."

It was inevitable that the real Israel would disappoint them.

After the Holocaust, the modern state of Israel afforded American Jews an opportunity to atone. American Jews had done virtually nothing for European Jews during those years; even public protests about American inaction were rare. One scholar of the period has called American Jewish response to the Holocaust "a deafening silence."

With Israel's creation, American Jews were determined not to fail again. This time they would stand beside their fellow Jews. Now, of course, these fellow Jews were different. They were the new Israelis, bronzed and muscular, self-assured and powerful, utterly unlike the European victims whom American Jews had failed.

Given the horrifying images of defenseless Jews being slaughtered during the Holocaust, American Jews relished those photographs of Israeli soldiers who represented something entirely different. There were photos of soldiers standing beside their tanks adorned with prayer shawls and phylacteries during morning worship. There was David Rubinger's famed photograph of three paratroopers standing shoulder to shoulder after the battle for the Old City in the 1967 Six-Day War. How different was this new Jew from the image of the little boy in the Warsaw ghetto, holding up his hands in surrender while a Nazi pointed a weapon at him!

In many ways, Israel was the fresh start that American Jews needed.

So American Jews raised many millions of dollars for Israel. Especially after the Six-Day War, they unabashedly expressed wholehearted solidarity with the Jewish state. American Jews learned Israeli dances at summer camp and sang Israeli songs with romantic pride. International fund-raising organizations printed posters with images of the tanned Jewish farmer, handsome male Israeli soldiers, and tough yet pretty female soldiers. Israelis were making the desert bloom and bravely defending their newfound homeland. They were "sabras"—a reference to a cactus fruit that is prickly on the outside but sweet inside. True, Israelis had to be tough to survive, but slice them open and they would ooze sweetness.

This lovefest with Israel extended even to the perception of the Jewish state as a successful example of socialism. If American Jews were self-conscious about their comfortable lifestyles, their complacency, and their materialism, then the kibbutz—

seemingly a place of economic and gender equality, social values, hard work, and ideological seriousness—was a natural object of adoration.

Saul Bellow is the American Jewish novelist who best captured American Jews' desire for a respite from history, but it is Philip Roth, and particularly his novel *Portnoy's Complaint*, who understood their adoration of Israel, which he thought was coupled with a profound self-loathing. A highly controversial figure ever since the appearance of his early collection of stories, *Goodbye, Columbus*, Roth rankled American Jews further when he published *Portnoy's Complaint*, a monologue of a young, angry, self-hating, sexually tormented Jewish man who tells his psychiatrist that he is "living in the middle of a Jewish joke."

Toward the end of the book, Alexander Portnoy, the narrator and main character, goes to Israel, where he meets a young kibbutznik named Naomi. He instantly becomes obsessed with her. Naomi, who is Roth's tool for expressing his Jewish self-loathing, has nothing but disdain for the Jewish world that Alexander inhabits. She says to him, "American society . . . not only sanctions gross and unfair relations among men, but it encourages them. . . . Rivalry, competition, envy, jealousy, all that is malignant in human character is nourished by the system." Naomi is a reminder to American Jews of what they hate about themselves.

Then, positioning herself coquettishly on the bed, she tells Portnoy that Israelis are revolutionaries, while American Jews are essentially collaborators:

> You are not the enemy of the system. You are not even a challenge to the system, as you seem to think. You are only one of its policemen, a paid employee, an accomplice . . . you think you serve justice, but you are only a lackey of the bourgeoisie.

You have a system inherently exploitative and unjust . . . and
your job is to make such a system appear legitimate and moral.

The kibbutz is the antidote to all that is wrong with America and
its Jews. "The system in which I participate . . . is humane and
just." Then comes her Marxist (read: kibbutz) jargon. "As long as
the community owns the means of production . . . as long as no
man has the opportunity to accumulate wealth or to live off the
surplus value of another man's labor, then the essential character
of the kibbutz is being maintained."

Portnoy's reply is brief and telling. "Naomi, I love you." He
propositions her, and she turns him down with a cutting, con-
descending dismissal. When he tries to grope her, she headbutts
his jaw.

"Where the hell did you learn that," he screams in pain, "in
the army?"

"Yes," Naomi replied. A minute later, she says to him, "There
is something very wrong with you. . . . You are the most unhappy
person I have ever known." Then, a few pages later, Naomi says
to him, "You should go home."

He should go home, she intimates, because he is nothing like
the Israelis he has come to visit. He should go home because
Israelis actually stand for something and he does not. He should
go home because Israelis are a people physically revived, to
which Roth contrasts Portnoy's pathetic sexual torment. Israelis
and Americans, Roth is saying, have become entirely different—
and American Jews feel envious and inadequate.

EVENTUALLY, THOUGH, THAT IDEALIZED American-Jewish
image of Israel shattered.

In the early 1950s, Arab *fedayeen* (Arabic for "self-sacrificers"—gunmen who were supported and equipped by their host governments, particularly the Egyptian military) were crossing Israel's border regularly, leaving death and mayhem in their wake. In 1953, an Israeli woman, Suzanne Kinyas, and her two children were murdered when a grenade was thrown into their house in the town of Yehud, some six miles inside the border. The IDF launched a reprisal attack on the Jordanian village of Qibya. The attack, which was carried out by the (in)famous Unit 101 under the command of Ariel Sharon, did not go as planned. Soldiers did not inspect the homes they dynamited, and the reprisal left in its wake sixty-nine dead Arab civilians, most of them women and children.

The American Jewish community expressed dismay over the attack, and Israel's image among American Jews suffered serious damage. Jacob Blaustein said to the AJC, "The Qibya incident was a tragic and clearly reprehensible affair . . . under no circumstances can it be condoned. The claim that it was retaliatory, no matter how well substantiated, does not excuse it." Abe Harman, Israel's consul general in New York, flew back to Israel to let the government know that one more incident like Qibya could well end American Jewish support for Israel. Subsequently, as relations with the Eisenhower administration soured, a few American Jewish philanthropists ended their contributions to the United Jewish Appeal; truthfully or not, they attributed their change of heart to Qibya.

Qibya was soon forgotten, but the next incidents would be worse.

When the 1982 massacre of Muslims in Sabra and Shatila (see chapter 1) became known, Rabbi Alexander Schindler, one of America's leading Jewish personalities and a leader of the Reform Movement, went to speak to Prime Minister Begin to express his horror. After the meeting, he asked, rhetorically, "What has given us, historically, the strength to stand the attacks of the world?" What had enabled the Jews to survive, he said, was "our sense of rightness. The only thing that enabled us to withstand the torments of the centuries, the martyrdom, was our sense of moral superiority."

Letty Cottin Pogrebin was absolutely right when she later said that 1982 became the moment of a major shift. The damage to idealized Zion was severe and permanent. Sabra and Shatila marked a major turning point; after 1982, the image of Israel as the embodiment of a dreamlike Jewish state became very difficult to embrace wholeheartedly. The floodgates of criticism creaked open—and with time, a trickle became a torrent.

IS HAVING POWER GOOD for the Jews? Or is powerlessness ironically preferable?

As the idyllic image of Israel began to crumble, that question became more pressing in American Jewish circles. Not surprisingly, though, there was nothing new about that question; it, too, was an ancient one. Just as the tension between universalism and particularism, which we saw in the previous chapter, first emerged in the pages of the Bible, so, too, does the Jewish preoccupation with the messiness of history. Should Jews stay above the fray and get a "good night's rest," or should they grab history by the horns, as did the other peoples of the region?

The debate about Jewish power begins, perhaps, in the Book of Exodus, after the Israelites have escaped Egyptian slavery and made their way into the desert on their way to the Promised Land. There we encounter a peculiar command: "Now if you make an altar of stones for Me, you must not build it with stones shaped by tools; for if you use a chisel on it, you will defile it."

Obviously, it would have been much easier to construct an altar if one could chisel the stones to fit. So what was the problem with chiseling? Rashi, the Jewish tradition's preeminent medieval biblical commentator, explains: "The altar was created to lengthen man's days, while iron tools are used to shorten them. It is not appropriate that that which shortens life shall have dominion over that which extends it." Anything that smacks of killing, of war, of cutting short human life, that stream of the Jewish tradition has long insisted, has no place in the life of the spirit.

Some four hundred years later, what had been true for the construction of the altar remained in effect for the building of the Temple in Jerusalem. The Book of Kings reports that in the Temple, "only blocks dressed at the quarry were used, and no hammer, chisel or any other iron tool was heard at the Temple site while it was being built." As if to ensure that everyone reading that narrative would understand the message, King David himself explains why he was not permitted to build the Temple in Jerusalem but had to leave that task to his son, Solomon, who would reign after him. David reports: "God said to me, 'You are not to build a house for my Name, because you are a warrior and have shed blood.'"

When Albert Einstein had said that Jews could—and should—do without temporal power, he was accurately reflecting one major theme of Jewish tradition.

Of all Judaism's commonly used texts, none is a better barometer of the sentiments of each generation than the Haggadah, the text traditionally recited at the Passover Seder. The most published Jewish text after the Bible, the Haggadah is also the most frequently updated, interpreted, and illustrated. The literally thousands of editions of the Haggadah, in languages too numerous to count, offer unparalleled glimpses into the worldviews of the communities that produced them.

It should therefore not surprise us that perhaps the most interesting artistic representation of this Jewish discomfort with power can be found in classic editions of the Passover Haggadah. A section toward the beginning of the Haggadah refers to four different dispositions in children, whom it calls the Wise Son, the Wicked Son, the Simple Son, and the Son Who Knows Not How to Ask. Though the Haggadah's point is that each of these children needs to be taught in a different manner appropriate to his nature, commentators and illustrators over the centuries have often gone further, telling us what they thought made a person "wise" or "wicked."

In the Middle Ages, European Jews lived without military power. Soldiers were Christian crusaders or officers of the Inquisition. Men bearing arms were representatives of the government, which Jewish communities always feared to one extent or another. It is therefore not surprising that numerous medieval Haggadah texts portray the Wicked Son as a soldier. A fourteenth-century Haggadah from Prague shows the Wicked Son as a man dressed in medieval battle garb, holding a spear in one hand while his other hand cradles the handle of a sword. The Rothschild Haggadah, from 1450, depicts the Wicked Son as a man holding a sword in his outstretched arm. Other well-known editions of the Haggadah, including a fifteenth-century Sarajevo Haggadah and a seventeenth-century edition from Amsterdam, have similar depictions. Military power, to put it bluntly, was for Gentiles, not Jews.

Some Jews actually transformed powerlessness—or at least the lack of military power—into nothing less than a Jewish ideal. In the Talmudic period, some sages said that there were three oaths that God demanded of the world. One, that the Jews were not to ascend to the Land of Israel "as a wall," but little by little, in smaller groups. Second, God warned the Jews that they must not rebel against the rule of the nations of the world. And finally, God demanded of the nations of the world that they not subjugate the Jews excessively. The nations should leave the Jews alone, and in return, the Jews should not "rock the boat," seeking to turn history on its head. Of course, the nations did not leave the Jews in peace, and Zionists *did* take the world by storm—but as an ideal, at least, this Talmudic passage seems to have eschewed the power that Jews would have needed to rebel. They were better off, it suggests, accepting whatever history had to offer.

Some contemporary scholars share this idealization of powerlessness. One fascinating example is Jewish historian David Biale (cited in the previous chapter). In his book *Power and Powerlessness in Jewish History*, Biale argues that the binary division of Jewish history into periods of power or powerlessness is far too simplistic. In periods when the Jews did have sovereignty and military power, their freedom of action was anything but unfettered. Conversely, when Jews seemingly had no military or governmental power, they instead managed a surprisingly nuanced balancing act and ended up wielding a great deal of political and economic power.

Obviously writing with Israel and Zionism in mind, Biale stresses that having military power can actually be disadvantageous in the long run. Because the Hasmoneans (Maccabees) focused on their military prowess, they failed to establish a stable government. Chaos ensued, and eventually they were defeated.

In fact, "ultimately," he says, "the victory of the Hasmoneans led to the destruction of the temple itself." Conversely, counterintuitive though it may seem, "the failure of the revolt against the Romans ultimately led to greater stability and greater Jewish power."

Lest his readers miss his point about Zionism, Biale makes it explicit. He reminds us that "the reestablishment of Jewish sovereignty under the Hasmoneans—an event often compared to the success of Zionism—had unexpected negative consequences." It led to utter destruction under the Romans.

The appearance of *Power and Powerlessness* in the 1980s, when Israel's fighting force reminded American Jews of the Maccabees, conveyed an implicit warning: this resumption of Jewish military might was not going to end well. Nor, by the same token, did seeming defeats have to be seen in wholly negative terms. Taken to its logical conclusion, Biale could have been read to suggest that if Israel were to fall, Jews would have greater stability, not less, and however counterintuitive, the Jews might possess even more power.

Even if Biale did not intend so radical a conclusion, his book channeled Brit Shalom, Ahad Ha'am, and even the Bible's antiwar ethos; by remaining on the academic playing field and staying mostly out of the political arguments about Israel, Biale was able to remain a bit above the fray of fiery Jewish communal arguments about the Jewish state. But there was no doubt that, like Albert Einstein, Hannah Arendt, and Judah Magnes, all of whom understood that history had always been a mess and that getting into history would get the Jews dirty, he harbored grave doubts about whether a Jewish state—and the power it both required and created—was a good idea at all.

ZIONISM, THOUGH, HAD AN entirely different understanding of Jewish power. Classical, mainstream Zionists desperately wanted to rejoin history, the mess and the pain notwithstanding. Their position, too, has its roots in the Bible.

In the Book of Numbers, as the Israelites approach the Promised Land and prepare to conquer it, the tribes of Reuben and Gad decide that they would prefer not to cross the Jordan. They would rather remain on its eastern side, with its verdant fields for their flocks. "'If we have found favor in your eyes,' they said [to Moses], 'let this land be given to your servants as our possession. Do not make us cross the Jordan.'" Though he is initially angered by their request, Moses eventually relents. But his consent comes with an important stipulation:

> If you will do this—if you will arm yourselves before the Lord for battle and if all of you who are armed cross over the Jordan before the Lord until he has driven his enemies out before him—then when the land is subdued before the Lord, you may return and be free from your obligation to the Lord and to Israel. And this land will be your possession before the Lord.

To be part of the Israelite nation is to commit to joining the conquests of the land. Warfare is not just one legitimate option. Later Jewish law on warfare even included a concept of "obligatory war": there are wars that one is obliged to fight.

Faced with these two deeply embedded Jewish traditions, American Jews tended to embrace the ideal embodied by the Temple, which a warrior was not permitted to build, while classical Zionists (and later, Israelis) embraced the story of the two tribes who were told that to be Israelites, they had to fight for their people.

Here, again, Haggadah texts that *Zionists* published are very telling. The cover of the Haggadah put out by the Palmach (the strike force of the Haganah, the pre-state military organization that became the IDF after Israel was created) shows a young man, the fields of the farm or kibbutz behind him, gazing intently at the rifle in his right hand. Now the person with the weapon is not the Wicked Son, as in the medieval Haggadot; now the fighter is center stage, on the cover. Here the person armed is the ideal; he is the one the entire Passover Seder is meant to celebrate.

In an Israeli-illustrated Haggadah from 1955, several decades after the Palmach's Haggadah, the Wicked Son is shown wearing dress clothes (a shirt and a tie, very unusual in Israel back then) and leaning *away* from a scene that includes a shovel in the earth and a guard tower. The point is clear. For Zionists, the Jews were going to redeem their people through working the land and protecting themselves, obviously armed. What makes the Wicked Son in the 1955 Haggadah wicked is that he is a dandy. He refuses to dirty himself by helping to build and defend the state.[*]

The Wicked Sons of medieval European and Israeli Haggadah texts are precise opposites of each other. So, too, are Diaspora and Israeli views of the Jewish use of power.

DESPITE THESE ANCIENT ANTECEDENTS, it was modern history—and a poem—that set in stone Zionism's attitude to

---

[*] Jews in America also employed the image of the "wicked son" for editorial purposes. In 1945, Arthur Szyk, the famed Polish-Jewish political artist who fled Europe for the United States (and who was a passionate Zionist), illustrated a pamphlet titled "There Were Four Sons." In his rendering, the "wicked son" bears an uncanny resemblance to Joseph Proskauer, the leader of the anti-Zionist flank of the American Jewish Committee.

power. Zionists had understood from the get-go that creating a state would entail getting into the mud of history, but the real wake-up call came with the Kishinev pogrom of 1903, six years after the First Zionist Congress. The horror began in this Russian city on Easter Sunday, April 19. There was

> murder and massacre during the night . . . 50,000 Jews (a third of the population) now fell prey to barbarism . . . a boy's tongue was cut out while the two year old was still alive. . . . Meyer Weissman, blinded in one eye from youth, begged for his life with the offer of sixty rubles; taking this money, the leader of the crowd destroying his small grocery store gouged out Weissman's other eye, saying "You will never again look upon a Christian child." Nails were driven through heads; bodies, hacked in half; bellies split open and filled with feathers. Women and girls were raped, and some had their breasts cut off.

Shortly after the pogrom, Hayim Nahman Bialik was sent to Kishinev by the Jewish Historical Society of Odessa to interview survivors and to tell their story. Bialik was a natural choice for the assignment. By the time of the pogrom, he was widely considered one of the greatest—if not *the* greatest—Hebrew writers of his generation. Ze'ev Jabotinsky, another Zionist leader and himself a gifted author, said that Bialik was "the one poet in all of modern literature whose poetry directly molded the soul of a generation."

What Bialik saw and heard when he arrived in Kishinev shocked him to his very core. He kept copious notes for a lengthy report, notes that he never touched again; instead, he wrote an epic poem that catapulted him to worldwide Jewish fame. Titled "The City of Slaughter," the poem is "still seen as the finest—certainly the most influential—Jewish poem written since medieval times." In that poem,* Bialik directs his fury not only at the marauding, raping, murdering mob but also, surprisingly, at the Jews themselves. In the middle of the lengthy and complex poem, Bialik describes the basement of a house where a gang of Cossacks repeatedly and mercilessly rape the Jewish women. While the savage assault is unfolding, according to Bialik's rendition, the Jewish men hide behind casks, unable to stop the attackers, too frightened to even try. These "sons of the Maccabees," as Bialik calls them, with bitter irony, are the very symbols of what Bialik believed had gone wrong with European Jewry.†

Then Bialik turns his rage on the Jewish tradition itself. With implicit reference to the Jewish tradition's rule that if the wife of

---

* Bialik wrote another poem in response to Kishinev, "On the Slaughter," which also became a classic. Bialik's Kishinev poetry has become almost liturgical in Israeli life, and some of its subsequent uses have been chilling.

In April 1979, Palestinian terrorists landed on the beach near the Israeli city of Nahariya and broke into the apartment of the Haran family. They shot the husband, Danny, on the beach and, grabbing four-year-old Einat by her hair, smashed her head repeatedly against the rocks until she died. Meanwhile, Smadar, the mother, hid in a crawl space in her apartment with her hand over the mouth of Yael, her toddler, so the young child would not cry out and reveal their location. In her fright and her desperation to keep Yael quiet, Smadar inadvertently smothered her to death. When he spoke at their funeral, Prime Minister Menachem Begin, who tended to quote biblical sources at moments such as these, quoted Bialik's "On the Slaughter": "Revenge for the blood of a small child / [even] Satan has not yet devised."

† It is likely that the scene as he describes it did not unfold precisely that way. What Bialik did was to combine elements of actual scenes that he heard recounted as he did his research. The number of rapes was shockingly high, and many took place in front of the victim's family. Some men did acknowledge that they had hidden (but watched) as their families were raped or butchered. And though there *was* some Jewish resistance, there were many attacks in which the Jews were so vastly outnumbered that resistance would likely have been both futile and suicidal.

a Kohen (a man of priestly status) has sex with another man, she is forbidden to him, Bialik describes how after the attack, these men of priestly descent stepped over the broken bodies of their still-living wives and ran to the rabbi to ask, "Is my wife still permitted to me?"

"*That* is what worries you?" Bialik virtually screams. The people you love are broken, wounded, raped, and sprawled on the ground, and all that concerns you is a question of Jewish law, the matter of whether your wives are still sexually permitted to you? What has happened to your humanity? What have you become?

Note how different is the shame at the core of Bialik's rage and the shame that many American Jews feel about the Jewish use of power. Bialik is enraged at the weakness, passivity, and cowardice of European Jews. For many Diaspora Jews, however, shame comes from having and using power. Here is George Steiner, the Jewish literary critic whose well-known monograph "Our Homeland, the Text" has become something of an anti-Zionist classic: "It was, during two millennia, the dignity of the Jew that he was too weak to make any other human being as un-housed, as wretched as himself." Steiner locates Jews' dignity in weakness, because Jews were then unable to make anyone else as miserable as they were. Zionists wanted none of that "dignity." To them, not only was Israel's amassing power legitimate, given the ongoing security challenges it faced, but in a way it was the redemption of the Jewish people from the humiliating, religion-induced weakness of European Jews.

Steiner was not entirely wrong when he wrote that Israel "has been compelled to make other men homeless, servile, disinherited, in order to survive day to day." But if that is true, is the price of Zionism justified? Classical Zionism, of course, took no pleasure in making others homeless, and it was certainly not Zionism's goal to make anyone servile. The point of Zionism, however, was that if people attacked the Jews, it was the attackers who would now risk becoming homeless or disinherited; the days of Jewish victimhood were over. The whole point of the movement was to shed that "noble" dignity of victimhood, powerlessness, and fear for which Steiner longed but of which Zionists were ashamed and tired.

The problem, as Bialik diagnosed it, was exile. The exile of the Jews from their own land had more than robbed the Jews of their strength and their courage. It had eroded their capacity to feel. Exile had eviscerated the Jew. For Bialik, therefore, and for many of his contemporaries, the point of Zionism, of the return to the Jewish homeland, was not merely to create a refuge or to fix the "Jewish problem" in Europe. Jews needed to return to their land because it was only there that they could fashion a "new Jew." Unlike Einstein, who thought that Judaism had outgrown its Maccabean period with its focus on military power, Bialik and his fellow revolutionaries believed that it was time to re-create the Maccabees of old. It was time for the Jewish nation to be reborn, it was time for Jews to reenter history—and it was time, when necessary, to fight with no apologies.

THIS NOTION OF A "new Jew" would become one of Zionism's most defining ideas. In 1942, some three decades after Bialik wrote "In the City of Slaughter," a writer in the Yishuv named Hayim Hazaz wrote a short story—"The Sermon"—that has become an Israeli classic. The narrator of the "sermon" is Yudke, one of the founders of the kibbutz on which he lives. Yudke is trying to explain to his fellow kibbutzniks why he believes that they should not teach Jewish history to their children. His main reason is that "we really don't have a history at all. . . . You see, we never made our own history, the gentiles always made it for us . . . it wasn't ours, it wasn't ours at all!"

Yudke's view of Jewish history is classic Zionist fare. "Persecutions, massacres, martyrdoms and pogroms. And more persecutions, massacres, martyrdoms and pogroms. And more, and more, and more of them without end." The Jews have been so weak and pathetic (and here Hazaz is almost identical to Bialik) that Jewish children find nothing of interest in Jewish history. "Children love to read historical novels. Everywhere else, as you know, such books are full of heroes and conquerors and brave warriors and glorious adventures. In short, they're exciting." The problem is that these children "read novels, but ones about gentiles, not about Jews. Why? You can be sure it's no accident. Jewish history is simply boring . . . it has no adventures, no conquering heroes, no great rulers or potentates."

Jews in history are not potentates. They are "a mob of beaten, groaning, weeping, begging Jews"—the opposite of inspiring. That is why, says Yudke, "if it were up to me, I wouldn't allow our children to be taught Jewish history at all. Why on earth should we teach them about the shameful life led by their ancestors? I'd simply say to them 'look boys and girls, we don't have any history. We haven't had one since the day we were driven into exile. Class dismissed, you can go outside and play.'"

Hazaz's implication that the kids should play now but (unlike their forebears) fight later would strike future Israelis as sad, but not debatable. By the time Israel was created, it was clear, sadly, that "the fight" would be part of the Israeli landscape for as far as the eye could see. (Ironically and tragically, Hazaz and his wife lost their only son in the War of Independence.) It was not that Zionists relished the conflict, Israel's most thoughtful authors reminded their readers; it was that there was no alternative. Anyone who imagined that the conflict could be settled peacefully was just dangerously naive.

Hayim Hazaz and George Steiner could not have disagreed more.

No one was more direct in noting the inevitability of a protracted conflict than Ze'ev Jabotinsky, the founder of Revisionist Zionism. In 1923, Jabotinsky wrote a pamphlet titled "The Iron Wall," which he followed up with "Beyond the Iron Wall," in which he argued that it was a mistake to underestimate the Arabs. The Jews would be foolish to imagine that they loved their Land of Israel more than the Arabs loved their Palestine. The Arabs, insisted Jabotinsky, were as attached to Palestine as any other people were to the land on which they lived, and ironically, those Zionists who believed that the Arabs could easily be bought off were being paternalistic, even racist. Both morality and reality demanded that the Zionists look the situation right in the eye:

Our Peace-mongers are trying to persuade us that the Arabs are either fools, whom we can deceive by masking our real aims, or that they are corrupt and can be bribed to abandon to us their claim to priority in Palestine, in return for cultural and economic advantages. I repudiate this conception of the Palestinian Arabs. Culturally they are five hundred years behind us, they have neither our endurance nor our determination; but they are just as good psychologists as we are, and their minds have been sharpened like ours by centuries of fine-spun logomachy. We may tell them whatever we like about the innocence of our aims, watering them down and sweetening them with honeyed words to make them palatable, but they know what we want, as well as we know what they do not want. They feel at least the same instinctive jealous love of Palestine, as the old Aztecs felt for ancient Mexico, and the Sioux for their rolling Prairies.

That meant, he said, that the Arabs would never voluntarily come to agreement with the Zionists. If the Zionists wanted a foothold in Palestine, Arab violence would have to be met with an "Iron Wall":

> This does not mean that there cannot be any agreement with the Palestine Arabs. What is impossible is a voluntary agreement. As long as the Arabs feel that there is the least hope of getting rid of us, they will refuse to give up this hope in return for either kind words or for bread and butter, because they are not a rabble, but a living people. And when a living people yields in matters of such a vital character it is only when there is no longer any hope of getting rid of us, because they can make no breach in the iron wall. Not till then will they drop their extremist leaders, whose watchword is "Never!"

In what would become the guiding spirit of Israel's political right in decades to come, Jabotinsky said, "The only way to obtain such an agreement, is the iron wall, which is to say a strong power in Palestine that is not amenable to any Arab pressure. In other words, the only way to reach an agreement in the future is to abandon all ideas of seeking an agreement at present."

Jabotinsky sadly proved prescient. In 1929, Arab rioters murdered 133 Jews and destroyed the centuries-old Jewish community of Hebron over one weekend, and in 1936 renewed Arab riots erupted. Then, it was not Jabotinsky but Joseph Klausner, a historian at Hebrew University and a Revisionist with a fiery pen, who echoed Bialik. (Earlier, Klausner had written Bialik to tell him that he thought that "In the City of Slaughter" was a "greater achievement than Ecclesiastes.") Klausner cried that Jewish passivity (of the sort that George Steiner relished) in the face of Arab attacks in Palestine was the very opposite of what Palestine was supposed to evoke in the Jews. Excoriating Ben-Gurion's policy of restraint in the face of Arab attacks, Klausner exclaimed that the Jews should have responded with infinitely greater force, "for it is possible that a reaction of this sort from the very outset would have put an end to the attacks from the very get-go." In what was almost certainly a reference to the Brit Shalom group, he continued: "For even the Arab-lovers in our midst admit and acknowledge that Arabs understand only power and retreat only in the face of force."

Klausner's was the sort of language that makes today's American Jews, as well as many Israelis, cringe with discomfort, but that would not have troubled him in the least. Like many other Zionists, Klausner was a passionate believer in the new Jew. Life in Palestine was intended to allow a new, liberated, strong, self-confident Jew to emerge—but Jews in Palestine were failing that vision. "We allowed ourselves to believe that in the Land of Israel the matter would be different. Here there would be no 'court Jews,' here we would not run to the local ruler [for protection]." Yet that had not happened. Because Jews of insufficient ideological fervor had moved to Palestine, the entire enterprise had been weakened:

The Land of Israel has become a refuge for masses of non-Zionists and anti-Zionists, for whom the Land of Israel is nothing more than a place to earn a living or a place to which they came for lack of any other options. All of these have weakened . . . the ideological unity of the Jewish majority. And in a place where there is no wholeness and unity of that sort, there can be no spiritual-physical might, which is needed if we are to have any hope of standing up to enemies who yearn for battle. For the sword is their beloved friend and they use the pistol as an ornament, as a European places a flower in his lapel.

To the Revisionists, celebration of powerlessness was defeatist and dangerous; not to use force when Jews finally had that option was a failure of epic proportions.

MAINSTREAM ZIONISTS DID NOT relish living by the sword, but they also intuited that they would have no alternative. Amos Oz, who died in 2018, one of Israel's greatest novelists and often mentioned as a contender for the Nobel Prize, was Joseph Klausner's great-nephew. Decades after Klausner penned his fiery invective, Oz began to question the Revisionist ideology on which he had been raised. But he was living in the Israel of the 1950s, when cross-border incursions by Arab fedayeen were a daily affair. Decades later, when he wrote his autobiography, Oz described a conversation he had with an older fellow kibbutz member, Ephraim. Guarding the kibbutz's perimeter at night, Amos asks Ephraim if he had ever shot "one of those murderers" while guarding or in war.

Ephraim, to Oz's surprise, refuses to call the Arabs "murderers." He understands how furious they are at the way history played out for them. "What d'you expect from them? From their point of view, we are aliens from outer space who have landed and trespassed on their land, gradually taken over parts of it. . . . Is it any wonder that they've taken up arms against us?" The Arab loss in Israel's War of Independence only made matters worse, Ephraim reminds Amos. "And now that we've inflicted a crushing defeat on them and hundreds of thousands of them are living in refugee camps—what, d'you expect them to celebrate with us and wish us luck?"

But if that's the case, Amos asks with more than a grain of cynicism, "what are you doing here with your gun? Why don't you . . . take your gun and go fight on their side?"

And that invites Ephraim's history lesson, a lesson that echoes Bialik, Hayim Hazaz, and Jabotinsky's Revisionists all at once. "Their side? But their side doesn't want me. Nowhere in the world wants me. Nobody in the world wants me. That's the whole point." So, Ephraim believes, the Jews have to fight. "Where is the Jewish people's land if not here? Under the sea? On the moon? Or is the Jewish people the only people in the world that doesn't deserve to have a little homeland of its own?"

With that attitude, Amos wants to know, what should they do if the Arabs attack? Says Ephraim, "We'll just have to lie down in the mud and shoot. And we'll try our damndest to shoot better and faster than them. But we won't shoot at them because they're a nation of murderers, but for the simple reason that we also have a right to live and we also have a right to a land of our own."

The question that matters most may not be whether force is good or evil; the real question is whether the Jews deserve to have a state. One of J Street's founders, as we saw in the previous chapter, said no; if maintaining a Jewish state requires endless conflict, then the state is a bad idea. Only a Jewish state at peace is a Jewish state worth having. Moderate Zionists, however, do not go there. Yes, they admit. The fight is horrific, the costs often unbearable to all, but if not fighting means the end of the state, then the alternative is worse.

The classic statement of this worldview is a eulogy that Moshe Dayan delivered in memory of a young man named Roi Rotberg. On April 29, 1956, twenty-one-year-old Rotberg was patrolling the fields of Nachal Oz, the Gaza-adjacent community in which he lived, on horseback. Accustomed to seeing Gazans picking the kibbutz's fields, Rotberg, seeing a group of Arabs in the fields, rode toward them to get them to leave. But it was an ambush, and as Rotberg approached the "farmers," they shot and killed him, then dragged his body into Gaza, where it was horrifically mutilated.

Coincidentally, Dayan had met Rotberg a few days earlier. He attended the funeral and delivered a brief eulogy (merely 238 words in total) that became one of Israel's classic speeches, still oft-quoted. Dayan reminded his listeners that there was nothing surprising about Arab resentment and violence. "Let us not cast the blame on the murderers today," he said. "Why should we deplore their burning hatred for us? For eight years they have been sitting in the refugee camps in Gaza, and before their eyes we have been transforming the lands and the villages, where they and their fathers dwelt, into our estate."

Yet if mere Israeli survival was going to evoke Arab anger, Dayan warned both his listeners and his entire newborn nation, Israelis had better be prepared to live by the sword. In language filled with biblical imagery, as if to remind his listeners that the battle to stay in the land was not new but was a story that had begun thousands of years earlier, Dayan continued: "Let us not fear to look squarely at the hatred that consumes and fills the lives of hundreds of Arabs who live around us. Let us not drop our gaze, lest our arms weaken. That is the fate of our generation. That is our choice—to be ready and armed, tough and hard—or else the sword shall fall from our hands and our lives will be cut short."

Some forty-five years later, from 2000 to 2004, Israel was embroiled in the Second Intifada. It had been many years since Amos Oz and his fellow kibbutznik Ephraim abandoned the fire line, and Israel had fought many wars by then. At that point, one of the intellectual darlings of Israel's left was Ben-Gurion University professor Benny Morris, whose research on the War of Independence and Israel's early years had exploded the myth that the Arabs had "fled" Palestine. No, Morris showed, they had left for many reasons. Some fled, some were intimidated into fleeing, and others, though many Israelis did not want to hear it, had been forcibly exiled as part of Ben-Gurion's explicit desire to address security issues during the war and diminish the number of Israel's Arabs so that the state he was creating would have a Jewish majority.

In a 2004 interview in *Ha'aretz*, Morris was clear about what Ben-Gurion did. "Ben-Gurion was a transferist. He understood that there could be no Jewish state with a large and hostile Arab minority in its midst. There would be no such state. It would not be able to exist."

What was astonishing about the interview was the fact that Morris, then the doyen of Israel's New Historians (a group of scholars—embraced by the left and reviled by the right—who had upended much of the mythology on which generations of Israelis had been raised and sought to "strip Israel's history of its grandeur," as historian Martin Kramer puts it), seemed unwilling to critique Ben-Gurion. "Ben-Gurion was right," Morris insisted.

"If he had not done what he did, a state would not have come into being. That has to be clear. It is impossible to evade it. Without the uprooting of the Palestinians, a Jewish state would not have arisen here."

Morris further insisted that what happened was not a war crime. "In certain conditions, expulsion is not a war crime. I don't think that the expulsions of 1948 were war crimes." He continued: "A society that aims to kill you forces you to destroy it. When the choice is between destroying or being destroyed, it's better to destroy."

Here was Benny Morris, the intellectual hero of Israel's left, echoing sentiments usually associated with Jabotinsky and Klausner. And herein lies one of the core differences between Israelis and many American Jews. American Jews, and particularly progressives and millennials, are so deeply troubled by Israel's use of force that they would give up the state in order to end the violence. So said J Street's Daniel Levy. So, implicitly, said the leadership of If Not Now in 2014 when they demanded that Israel "stop the war on Palestine" without mentioning that there was also a war on Israel. So many others feel, even if they do not articulate it. Simply put, for American progressives, the conflict is a human rights issue.[*] For Israelis, even Israelis on the political left, it is first and foremost about security and survival.

---

[*] Decades ago, this ideological purity was less common, even among Jews who had long been ambivalent about Zionism. Jacob Blaustein, for example, urged President Harry Truman, at the conclusion of Israel's War of Independence, not to pressure Israel to take back all the Palestinians who had become refugees. "It would be unrealistic to expect the young state to repatriate all of them," he told the president, *"especially since it was Arab aggression that had put them into their present plight."* Today such descriptions of the conflict are considered gauche in most American Jewish circles.

In language that would infuriate many American Jews, even those committed to Israel, Morris minced no words. If Ben-Gurion wanted to found a Jewish state, some of the Arabs had to go, he said. "You can't make an omelet without breaking eggs. You have to dirty your hands." To a large extent, the divide between American Jews and Israelis is over who is willing to say that, and who is not.

THE WORLD'S TWO LARGEST Jewish communities are therefore divided by radically different instincts about universalism versus particularism as well as by their opposing attitudes toward Jews' involvement in the messiness of history. These differences alone would be cause enough for a gaping chasm between the two. As we will now see, however, there is still more that divides these communities, including a disagreement about what Judaism at its essence is meant to be.

5

PEOPLE OR RELIGION:
WHO AND WHAT ARE THE JEWS?

I t's not every day that *Time* magazine puts a rabbi on its front
cover. The year was 1951, and the rabbi was Louis Finkelstein,
who served as chancellor of the Jewish Theological Seminary
(JTS), the academic center of Conservative Judaism, then the
largest movement in American Judaism.

Time was enthralled by Rabbi Finkelstein. "With his flashing
eyes, floating hair and black beard heavily streaked with grey, he
looks, at 56, like a reasonable modern facsimile of an Old Testament patriarch," the magazine said. Like many other American Jews of the period, Finkelstein was of European origin. And
Finkelstein was enthralled by America, where, he gushed, Judaism was seeing a revival that few had thought possible. "For he
believes—and on abundant evidence—that U.S. Jews are returning to their synagogues and temples as never before."

Here is how *Time* described what was happening in American Jewish life:

The old, half-deserted synagogues are filling up again, new congregations are forming, new synagogues are being built. Young married couples are sending their children to religious schools to learn the fundamentals of their faith—then forming study groups so that they will know what their children are talking about. The word that such young Americans use, over & over again, when they are asked what they are looking for, is "heritage."

"When I was a seminary student 40 years ago," Finkelstein told *Time*, "it seemed so clear to us that our faith could not survive here that we even wondered for what purpose in the Divine Economy the Jews had been brought to the New World." But after the Holocaust, American Jews were desperate to belong again, and Finkelstein, like many Jewish leaders, was brimming with optimism.

The *Time* article did hint at a fly in the ointment. Louis Finkelstein "was definitely a non-Zionist—a stance which looked to Zionists like anti-Zionism. At least one large contributor to the seminary tore up his usual check." The article also noted that "when [Finkelstein] refused to let the students sing the Israel national anthem at commencement in 1945, on the ground that a political song has no place at a religious ceremony, the seminary nearly split apart."

Time suggested, however, that all that was resolved. "Today, now that the issue has simmered down, Finkelstein feels that perhaps he was mistaken, and that the State of Israel may turn out to be a good thing, after all. Relations between the seminary and Israel are now cordial."

Even at face value, it was an extraordinary admission. The rabbi at the helm of the largest, most dynamic movement in

American Judaism refused to allow the singing of "Hatikvah" at graduation, and the best he could muster was an admission that "the State of Israel may turn out to be a good thing, after all."

But *Time*, enraptured and in awe, gave Finkelstein a bit of a pass. It neglected to note that Finkelstein had said as recently as 1943, at a meeting of the American Jewish Committee, that "there isn't one possibility in one hundred that there will be established in the course of the next twenty-five years what is called a Jewish state in Palestine. . . . That cannot possibly be done in our time."

There was much more to the story that *Time* did not report. In 1944, JTS awarded an honorary doctorate to Chaim Weizmann, but at the ceremony the rabbinical school's citation tellingly mentioned only his scientific accomplishments and ignored his leadership of the Zionist movement. In 1946, as mentioned, the JTS graduating class pleaded with Finkelstein to allow "Hatikvah" to be sung at the conclusion of the ordination ceremony, but the chancellor again refused. In 1948, when Israel was created, JTS refused requests from several faculty members that it take out an ad in the *New York Times* celebrating the creation of the first Jewish sovereign state in two thousand years.

The following year, in 1949, even after the creation of the State of Israel, JTS remained hesitant to show its support. So three students climbed the seminary's iconic tower at the corner of New York's Broadway and 122nd Street and hoisted an Israeli flag. The seminary had it taken down. Perhaps most ironically, for several years around the time of Israel's creation, when seminary students wanted to ensure that "Hatikvah" would be heard during commencement, they enlisted the help of Christian students at Union Theological Seminary (UTS), across the street. Accommodating their Jewish colleagues' request, the Christian theology students played "Hatikvah" on the UTS carillon during or after the commencement ceremonies.

With the embers of the Holocaust still aglow, the Jewish people were building a state in a dramatic statement of symbolic rebirth—but Finkelstein would have none of it at his flagship institution.

Some three miles north of the JTS Manhattan campus sat the campus of Yeshiva University (YU), the academic and intellectual headquarters of American Orthodoxy. In 1947, with the Holocaust seared into Jewish consciousness and the Yishuv desperately fighting to create a Jewish state, Rabbi Joseph B. Soloveitchik, the intellectual giant who almost single-handedly defined American Modern Orthodoxy, then served as the head of the YU rabbinical school. He called in three students who were just about to be ordained. Two of them were from the Twersky dynasty of scholars, and the third was named David Smith. "Smitty," as he was known, was an orphan, a brilliant Talmud student, and a passionate Zionist and member of Betar, the Revisionist group inspired by Ze'ev Jabotinsky.

To the consternation of YU's faculty, as the entire story was related decades later by David Krakow, who had been involved in Betar and was friendly with several of those YU students, Smitty had begun to agitate on behalf of Betar among his fellow students and sought a venue at which Betar could make its case. Eventually, YU's faculty reluctantly relented and agreed to let the Betar members invite a speaker on a Sunday for an event to be held in the cafeteria, on the condition that whoever came to speak would be willing to debate the university's leading faculty.

Determined not to "lose" the debate, the students invited Benzion Netanyahu (father of Benjamin Netanyahu, who was not yet born), then a budding scholar of Jewish history at Philadelphia's Dropsie College. As Krakow, who attended the Sunday session, recalled some seventy years later, Netanyahu's most memorable comment during his YU visit was that pacifism is not a Jewish value; it is, he insisted, a Christian value, but one that even Christians do not abide by. Netanyahu "destroyed" the debaters on the faculty, said Krakow.

But there were consequences to their humiliation. Rabbi Soloveitchik called in Smitty and the two Twerskys and warned them: unless they abandoned their support for Betar, they would not be ordained.* Smitty, recalled Krakow (who was himself a leader of Betar in the United States), defied Soloveitchik. He left Yeshiva University and after a few stops ultimately set sail for Israel on the *Altalena*, a ship purchased by Jabotinsky's followers that was headed from Europe to the new Jewish state.

Prime Minister David Ben-Gurion saw the ship as a threat. He had ordered that all the Jewish paramilitary groups be folded into the army, but the *Altalena* was carrying arms specifically for the Irgun, the paramilitary group that had been commanded by Ben-Gurion's nemesis, Menachem Begin. So Ben-Gurion ordered his troops to fire on the ship. The boat, filled with highly explosive cargo, exploded and sank, and a few men were killed.

---

* Rabbi Soloveitchik had a complex relationship with Zionism, which began with a strong antipathy to the movement but ultimately morphed into much greater acceptance. By 1956, "the Rav," as he is known to his disciples to this day, had changed his view dramatically, and the address that he delivered on Israel Independence Day in 1956 ("Kol Dodi Dofek [The Voice of My Beloved Knocks]") has become a Zionist and theological classic, even though he continued to have reservations about some of the ways in which Israel was developing. Why, precisely, Rabbi Soloveitchik took such a dim view of his students' being members of Betar is not entirely clear. It could have been Betar's secularism, to which he remained opposed, or its militarist posture.

Smitty survived, however, fought with the Irgun in the unsuc-
cessful attempt to retake the Old City of Jerusalem in the War
of Independence, married a Yemenite woman, had children, and
became a leading lawyer in Israel, where he remained for the
rest of his life.

Years later, Rabbi Soloveitchik, after much lobbying by
Smitty's friends, granted David Smith his ordination. But in the
late 1940s, even after the Holocaust and the loss of one-third of
the Jewish people, being a Revisionist Zionist prevented him
from getting his degree.

At around the same time that Rabbi Finkelstein was prohib-
iting the singing of "Hatikvah" at JTS and YU's Rabbi Soloveitchik was refusing to grant Smitty his ordination, similar pressure
was brought on students at Cincinnati's Hebrew Union College
(HUC), the center of Reform Judaism. Rabbi Richard Hirsch recalled years later that when he informed HUC that he intended
to go to Israel to fight for the Haganah, Rabbi Nelson Glueck, the
president of the college, urged Hirsch not to go. When Hirsch
insisted, Glueck warned him that the college would grant him
no credit for any academic work he did there. Hirsch did eventually move to Israel and received his ordination, but at HUC, as
well, there was pressure on students not to join forces with the
just-emerging Jewish state.

In retrospect, all this seems incomprehensible. With the
Jewish people just climbing out of the abyss, how could it be that
American Jewish leadership and institutions did not show solidarity with the just-emerging state? There *was* no occupation
then, no accusation that Israel had abandoned liberal democratic
values, no resentment of Israel's rabbinate and its views of non-
Orthodox Judaism. None of this had arisen at all yet.

So how are we to explain this tepid, hesitant attitude toward Zionism in all three movements? To be sure, it was a period when many American Jews were immigrants, still focused on demonstrating their loyalty to America and on making their way into American society. Yet that is only a partial explanation. Just as with universalism versus particularism, or the messiness of history versus staying above the fray, a deeper issue is at play here. This time the issue was a disagreement over the very essence of Judaism. Is Judaism a religion? Or does being Jewish mean being part of a nation? To no small degree, that issue still lies at the heart of the divide between American Jews and Israel.

THE TENSION BETWEEN JUDAISM-AS-RELIGION and Judaism-as-nationhood is nothing new; it antedates Zionism by centuries. To get a glimpse of how deeply rooted this tension is in Jewish life, let's look at Hanukkah.

What is the story behind the holiday of Hanukkah? Even the Jewish tradition, it seems, is not certain. The Talmud itself asks "Why do we celebrate Hanukkah?" and gives what has become one of the standard answers. We celebrate the holiday because "when the Greeks entered the Temple, they polluted all the oils in the Temple, and when the Hasmonean dynasty overcame and defeated them, they checked and they found but one cruse of oil that was set in place with the seal of the High Priest, but there was in it only [enough] to light for a single day. A miracle was done with it, and they lit from it for eight days."

Hanukkah, says the Talmud, is about a miracle. God isn't explicitly mentioned in that passage, but it is obvious to the Talmud that it was God who wrought the miracle. Yes, the Maccabees (here called Hasmoneans, based on their family name) are mentioned, but the central dimension of the holiday is the miracle of the oil. Hanukkah is thus about a *religious* event.

The Jewish liturgy, however, suggests otherwise. In the prayer called "Al HaNissim" ("For the Miracles") that is added into the liturgy during Hanukkah, a different story takes center stage. There, the prayer book says, the critical part of the story is not the oil:

> [We thank you also] for the miracles, the redemption, the mighty deeds, and the victories in battle which You performed for our ancestors in those days, at this time.
>
> In the days of Mattathias, son of Yoḥanan the High Priest, the Hasmonean, and his sons, the wicked Greek kingdom rose up against Your people Israel to make them forget Your Torah and to force them to transgress the statutes of Your will. It was then that You in Your great compassion stood by them in the time of their distress. You championed their cause, judged their claim, and avenged their wrong. You delivered the strong into the hands of the weak, the many into the hands of the few, the impure into the hands of the pure, the wicked into the hands of the righteous, and the arrogant into the hands of those who were engaged in the study of your Torah. You made for Yourself great and holy renown in Your world, and for Your people Israel You performed a great salvation and redemption as of this very day. Your children then entered the holiest part of Your House, cleansed Your Temple, purified Your sanctuary, kindled lights in Your holy courts, and designated these eight days of Hanukkah for giving thanks and praise to Your great name.

In this prayer, the miracle of Hanukkah is not the religious miracle-of-oil, but the Maccabees' victory in their battle against the Greeks. This is Hanukkah as *national* event. Though the praise is addressed to God (not surprising for a prayer, of course), the heroes of the story are the warriors. What is miraculous is their victory, the triumph of the few over the many, the seemingly weak over the seemingly powerful. Here Hanukkah is about the survival of the nation and the restoration of sovereignty.

In the "conversation" between these two classic Jewish texts and their implicit debate about what is the essential dimension of Jewish life, we have an early version of the tensions that surfaced at those American rabbinical schools almost two thousand years later. Zionism did not invent the argument, but it did put it in sharp relief; suddenly, for the first time since the Maccabees, the Jewish people were being afforded a version of Jewish engagement that was not about religion but about statehood. As long as sovereignty was nowhere on the Jewish horizon, the default assumption that Judaism was a religion had prevailed mostly unchallenged. The awakening of a Jewish political movement, however, changed all that.

The Zionists were by no means oblivious to the fact that they were reigniting an old conversation. In some ways, in fact, their work was a declaration of ideological war on Judaism-as-religion.

If the classic debate unfolded in the folios of the Talmud and the volumes of liturgy, in the Yishuv the battle was often fought with music: Zionists were writing songs as they struggled to build their state. In 1924, Menashe Ravina, a German Jewish composer—and both a Zionist and a Communist—immigrated to Palestine. Twelve years later, in 1936, he wrote a Hanukkah song that became an Israeli classic. While basing his song on a verse from the biblical book of Psalms, "Who can express the mighty acts of the Lord, or cause all His praise to be heard?" (106:2), Ravina actually rejects the Psalmist. Instead of recounting the "mighty acts of the Lord," the secular Zionist Ravina has something else in mind; his poem refers to the "mighty acts of *Israel*." If the Psalmist believed that it was God who was the redeemer, Ravina disagrees: "In every generation, a hero arises / who redeems the nation."

For Ravina, and the Zionist world he represented, what mattered were the "mighty acts of Israel," not the "mighty acts of the Lord." Notice what else is missing from Ravina's account: there is no miracle of oil, and even the Temple is gone from the story. The Priests are gone. The Maccabees are military figures, nothing else. And God has been entirely excised. While faculty members at American rabbinical schools were certain that being a religion was what would save Judaism (recall Finkelstein's delight at synagogues in America filling up once more), Ravina and his colleagues believed that religion would destroy what was left of Jewish life. What would save Judaism was nationalism; what would save Judaism was Zionism.

The same attitude, perhaps even more extreme, features in another song from the 1930s, this one written by the Israeli poet and educator Aharon Ze'ev. Born in the Polish town of Sokołów Podlaski, Ze'ev had a colorful life, to put matters mildly. In 1920, during the Polish-Soviet War, he was charged with opening fire on soldiers from the conquering Red Army. Convicted and sentenced to death, Ze'ev was spirited out of harm's way at the very last moment and narrowly avoided execution. In 1925, he moved to Palestine, where, in addition to a series of other significant posts, he eventually served as the chief education officer of the IDF.

Given his colorful personality, the "in your face" tone of Ze'ev's song debunking the classic Hanukkah story should perhaps not surprise us. It begins with a not very well camouflaged attack on religion. Whoever is desperate for redemption, Ze'ev proclaims, "Should lift his eyes and his heart to us. / To the light—let him come!"

In traditional Jewish life, people who thirst for light—for the life of spirit—lift up their eyes to God. Not here, though. Yes, they should lift their eyes, but to the Zionists, and then join *them*, not God. The Hanukkah reference, which continues the assault on classic Jewish religious tropes, follows: "No miracle unfolded for us / We found no cruse of oil." Instead, Ze'ev insists, whatever redemption there was, was wrought by human hands: "We chiseled the rock until we bled / And there was light!"

It's all about what human beings do, Ze'ev insists. God is gone and so are miracles. Even the meaning of the light has changed. If light in classical Hanukkah is the light of the flame that was kindled in the Temple, now the light is the light of deliverance, the light of freedom, the light of independence so much on everyone's mind in the Yishuv in the 1930s when Ze'ev wrote his song.

Nation, not religion, said Ze'ev. Religion, not nation, said the heads of the American rabbinical schools. Here, too, a clash was bound to follow.

JUDAISM WITHOUT GOD? JUDAISM without mandated ritual rites? Judaism not as religion but as nationalism? This was completely new, a radical rewriting of Judaism. In some ways, this was a variation on the anti-passivity theme that Bialik displayed in his poem "In the City of Slaughter." Bialik stopped short, however, of rejecting religion altogether. For Bialik, religion was a complex matter. There was much about the religious world of his youth that he rejected, yet there were elements of Jewish religious life that he continued to love and to revere.

Such nuance was rare in Zionist circles, however. Though many of the early Zionists had grown up in religious homes with rich Jewish educations and were therefore in some ways always in dialogue with Jewish texts and traditions, many were deeply antagonistic to the way of life in which they had been raised. It is that antagonism to religion that figures in Ravina's and Ze'ev's songs. At the heart of their work lies a rejection, not just of Jewish weakness, but of everything having to do with religion. For decades, that dismissive attitude toward religion was a defining dimension of what Zionism was all about. To be sure, there were religious Zionists who did not share this orientation, and equally important, in recent decades a new openness to religiosity has begun to filter into parts of Israeli society. Yet we can now understand better rabbis like Louis Finkelstein and Joseph Soloveitchik who were troubled, to varying degrees, by movements that stressed peoplehood over religion, land over God, rebellion over tradition.

No work of literature captures Zionism's rebellion against religion more explicitly than Nathan Alterman's famous poem "The Silver Platter." Alterman, one of the great poets of the period of Independence (and after Bialik's death in 1934, almost universally recognized as the poetic voice of the Zionist movement), wrote "The Silver Platter" in response to the pithy remark by Chaim Weizmann that "a state is not handed to a people on a silver platter." He wrote this poem in December 1947, a month after the UN vote to partition Palestine and just months before Ben-Gurion would declare Israel's independence.

To fully appreciate Alterman's poem, we need to see how it plays off the biblical text to which he was responding. The poem describes the nation assembled, waiting for a "miracle, the one miracle and only." To traditional Jews, when the nation assembles waiting for a miracle, it is clear that it is awaiting the revealing of the Torah at Mount Sinai. Not so for Alterman, as the date of the poem suggests. Now the miracle, the "one and only," is the creation of the state.

Alterman's poem is riddled with a subtle derision of Jewish ritual practice. In the biblical account, as the nation prepares to receive the Torah, Moses tells the men not to approach a woman. But "The Silver Platter" features a boy and a girl, who are apparently inseparable and virtually indistinguishable. There would be no old-fashioned separation of the sexes in the new world that Alterman foresaw. In the Torah, the Israelites are commanded to wash their clothes as part of their preparation for revelation, but in the poem, the boy and the girl are caked with dirt, and they do not wash. Saving the Jews, Alterman wants to suggest, will require getting dirty. Not only is history a messy business, but cleanliness, purity, and holiness—religion, in other words—will not keep the Jews alive.

For Zionists, Judaism was the nation, and the revival of Judaism meant the restoration of the homeland. Not so for American Jews. For them, Judaism represented primarily a religion. That is why when Israelis are asked to complete the phrase "Jews and . . . ," they reply, "Jews and Arabs." They do not say, "Jews and Muslims," even though most of the Arabs of the region are Muslim. They say "Jews and Arabs" because when they think of themselves as Jews, they think primarily of peoplehood. So that is how they think of the others around them too.

MEANWHILE, AMERICAN JEWS WERE also engaged in their own dramatic rewrite of what Judaism was meant to be. Their claim that Judaism was "no longer a nation, but a religious community," and that they sought no return to Palestine, was precisely the opposite of what Zionism was doing in redefining Judaism as nationhood without religion. Thus, the Pittsburgh Platform, written in 1885, was deeply at odds with Zionism's fundamental commitments. Religion—and not nation—was the core of this emerging American Judaism. The stained-glass window of Congregation Sherith Israel in San Francisco depicting Moses descending, not from Mount Sinai, but from Yosemite's El Capitan captured matters perfectly. To Americans, the revolutionary spirit of that image was the claim that Sinai had come to California and revelation could be had in the United States. What Alterman was saying was that that revolution was far too tepid, far too meek, and ultimately useless given what the Jewish people needed. There is no need for Mount Sinai *anywhere*, he was saying, and it was time to forget revelation. It was time to build the Jewish future, to work the land, and to take up arms. Religion of any sort, Reform or Orthodox, was the enemy of Jewish progress.

While Alterman was arguing that it was the Land of Israel, soaked with Jewish blood if need be, that would redeem the Jewish people, American Jews often saw *America* as the new Promised Land. Rabbi Kaufmann Koller, who spearheaded the 1885 Pittsburgh Platform, said that in "the jubilant tocsin peals of American liberty" he heard "the mighty resonance of Sinai's thunder."* The Jews had a new promised land: "Here is the land where milk and honey flow for all. . . . This is the land of promise of a great and new human race."

Reform's rewriting of Judaism's essence, as we saw, was well suited to the American worldview that Woodrow Wilson would express several decades later. This reconceptualization of Judaism worked well for yet another reason: it made Judaism a better fit for an America in which religion was seen as a central and positive societal force.

No one articulated this better than Alexis de Tocqueville, the French diplomat and scholar best known for his two-volume study of the United States called *Democracy in America*. De Tocqueville believed that religion was critical to the perpetuation of the unusual democracy that had taken root in America. Unlike his French compatriots, who feared that the Catholic Church remained a threat to democracy even after the French Revolution, de Tocqueville felt that in America democracy's success actually *depended* on religion. By reminding human beings of values beyond their own needs, he believed, religion resisted the tyranny of the majority, individualism, materialism, and democratic despotism. Christianity "exerted 'a greater influence over the souls of men . . . in America' than anywhere else in the world," de Tocqueville said. He believed "that only in the United States was

---

* Even when the Reform Movement broke from the radical positions of the Pittsburgh Platform, it still did not abandon its antinationalism. The 1937 Columbus Platform, which tempered Pittsburgh's text somewhat, once again described Judaism as a religion, not a people. True, it mentioned the "Jewish people" in its first sentence, but even that was in the context of defining Judaism as a religion: "Judaism is the historical *religious* experience of the Jewish people." There was still no place for Zionism's fierce nationalist particularism. "Though growing out of Jewish life, its message is universal, aiming at the union and perfection of mankind under the sovereignty of God."

religion linked to 'democratic instincts' and the 'spirit of individual independence.'"

To side with religion, de Tocqueville said, was to side with America. To commit to religion was to commit to what made America great. By describing Judaism as a religion and not as peoplehood, the Reform rabbis were both avoiding the pitfall of stepping afoul of what would be Wilson's conditional welcome *and* defining Judaism in a way that it was, as far as de Tocqueville was concerned, a contribution to America's greatness.

That is why when American Jews complete the phrase "Jews and . . . ," they say, not "Jews and Arabs," as do Israelis, but "Jews and Christians," or "Jews and Gentiles." For in America, Judaism has become religion.

That strategy of conceiving of Judaism as a religion served American Jews well for a long time. "The newcomer," wrote Will Herberg, the Jewish American sociologist of religion, in 1955, "is expected to change many things about him as he becomes an American—nationality, language, culture. One thing, however, he is not expected to change—and that is his religion." Defining Judaism as a religion gave Judaism a kind of protected status: it was not something America would demand that Jews jettison in order to be seen as thoroughly American.

The transformation of Judaism into a religion served American Jews' interests in yet another way. America, after all, is corrosive of ethnic identity. Four generations after Italian immigrants arrived on America's shores, how Italian are their descendants? Do they speak Italian? Are their homes distinctively Italian in any meaningful way decades later? When a descendant of an Italian immigrant who came to the United States in 1910 marries a descendant of a German immigrant from the same period, is any cultural adjustment required? Rarely. Aside from ethnic identities related to physical appearance (African Americans, Asian Americans, Hispanic Americans, and the too often ignored Native Americans, among others), most other ethnicities have long since disappeared.

Even the ethnic dimension of Jewish life has mostly dissolved. Few American Jews speak Hebrew, Yiddish, or other Jewish languages. For the most part, cuisine in Jewish homes is scarcely different from that of other American homes. American progressives are culturally almost indistinguishable from progressives of other backgrounds. Jews were perhaps the last to give up the ethnic ghost, but even among American Jews, ethnicity is finally disappearing. If anything has survived, it has been a sense of Judaism as a faith tradition, Judaism as religion, no matter how profound or casual a person's faith and no matter what particular form religious participation takes.

IRONICALLY, THEN, BOTH ZIONISTS in Europe and the Yishuv and Jews in America were engaged in a thorough rewrite of Judaism. While each is understandably critical of the other's revision, both would do well to acknowledge their own radicalness and, at the same time, to recognize that what the other has done is an ancient and hallowed Jewish strategy for survival. There have been several prior dramatic "rewrites" of Judaism, including the advent of Hasidism in eighteenth-century Ukraine, but the paradigmatic example is the response of a small group of scholars to the destruction of the Second Temple.

When the Romans sacked Jerusalem in 70 CE, they essentially ended an entire Jewish way of life. In the poetic words of Lord Rabbi Jonathan Sacks, "All the institutions of national Jewish life were now gone. There was no Temple, no sacrificial order, no priests, no kings, no prophets, no land, no independence, and no expectation that they might soon return. With the possible exception of the Holocaust it was the most traumatic period in Jewish history. . . . Where in the despair was there a route to hope?"

The genius of the rabbis of the Talmud, who essentially created a new form of Jewish religious life, was being able to recognize the enormous crisis they faced and having the courage to reimagine a Judaism that could survive in the new world order. According to a Talmudic legend, Rabbi Yoḥanan ben Zakkai had predicted to the Roman general Vespasian that he, Vespasian, would one day rule Rome. Vespasian scoffed, but when he was eventually called back to Rome to assume the position of emperor, he said to ben Zakkai:

> "I will be going to Rome to accept my new position, and I will send someone else in my place to continue besieging the city and waging war against it. But before I leave, ask something of me that I can give you." Rabban Yoḥanan ben Zakkai said to him: "Give me Yavne and its Sages and do not destroy it and spare the dynasty of Rabban Gamliel and do not kill them as if they were rebels."

What ben Zakkai asked was that Vespasian spare the small band of scholars (of which he was a part) who would become the core of the new version of Jewish life that was already emerging, and Yavne, their seat of learning. That was, of course, a rather strange request, as even the Talmud notes. After all, why did he not just ask Vespasian to leave the Jews alone? Why did he not beg the Romans to end their war against the Jews?

We can take a very educated guess. Just as Louis Brandeis

understood that he had to do the best that he could to endorse Zionism in the particular American context in which he was working, so, too, Rabbi Yohanan ben Zakkai understood that there were concessions that Vespasian could make, and others that he would simply not consider. Ben Zakkai understood that the war against the Jews was not going to be suspended, and he intuited that it would be pointless—and perhaps dangerous—to request that of the emperor-to-be. He asked, therefore, for the best that he thought he might get, which was that Rome spare the lives of the scholars who were busy reinventing Judaism.

Yohanan ben Zakkai and his colleagues were reimagining Jewish life in light of the harsh realities of the world in which they lived. Chief Rabbi Lord Jonathan Sacks once more: "Every synagogue became a fragment of the Temple. Every prayer became a sacrifice. Every Jew became a kind of priest, offering God not an animal but instead the gathered shards of a broken heart."

That strategy not only worked in the first century but preserved Judaism for two millennia. Then the world changed again, Europe darkened, and to many Jews it became clear that the rabbis' strategy might no longer be able to preserve Jewish life. As the sun was setting on European Jewry, Jews in America and Palestine both reached the same conclusion—it was time for a reinvention of Judaism. How ironic it therefore is that their respective reconceptualizations of Judaism sparked the crisis between the two.

HOW DOES THIS RADICAL conceptual divide over whether Judaism is a religion or an ethnicity play out in relations between the two communities? One manifestation is the lack of political cooperation between Israeli and American Jewish progressives. Though right-of-center American Jews are often active in supporting Israel's right-leaning parties and offer financial support through American Friends of Likud and other organizations, there has been surprisingly little alignment between liberal American Jews and the Israeli political left.* There is, of course, some American organizational support for Israel's left-leaning parties, but the relationship on the left is not nearly as vigorous as it is on the right. Why is that?

Once again, the answer lies largely in the Judaism-as-religion issue, which makes it difficult for the two communities to understand each other. Einat Wilf—a secular and unabashedly nationalist former Knesset member and outspoken voice for liberal causes—is a compelling example of how Judaism-as-religion versus Judaism-as-nation creates a disconnect between the two communities. In 2018, she published a book titled *The War over the Right of Return*, in which she argues that the fundamental reason the Israeli-Arab conflict has never been settled has been Israel's refusal to reject outright the Palestinian demand for a "right of return" of 1948 refugees and their descendants.† The

---

* This was not always the case. In the pre-state era, and continuing even after Israel's establishment, there were worldwide movements, such as the Ichud Olami, that represented Israel's socialist parties and like-minded Jews throughout the world.

† UNRWA (United Nations Relief and Works Agency for Palestine) is the only UN body devoted to refugees of a particular region. Refugees in other parts of the world are all served under the aegis of the United Nations High Commissioner for Refugees (UNHCR). This is critically important, since UNRWA defines "refugee" for Palestinians differently from the definition used by the UN for any other group: it defines as refugees not only those who left Palestine during the 1948 War of Independence but their descendants as well. Because most of the original refugees are no longer alive, using the usual definition of "refugee" would yield a very small number. But by including the

fact that millions of Palestinians still harbor a hope of returning to "Palestine," argues Wilf, leaves open in their minds the possibility that Israel as a Jewish nation-state can still be ended. End that charade, she argues, and one major obstacle on the road to settling the conflict will have been removed.

What matters for us is not whether Wilf's analysis is right or wrong. What we need to note is that there is scarcely an American Jewish liberal who would dare speak aloud about denying the Palestinian right of return once and for all. How does Wilf straddle the fence, some might ask? How can she be both a liberal and such a committed nationalist? To Wilf, as to many Israelis, there is simply no fence to straddle. For many Israeli progressives like her, there is no tension at all between liberal values and Judaism-as-nation. But for American Jews who see themselves primarily as a religion and not a nation, Wilf's value set is a much more difficult position to adopt. The disconnect is between Judaism-as-justice and Judaism-as-survival. Those are obviously not always incompatible, but they *are* profoundly different instincts.

In the summer of 2018, when Palestinians began massive protests along the Gaza border, Israeli troops were forced to use live fire to keep masses of Gazans from approaching and then trampling the fence; had the fence been overrun, hundreds or even thousands of Gazans could have spread out across the area along the border, which is dotted with dozens of Israeli towns, kibbutzim, and even cities. There were concerns that a bloodbath might ensue.

To prevent that eventuality, the IDF ordered soldiers not to let anyone approach the fence. Tragically, some Gazans, especially

---

descendants of those 700,000 people, UNWRA claims that there are several million such Palestinian refugees.

the young, heeded the call of Palestinian leaders to attack the fence, and many were shot.* On a particularly horrific day in May 2018 (not coincidentally, the very same day that the American embassy in Jerusalem officially opened), some sixty Palestinians were killed trying to approach the fence. It was a grim day for Israelis, who were saddened by the loss of life. Nonetheless, even among Israel's left, there were no mass demonstrations, no widespread calls for investigations of the army's policy or its execution, and no calls for a change in government as a result of what had happened.

Israel's left understood what was at stake. When Hamas's leader, Ismail Haniyeh, had said in March, a few months prior, that the protests along the Gaza border were the beginning of the Palestinian return to "all of Palestine," Israeli leftists believed him. They similarly understood that if Haniyeh was cynically going to send dozens of young Palestinians to trample a border that Israel has always defended with lethal force (while he sat comfortably many kilometers away), he was knowingly sending his own citizens directly into harm's way. The Israeli left remained saddened and frustrated but, for the most part, quiet.

It was then that, in the United States, *The Forward* ran the above-mentioned piece with the headline "Israel's Choice to Shoot Palestinians Should Horrify—But Not Surprise Us." *The Forward*'s editors most likely did not know that Israeli liberals saw matters very differently (after all, most of those editors could not read and understand a Hebrew newspaper), and they did not bother to ask themselves why there was no outcry there.

---

* There were accusations that in a small number of cases, Israeli snipers also shot Palestinians who were not approaching the fence or committing any other act of violence, prompting the IDF to open several investigations.

Had they wondered about that, however, they might have come to understand that their visceral response to what had unfolded at the border was in large measure the product of Judaism-as-religion, while the sad but stoic response of the Israeli left stemmed from their lives being fashioned around Judaism-as-nation.*

That disconnect also explains the lack of real cooperation on matters of religion. This, too, Einat Wilf seeks to explain to American Jews frustrated that Israelis are not joining their calls for an egalitarian prayer space at the Western Wall, more support for Reform and Conservative Judaism in Israel, and the like. As Wilf explains, "The notion that praying to a god that does not exist next to the ruins of an outer support wall somehow matters more than doing it anywhere else [is] entirely alien to me." Israe-

---

* A particularly unfortunate instance of the divide over nationalism causing a rift between American and Israeli progressives, which also shed light on *The Forward*'s universe, unfolded in September 2018. Shortly after Ari Fuld, an American immigrant to Israel and a prominent speaker and activist on Israel's behalf, was stabbed to death by a teenage Palestinian terrorist in the Gush Etzion area right outside Jerusalem, Daniel Solomon, who had until not long before been an editor for *The Forward*, tweeted: "I think it shows a kind of charmed, modern naivete that people who occupy the lands of others expect to walk around unmolested." He continued, "Hard to feel much sympathy when this happens to settlers. Sry."

The Israeli left did not react in any similar way. Even Israeli progressives know that Gush Eztion is not "the territories" in the same way that other areas are, since the Gush fell into Jordanian hands just hours before Israel's creation. Most Israelis see it as having been *re*-taken in 1967. Israeli progressives also know that terror attacks occur not only in the territories but inside the green line as well. They are under no illusions that Fuld's murder was about "occupation." It was about Israel's existence. After an onslaught of horrified responses to his tweet, Solomon deleted it and apologized. By then, however, screenshots were ubiquitous and were being used by many across social media (whether fairly or not) as a reminder of how far some leading American progressives had drifted from any sense of identity with Israel, or even with the basic value of the lives of Jews.

lis vote first on security and the economy, she says, and even if
the issues that American Jews care about do matter to Israelis on
some theoretical level, those are the issues on which Israelis will
always compromise:

> Ever since Israeli Prime Minister Benjamin Netanyahu scuttled
> a deal that would have allowed Conservative and Reform Jews
> to pray at the Western Wall, Diaspora Jews have been loudly
> condemning Israel for its lack of religious pluralism. In fact,
> these accusations are nothing new; for years, American Jews
> have argued that the "State of the Jews" is not truly a home to all
> Jews, lacking the religious pluralism they find in the Diaspora.
>
> And yet, most Israeli Jews have no idea what they're talking
> about. As far as Israelis are concerned, they have an incred-
> ibly pluralistic society reflecting multiple religious practices,
> sects, sub-sects and ethnicities. Israeli Jews are remarkably
> tolerant of a host of different modes of practical ritualistic ex-
> pression. One can be a devout atheist-shrimp-eating-Shabbat-
> driving Jew or a fanatical, carry-out-all-the-Mitzvas one, and
> all are citizens of the Jewish state.
>
> As a society, Israelis really could care less how citizens ex-
> press their religious identity, Jewish or otherwise.
>
> Of course, this is not what liberal American Jews want
> when they ask for more "pluralism." What they mean is having
> equal standing in the public and political sphere for Conser-
> vative and Reform Judaism, which are all but foreign con-
> cepts to Israelis.

It is not that Israeli progressives disagree with their American
progressive counterparts. The reason that American progressives
are making no progress on the issues that matter to them in Israel

is that they have adopted a fundamentally religious agenda, when Israeli progressives tend to spend their political capital on issues related to foreign policy and social equality. That, too, is derivative of a reality in which one community is focused on nation while the other sees Judaism as essentially religion.

ANOTHER RELATED FACTOR DEEPENING the divide between American and Israeli Jews is also derived from the tension between Judaism-as-nation and Judaism-as-religion. That factor is the Hebrew language. Hebrew, obviously, is the language of discourse in Israel, and American Jews, for the most part, have decided not to speak or to understand it.

This blunt formulation is intentional: it's not just that American Jews do not speak Hebrew, but that over the years Jewish educators consciously chose to remove significant Hebrew-language education from their curricula. To be sure, learning a language takes time and effort, so they faced a significant pedagogical challenge given the limited number of hours with which they had to work. Yet, there are some schools (both Orthodox and non-Orthodox) that do teach Hebrew rigorously and give their students at least a good grounding. Most do not try; the decision not to teach Hebrew, say some scholars, was also a conscious decision not to highlight the peoplehood dimension of Judaism. Doing so would have made American Jews feel like outsiders in America.

Think about it. French citizens have a language that unites them. So, too, do Italians, Germans, Spaniards, Russians. We're not at all surprised by that—the fact that language is key to a country's culture is obvious. But it's also worth noting that people of the same *religion* need *not* share a language. Catholics in Peru have no language in common with Catholics in America. Protestants in Taiwan have no language in common with Protestants in Germany. And though many Israelis have learned English, the fact is that Jews in America have no language in common with Jews in Israel.

Language is an instrument not only of culture but also of nationhood. Jews have been aware of this since the time of the Bible. When Ezra and Nehemiah led the Jews who had returned from Babylonian exile back to Judea, they found the community there not only in disarray but on the verge of extinction. Nehemiah, describing what he saw, points to two issues relevant to our time as well. "I saw that the Jews had married Ashdodite, Ammonite and Moabite women; a good number of their children spoke the language of Ashdod and the language of those various peoples, and did not know how to speak Judean." As if he could have foretold our own time, Nehemiah worried about intermarriage and the loss of a distinct Jewish language; he understood that what defines a people is largely family and language.

The early Zionists understood this too. They revived ancient Hebrew—a language that for thousands of years had not been used as a language of daily discourse—not only because they needed a language to bind together all those who would gather together to build the Jewish state, but because Hebrew was the language of the Jews when they had last been sovereign.

Yehuda Alkalai, an early Zionist thinker and Sephardic rabbi, felt that among the many mistakes his ancestors had made in exile, the abandonment of language was central. "I wish to attest to the pain I have always felt at the error of our ancestors, that they allowed our Holy Tongue to be so forgotten. Because of this our people was divided into seventy peoples; our one language was replaced by the seventy languages of the lands of exile. . . . We must redouble our efforts to maintain Hebrew and to strengthen its position."

Similarly, when Leo Pinsker, one of Zionism's earliest important theorists, wrote *Auto-Emancipation: An Appeal to His People by a Russian Jew* in 1882, he noted, "The Jewish people lacks most of the essential attributes which define a nation. It lacks that authentic, rooted life which is inconceivable without a common language and customs and without geographic cohesion." A. D. Gordon, who would come to be seen as one of the spiritual fathers of the labor Zionist movement, also believed that Diaspora life had rendered an emaciated version of Jewish peoplehood—but the good news, he said, was that the Jews at least understood what was wrong and were intent on fixing it. "We are a people without a country, without a living national language, without a living culture—but that, at least, we know and it pains us, even if only vaguely, and we seek ways and means of doing what needs must be done."

Indeed, when Joseph Klausner sought to describe the great accomplishment that was the establishing of a new city named Tel Aviv, what he loved perhaps more than anything was the fact that it was a Hebrew-speaking city:

Have you seen in the Diaspora an all-Jewish city like Tel Aviv? . . .
Have you seen in the Diaspora an entire city built almost exclusively by Jews, from road and street to house and garden, where everything continues to be done by Jews right now, from water and power supply to waste removal?—No, no, you have not.

What made this Jewish rebirth possible, Klausner believed, was a Jewish spirit embodied in the revival of—of all things— language. It was Hebrew that was key to this new Jew, to the brimming sense of potential that characterized the entire Zionist enterprise in pre-state Palestine. What most struck Klausner about the Yishuv, more than any of its other manifold accomplishments, was what the Hebrew language had done to and for the Jew. "Klausner went on to enumerate the many facets of the Tel Aviv miracle; a city whose systems of government and justice are in Jewish hands; whose educational institutions operate strictly in Hebrew and whose literature and journalism are printed exclusively in Hebrew; whose language is Hebrew, as heard on every street and used for all common purposes."

In the United States, however, though there were pockets of Hebraists among American Jews, especially in the 1930s and 1940s, who raised their children in Hebrew-speaking homes, they were the small exception to the prevailing rule. Even Arthur Herzberg, perhaps the greatest American scholar of Zionism in his day, noted that the devotion to Hebrew so characteristic of Zionism was never going to take in America. "There is no great likelihood that for Jewish national reasons American Jewry will swim upstream and steep itself in Hebrew language and Hebrew culture. Israeli national culture will be admired by world Jewry, but not really shared, for we are not in the mood for becoming artificial cultural irredentists."

When the Conservative Movement explicated its fundamental principles in 1988, it noted the centrality of Hebrew to the Israeli experience and then went on to say that American Jews, unlike Israelis, did not see Judaism as a nation but as a religion in which ethics were central. The movement did not believe that Hebrew needed to be a pillar of Jewish identity:

> Israel and the Diaspora enjoy different advantages while facing unique challenges. Only in Israel may a Jew lead an all-

encompassing Jewish life. There . . . Hebrew is the nation's language and the Bible is studied in every school. Paradoxically, the very ease with which Jewish identity may be expressed in the Jewish state may give the false impression that religion is not needed in Israel for Jewish survival as it is in the Diaspora. We do not believe that Jewish identity can be replaced by Israeli identity or the ability to speak Hebrew. We are convinced that Jewish religion is essential as a source of ethical and moral values.

By the time this statement was written, American Judaism's move away from Hebrew was long under way. As early as 1906, Solomon Schechter, the Romanian-born British scholar who led the Jewish Theological Seminary and thus served as the titular head of Conservative Judaism, wrote, "It is a tragedy to see the language held sacred by all the world, in which Holy Writ was composed, and which served as the depository of Israel's greatest and best thought, doomed to oblivion and forced out gradually from the synagogue." The synagogue was hardly the only place where Hebrew was forced out; Hebrew as a spoken language was essentially excised from American Jewish life altogether.

David Ben-Gurion, realizing early on what was happening to Hebrew in America, went so far as to say that a sine qua non for being a Zionist was an "inner need . . . to live a full Jewish life" in Israel, immersed in both Jewishness and Hebrew. As for American Zionists, he said, "you tend to translate Zionism into 'Americanese,' while my conception differs." Moshe Sharett, who succeeded Ben-Gurion as prime minister, thought that Diaspora Jews ought to have as a goal making the "Hebrew language the living and cultural language of Jews in the Diaspora," so that they would become bilingual communities, as had happened in parts of Canada.

When a leading Jewish foundation dedicated to the renewal of Jewish life in America solicited a series of papers on "Judaism as Civilizations" in 2008, one respondent, an editor of *The New Republic* and one of American Judaism's most important public intellectuals, chose to focus on the centrality of language. "The Jew's homeland is not only soil," he argued, "it is the language." In the uniquely impoverished conception of Jewish culture created by American Jews, he said, Hebrew is not required—but they are wrong. "America was the first major Jewish culture to decide that it is possible to develop and bequeath the Jewish tradition without the Jewish language. It is a crime. [Jews] believe that any Jewish expression is equal to any other Jewish expression. . . . I study Maimonides and they cook chicken soup, and we are all Jews together—but it isn't true."

The American Jewish community is the first great community in the history of our people that believes that it can receive, develop, and perpetuate the Jewish tradition not in a Jewish language.* By an overwhelming majority, American

---

* One particularly poignant indication of the role of Hebrew as the Jewish people's eternal language emerged from the Warsaw Ghetto during the Holocaust. Abraham Lewin, a Jewish educator, chronicled Jewish life in the ghetto by keeping a diary, which he wrote in Yiddish. In the summer of 1942, however, the Nazis began the Great Deportation, sending some 250,000 Jews to their deaths in Treblinka. As part of the Great Deportation, Lewin's wife and sixteen-year-old daughter were sent to Treblinka as well. Lewin briefly ceased writing, but when he resumed, he wrote in Hebrew, which he continued to do until he, too, was murdered. David Roskies, a scholar of Holocaust literature, suggests that once the Jews were no longer confined to a ghetto but were now being exterminated in mass numbers, Lewin switched to Hebrew because that was the language that

Jews cannot read or speak or write Hebrew, or Yiddish. This is genuinely shocking. American Jewry is quite literally unlettered. The assumption of American Jewry that it can do without a Jewish language is an arrogance without precedent in Jewish history.

Ironically, his argument continued, where American Jews have excelled has been in creating great communal institutions. But these institutions have made great cultural contributions to *American* culture, not to *Jewish* culture. As a result, "we are in danger of transforming American Jewish culture into an essentially commemorative culture," a culture that lives off the contributions of those who came before, with no substantial contributions from new generations to that ongoing chain of cultural exploration and development.

Given the centrality of Hebrew to the Zionists' sense of accomplishment, the abandonment of Hebrew in the United States was bound to create a rift, a sense of otherness. And on a much more utilitarian level, American Jews' decision not to learn Hebrew means that they have access to a very thin slice of Israeli culture. Everything that they know or feel about Israeli society is fed by a cultural trickle mediated by others who decide what should and should not be translated. If a citizen of France or Germany spoke no English, how deep an understanding could they possibly have of the United States, its culture, its struggles, and its nuances? Very little. No Frenchman or German who did not speak English could be said to understand America in any meaningful way, and any advice they offered would be ignored,

---

would transform his "private testimony onto a meta-historical plane" and "ensure the document's eternality."

swatted away like a pesky fly that, while annoying, was of no import at all.

Not speaking Hebrew is not a moral flaw, and today's American Jews have no access to Hebrew because of decisions that other people made. Nor can their lack of knowledge of Hebrew be fairly seen as an indication that American Jews are not wise or do not care. Their lack of facility with Hebrew, however, even on the most rudimentary level, limits them to encountering Israel through the lens of what the English-language press decides they should read, without direct access to Israel's press, literature, music, television, or culture. How passionate could any human relationship be if almost every interaction was lived through a filter someone else had constructed?

WHETHER JUDAISM IS A religion or a people is no mere academic matter. It is also not a matter of right or wrong. American Judaism had good reason to be attracted by Judaism-as-religion. Zionists had equally good reason for opting for peoplehood over religion. What is critical for us to understand is that the divide that Jews now confront reflects the roots of each of these communities and how Jews in each place define what it means to be a Jew.

These competing definitions of Jewishness have even further implications. How Jewishly infused should society be? How much religion ought to be allowed in the public square? Because of their radically different reads of what Judaism is, American Jews and Israelis instinctively have different reactions to these questions, too, as we shall see in the next chapter. And those different reactions, sadly, widen the divide even further.

6

HOW NAKED A PUBLIC SQUARE:
A LIBERAL OR ETHNIC DEMOCRACY?

In 2018, the Israeli Knesset passed a highly controversial bill declaring that Israel is the nation-state of the Jewish people. Even those Israelis who vociferously opposed the bill (either because of its timing or because of the wording of certain clauses) saw nothing terribly controversial about its central claim—that Israel is the nation-state of the Jewish people.

After all, when the British issued the 1917 Balfour Declaration, they stated: "His Majesty's government view with favour the establishment in Palestine of a national home for the Jewish people." A national home for the Jewish people did not mean just a democracy in which Jews would have no fewer rights than anyone else. (That is what the United States was meant to be.) The Balfour Declaration clearly intended the creation of an entirely different kind of country.

Israel's Declaration of Independence had made precisely that claim as well. The phrase "Jewish State"—not "state of the

Jews"—appears no fewer than five times in the Declaration. Even as the Declaration appeals to the United Nations for support, it asks that the UN "assist the Jewish people in the building-up of its State." And it reaches out to *Jews* around the world, asking them to join in the building of the state.

In 1958, ten years after independence, Israel passed a Basic Law (which has quasi-constitutional status in Israel) declaring that parties denying the "existence of the State of Israel as a Jewish and democratic state" would be prohibited from running for the Knesset. The 1992 Basic Law on Human Dignity and Liberty opens by stating that "the purpose of this Basic Law is to protect human dignity and liberty, in order to establish in a Basic Law the values of the State of Israel as a Jewish and democratic state." Given the Balfour Declaration, the Declaration of Independence, the 1958 and 1992 Basic Laws, and much more, Israelis—both left and right—failed to see anything terribly controversial about the central claim of the 2018 Nation-State Law.

Throughout the rest of the world, however, including among many Jews who care deeply about Israel, the reaction was entirely different. *Time* magazine announced that "A New Law Shifts Israel Away from Democracy." The *Atlantic* noted that "critics, especially Jews in the diaspora, see it as a definitive declaration in favor of a Jewish identity at the expense of a democratic one." One writer in *The Forward*, reflecting a view held by many American Jews, claimed that the major problem with the bill was that "enshrining Israel as the nation-state of the Jewish people makes constitutional the second-class status of Arab citizens."

Israelis were befuddled by the brouhaha. Yohanan Plesner, president of the Israel Democracy Institute and a former member of the Knesset, asked, "Why all the commotion over a law that seeks to affirm something most Jews fervently believe—that

Israel is the nation-state of the Jewish people?" Plesner actually opposed the law for a variety of reasons, but he saw nothing objectionable about the law's central claim that Israel is the nation-state of the Jewish people.

Many Israelis felt that the Nation-State Law was gratuitous, designed mostly to buttress the prime minister's political standing, and they wished that it had never come up. Given that it had, however, as much as they were appalled by the prime minister's political ploy, they were even more incredulous about the reaction that the law evoked. Calling Israel the nation-state of the Jewish people seemed to them to be belaboring the obvious.

WHY WERE THE ISRAELI and American Jewish reactions so different? At its core, just as we have seen with other conflicts throughout this book, this was a question of the radically different purposes at the heart of each of the two countries. The United States was created to welcome to its shores people from around the globe, whatever their backgrounds. Israel was created to foster the recovery and renewed flourishing of the Jewish people.

To American sensibilities, there is something deeply disturbing about the legal and cultural implications of a country being a specifically *Jewish* country. American Jews, after all, have long been "mentors of American pluralism," believing that their success in America has been due in no small way to the fact that America is not an explicitly Christian country. Though the principle of the separation of church and state is as old as the First Amendment, American Jews have long had to fight for the cultural equality that they now take for granted. That has made them all the more intent on preserving those rights, by keeping religion out of the public square.

"Blue Laws," which mandated the closing of businesses on Sundays, had put Jewish enterprises closed on Saturdays at a disadvantage. As those laws eroded, Jews felt that America was making progress, drawing ever closer to its founders' ideal. Early traditions of prayer in American public schools, which lent them a distinctly Protestant tone, also aroused Jewish concern. Jewish organizations fought the tradition and then, once they won, worked tirelessly to safeguard those gains. Many Jewish organizations also opposed government support for parochial schools, not because such support would necessarily put Jews at a disadvantage, but because Jews worried that government involvement in religious education would weaken the separation between church and state. That, they feared, risked everything they had achieved.

On some church-state issues, the Jewish community split. Most mainstream American Jewish organizations sought to eliminate sectarian celebrations of Christmas in public schools and argued that Christmas displays—in particular the cross and creche displays—ought to be banned from public property. When the Supreme Court ruled in *Lynch v. Donnelly* (1984) that the creche was not objectionable if it was in the context of other "secular" Christian symbols, many mainstream Jews were distressed. They worried that Christianity was creeping back into the public square. Although Chabad, like some other Orthodox groups, had no objection to the ruling—after all, they wanted to display Menorahs in public spaces, and if *Lynch* opened the door to Christian displays, it would do the same for Jews—most American Jews instinctively embraced what Richard John Neuhaus, a Roman Catholic priest and American public intellectual, called "the naked public square."

Ironically, in Israel, even *secular* Israelis implicitly agreed with American Chabad. They instinctively felt that for civic life to be meaningful, the public square should *not* be overly naked. Neuhaus agreed. He argued that a meaningful public moral discourse had to be based on tradition of some sort. Otherwise, he said, "politics becomes civil war carried on by other means." Either we have some shared, essentially agreed-upon tradition that sets the tone and content of our society, or internecine cultural warfare becomes virtually unavoidable.

American Jews instinctively disagree with Neuhaus's critique of the naked public square. They believe that the most effective way to protect an environment of tolerance is a kind of hyper-civility, in which as little as possible is said or done that might offend or cause discomfort to others. Yet there is a danger to such blandness, to a lack of cultural color and specificity. When Neuhaus retorts that "civility is the language of the uncertain," he is denigrating what America was becoming and, implicitly, *lauding* what the Jewish state was trying to do. Israel, especially given the radically secular roots of many of its founders, has never been about theological certainty. But it *has* been about what we might call a "certainty about a desire to belong." For that reason, for most Israelis, it was long clear—and remains so—that Israel should be not only the "state of the Jews" but a deeply "Jewish state" as well.

THIS QUESTION OF ISRAEL being a "state of the Jews" versus a "Jewish state" is as old as the book that launched political Zionism in the first place. Theodor Herzl titled his 1896 book *Der Judenstaat*. The German term, however, is ambiguous. Did Herzl intend by his title "The Jewish State" or "The State of the Jews"? In other words, did Herzl have in mind a state that would *comprise* mostly Jews, or a state whose very *content* would be Jewish at its core? Was Israel's Jewishness going to be *demography* or *essence*?

Surprisingly, some Israeli public intellectuals have argued that Herzl had demography in mind—or should have. Amnon Rubinstein, who has served as both education minister and chairman of the Knesset Law and Constitution Committee, once opined that "Herzl entitled his famous booklet *Der Judenstaat*, a state of the Jews, hardly a Jewish state." Shulamit Aloni, who until her death in 2014 was a leading public figure in Israel's political left, said even more contentiously, "I do not accept the idea of a 'Jewish state.' It is a 'state of the Jews' to be exact. Herzl wrote a book called *The State of the Jews*." And Amos Oz said, "Herzl's book was called *The State of the Jews* and not *The Jewish State*: A state cannot be Jewish, any more than a chair or a bus can be Jewish."

Oz, brilliant novelist though he was, was wrong about the impossibility of a state being Jewish. That states *can* be ethnic or religious is obvious; for instance, no one questions whether Saudi Arabia or Iran are Muslim states, both in name and in substance. The question is whether or not Israel *should* be. To some degree, the public intellectuals cited here began debating Israel's Jewishness after that train had already left the station. For long before there was a Jewish state, there was an implicit understanding in the Yishuv that Jewish substance should pervade Israel's "ether." Israel has codified a plethora of laws that, however odd or even offensive they may sound to American ears, knowingly impinge on Israelis' individual autonomy in order to protect and enhance the Jewish nature of the Israeli public square.

These laws cover a wide array of dimensions of Israeli life, especially in matters that pertain to religion, culture, and nationality. Those pertaining to religion are the most obvious.

Conversion to Judaism is controlled by the chief rabbinate, a law that the Knesset has been unwilling to overturn; since the chief rabbinate does not recognize conversions performed by non-Orthodox rabbis, this is a source of much American Jewish resentment. Intercity public buses do not run on Shabbat, and in most cities even local public transportation is suspended during Shabbat. In most cities (though Tel Aviv has been taking the lead in challenging this tradition), the law mandates that most commercial establishments be shuttered on Shabbat. The Israeli public square is profoundly different on Shabbat.[*]

Israel has also taken many nonlegal steps to ensure the Jewish nature of the public square. On Friday afternoons in Jerusalem, the air-raid siren sounds just as Shabbat begins. It is not nearly as loud as the "real" air-raid siren so that citizens know that what they are hearing is not the "real thing," but it is audible throughout the city nonetheless. Why sound the siren on Friday afternoons? At the time that the Temple stood, the shofar was sounded from the Temple Mount's southwestern corner rooftop as Shabbat began; today that "public announcement" of Shabbat is replicated by the air-raid siren. There is no Temple in Jerusalem anymore, but for a few seconds each week Jerusalemites live as if there were.

Though America's separation of church and state leads many to believe in a clear line between religion and culture, in

---

[*] Not all these "religious taboos" are legally mandated. In Israel, scarcely a car moves on the streets, even on the major highways, on Yom Kippur. Families can literally walk in the middle of an eight-lane highway on Yom Kippur, knowing that not a single vehicle will be moving—even though there is no law that says one cannot drive on Yom Kippur. Some social consensus about the Jewish public square is so universally held that there is no need to legislate it. Indeed, legislating it might raise objections and lead to the erosion of that tradition.

countries like Israel, the boundary between religion and culture is often very unclear, and what may seem like a religious edict may actually be a cultural one. Israeli law, for example, forbids the public display of *hametz* (leavened bread) during the Passover holiday. In 2008, when a municipal judge overruled the conviction of four merchants who had *sold* leavened bread on Passover, she justified that decision by pointing to a legal technicality, *not* by arguing that the state should have no say in what food citizens should or should not be able to sell because of a religious holiday.

Interestingly, even many secular Israelis agreed with her, in recognition of the tension between "freedom of religious expression" (or freedom *not* to observe the religious dictum) and the formation of a national identity with Judaism at its core. Foreign Minister Tzipi Livni, herself a secular Jew (and once a political darling of American Jewish progressives), was not concerned about the law's curtailment of Israelis' individual freedoms. A larger "good" was at stake. "Ostensibly, the ban on the public display or sale of bread on Passover is a minor and marginal issue, but I believe that this is not the case," she wrote and was quoted in the *New York Times*. "In my view, this prohibition is part of the substantive question of how we wish to characterize our identity in the national home for the Jewish people." The Israeli legal system's limitation on personal autonomy, Livni was saying, is a price that Israeli citizens should be willing to pay in order to create a richly Jewish public square.

Another example of Israeli legislators and courts embedding Jewish culture in the public square has been what is known as the "Pigs Law." To Jews, pigs have been a symbol of the "forbidden" since ancient times. As archaeologists have shown, "Bones recovered from the excavations of the small early Israelite villages in the highlands differ from settlements in other parts of the country in one significant respect: there are no pigs. . . . Though the early Israelites did not eat pork, the Philistines clearly did."

The Knesset has "channeled" this cultural artifice as well in its attempt to color Israel's public square with a Jewish hue. Enacted in 1962, the Pigs Law forbids raising pigs in Israel, except in Arab villages. Though public support for the law has eroded since then (largely because the chasm between religious and nonreligious Jews has deepened as the rabbinate's attempt to impose tradition on Israelis increases secular Jews' resistance to laws that appear to coerce them into Jewish observance), it has never been repealed. The "infringement" on the rights of those who might have wished to raise pigs was seen as justified in order to create a Jewish ambience in the Jewish state. Pigs being perhaps the paradigmatic symbol of forbidden food in Jewish tradition, even the vast majority of secular Jews in Israel's early years had no objection to the law.

Of course, the courts have also had to ensure that they do not intrude unnecessarily on citizens' individual autonomy. In 2004, for example, the Supreme Court overturned (pending further review) local statutes in Tiberias, Beit-Shemesh, and Carmiel that had prohibited the sale of pork anywhere in the city, specifically arguing that those rulings were an illegitimate limitation on citizens' autonomy. Justice Aharon Barak, widely acclaimed as one of Israel's greatest jurists, acknowledged that there was reason to view with some sympathy the intent of the law because pigs were not only a religious issue but a *national symbolic issue as well*. Still, he cautioned, the law impinged too draconically on the rights of citizens in those cities who might want to eat pork, so the court set aside the laws and demanded that the cities review them.

Another example of Israel using legislation to deepen the

Jewish color of the public square is the Ninth of Av, the day in Jewish tradition for mourning the destruction of the two Temples in Jerusalem (the first in 586 BCE at the hands of the Babylonians and the second by the Romans in 70 CE). Memory of the destruction of the Temples, both their literal destruction and their fates as a metaphor for what could happen to Israel in the future, looms large in Israeli life. On the Ninth of Av, much of Israeli television (another dimension of the public square in today's world) is devoted to programming germane to the Ninth of Av; some of it is always about the Holocaust, which invariably comes to mind for any Israeli who thinks about "utter destruction."

Recall, also, Moshe Dayan's aforementioned plan to describe Israel's possible military collapse in the early days of the Yom Kippur War as "the destruction of the third Temple." When Yehuda Amichai, one of Israel's leading poets and a deeply soulful secularist, wished to discuss Israel's propensity for self-destructive behavior, he also turned to the Ninth of Av as a metaphor, since the historic weight and meaning of the day are universally understood in Israel. Writing of Jerusalem's "suicide attempts," he penned a poem in which he said that Jerusalem "tried again on the Ninth of Av," and then predicted, with sadness, "She'll never succeed / but she'll try again and again." In Jewish (and now, Israeli) parlance, nothing conveys the propensity for self-destruction more than the image of the Ninth of Av.

That is why Israel has used legal restrictions to ensure that the Ninth of Av remains part of Israelis' historical and ethnic vocabulary. Local municipalities have legal authority to close restaurants, cafés, bars, and movie theaters on the Ninth of Av. The vast majority of Israelis do not fast on the Ninth of Av, and the law makes no suggestion that they should. What it does suggest, however, is that the destruction of the two Temples, each of which led to the Jewish people being exiled, is a critical memory for a state that has sought to undo exile. Even a relatively minor religious day like the Ninth of Av has secular legal status.

In a different vein, but essentially for similar reasons, Israeli law permits people to marry only people of their own religious tradition; that applies to Jews, Christians, and Muslims, among others. Imagine a U.S. law that officially sanctioned only marriages where both partners were of the same religion. Or an American congressman proposing a law stating that a political party that did not endorse the United States as a *Christian* country would be disqualified from running. The mere notion is preposterous.

Today intermarriage in the American Jewish community scarcely raises an eyebrow. When Chelsea Clinton married a Jewish man or Mark Zuckerberg married a non-Jewish woman, the reaction was more one of curiosity than anything else, and even that only because these were public figures. More generally, intermarriage in the United States has ceased to surprise even in the slightest. Some 70 percent of non-Orthodox American Jews intermarry.

In Israel, however, intermarriage is still a profound social taboo because in Jewish tradition, marriage and family are considered bulwarks of fashioning and transmitting identity. In 2018, when Tsahi Halevi, the Israeli actor and star of the series *Fauda*, married Lucy Aharish, an Arab anchorwoman, the wedding caused a (short-lived) storm of controversy. Interior Minister Aryeh Deri said in an interview that "assimilation is consuming the Jewish people" (keep in mind that he spoke about the phenomenon "consuming" the Jewish people while addressing one single instance of intermarriage), while Likud member of Knesset Oren Hazan, never known for subtlety, said, "I'm not accusing Lucy Aharish of seducing a Jewish soul in order to hurt our nation and prevent more Jewish offspring from continuing the Jewish line. On the contrary, she's welcome to convert." He even had a message for the bride: "Lucy, it's nothing personal, but know that Tzahi is my brother and the people of Israel are my people. Enough with assimilation!"

While it is possible that Aharish's being an Arab contributed to the sentiments of Deri, Hazan, and others, neither Deri nor Hazan said a word about her ethnic background. What they focused on was assimilation. It would be almost impossible to imagine an interfaith wedding in the United States causing such outrage, nor would one expect to hear government officials or community leaders reacting in that fashion.

Perhaps the most controversial of all of Israel's legal means of protecting a Jewish "public square" is the law (supported by two major Supreme Court rulings) that permits small communities to set up "admissions review boards" to decide who will be able to move into the town or village. Opponents of the rules argue that they are racist, since the fairly obvious intent is to allow Jewish communities to prevent Arabs from moving in.* But not even all Israeli liberal scholars agree with that assessment. Even if the goal is to prevent Arabs from moving into Jewish neigh-

---

* In one case, judges in the minority (including Supreme Court justice Salim Joubran, a Maronite Christian Arab), who wished to rule against the legitimacy of the law, pointed to public comments made by Knesset members who had supported the law and stated unabashedly that the goal of the law, despite its explicit nondiscrimination clause, was to prevent the admission of Arabs into villages that did not want them. The majority, who could not deny what the lawmakers had said, insisted that what mattered was what the law's wording actually stipulated, not opinions expressed by lawmakers as to the purpose of the law.

borhoods (or Jews moving into Arab neighborhoods, for that matter), the issue is not race, they insist, but the legitimate desire of a community (Jews in this case, though Arabs could want the same thing) to live in a setting where their culture does not have to compete in the public sphere. The whole point of leaving Diaspora and moving to a Jewish homeland, Zionists felt, was to end assimilation. The days of Jews having to accommodate their way of life to the sensibilities of those around them had to end. Israel, many scholars therefore argue, should give both Jews and Arabs the right to live in settings where pressures to assimilate will be tempered; Arabs should therefore likewise have every right to live in their communities knowing that Jews will not begin moving in.*

Interestingly, the debate over mixed communities predates Israel's establishment by decades. David Ben-Gurion, Israel's founding prime minister and (as a socialist for much of his life) long the hero of the American left, was opposed to mixed communities. In an essay he penned as part of his ongoing debate with Brit Shalom, he said: "We should strive to end mixed cities to whatever degree that is possible. Jerusalem should serve as a prime warning." He insisted that collusion between the British administration and the Arab effendis had reduced a large Jewish majority to a vulnerable minority, a phenomenon he did not wish repeated throughout the country. He told his readers that he was completely committed to fairness: "Just as I oppose discrimination

---

* The Israel Democracy Institute (IDI) came out strongly against including a clause to the same effect in the 2018 Nation-State Law. The IDI argued that such a clause was motivated by racist instincts, and that giving it the status of a Basic Law would skirt limitations that the courts had imposed on related laws.

against the right of the Jewish community in Jerusalem, so am I against any injury to the right of those who are not Jews." But in his mind, fairness did not have to mean integration. Liberal values did not have to supersede the right of Jews to have their own communities.

For Ben-Gurion, the ethnicity-blind commitments of American society were not as sacred in the Israeli setting. It was not that equality was unimportant. But it was critical, he argued, to create a space in which Jews could once again thrive as Jews without feeling constrained by others, as they had always felt in the Diaspora. As long as the rights of Arabs were not trampled, he saw nothing wrong with purposefully separate communities.

It bears noting that the desire for reasonably homogeneous communities is not only a Jewish-Arab issue. When asked if they would be willing to live in a neighborhood with ultra-Orthodox Jews, 78 percent of secular Israelis say no (though no one has proposed a law that would prevent a Jew from moving into another Jewish neighborhood). In a book on emerging trends in Israeli religiosity and identity, Shmuel Rosner, a noted Israeli journalist, summed up matters as follows: "In other words, everyone wants separation." The various *Jewish* groups in Israeli society—ultra-Orthodox, national-religious, traditional, secular, and others—each prefers to "keep for itself a space that feels appropriate to its way of life, without undue influence from other groups."

Such a sentiment may seem at odds with how Americans think of an ideal society (though in reality, of course, American neighborhoods are much less integrated than many would like), but unlike the United States, which sought to set ethnic ties aside, Israel is a country fundamentally committed to the flourishing of ethnic identity. The desire for separation feels to many Israelis as nothing other than equal opportunity for all to preserve a way of life and a set of cultural or religious traditions, without pressure to accommodate themselves to outside cultural pressures; this is part of the very purpose of the Jewish state.

ALL THIS SHOWS HOW fundamentally different a project Israel is from the United States, and in particular how radically different it is from what American Jews want *America* to be. Part of what stymies conversations between American Jews and Israelis when conflicts about the public square arise (the Nation-State Law, the Western Wall, and even asylum-seekers[*]) is that they never surface the fundamental disagreements about what type of society Israel was meant to be. When Israel takes steps that suddenly highlight Israelis' desire, not for a naked public square but for one infused with deep Jewish resonance, American Jews are often appalled. When Israel does something ethnocentric that strikes American Jews as antithetical to fundamental American values, many American Jews reflexively call those steps "antidemocratic" (since democracy, they believe, is one of America's most central values). Israelis, in turn, cannot understand why American Jews, who face overwhelming pressures to assimilate, do not understand the significance of what Israel is desperately trying to preserve.

---

[*] In 2018, a major controversy erupted in Israel when the prime minister announced plans to evict some forty thousand Sudanese and Eritrean asylum-seekers who had entered Israel illegally, seeking work. Many Israelis opposed the move, arguing that a country built for refugees from the Holocaust could not turn its back on people fleeing human disasters in Africa. Others argued, however, that not evicting them would set a precedent, leading to more illegal immigration, which would then erode the demographic Jewish majority Israel needed to remain democratic but also Jewish. In response to widespread objections to his plan, the prime minister backed down.

CONTRARY TO ALL THOSE critics of Israel's Nation-State Law, the real issue is not whether Israeli democracy is eroding but rather what kind of democracy Israel should be. To paraphrase George Orwell, not all democracies were created equal.

Indeed, Israeli legal scholars have been pointing that out for decades. Professor Ruth Gavison, a legal activist, a former professor at Hebrew University's law school, and once a nominee to Israel's Supreme Court, has pointed out that "the real tension is not between Israel's 'Jewish' and 'democratic' aspects, but between competing ideas within democracy, which are forced to find a balance between complete civic equality and freedom for the majority to chart the country's course." She points out, however, that "the Jewish character of the State of Israel does not, in and of itself, mean violating basic human rights of non-Jews or the democratic character of the country." Gavison is, of course, fully aware that the distinct Jewishness of the state makes many Arabs feel like second-class citizens, but she denies that this means that Israel is somehow not democratic. She writes: "Non-Jews may not enjoy a feeling of full membership in the majority culture; this, however, is not a right but an interest—again, it is something which national or ethnic minorities almost by definition do not enjoy—and its absence does not undermine the legitimacy of Israeli democracy."

As if she were echoing Neuhaus and his call for rooting a society's values in a particular tradition, Gavison says:

> The idea of national self-determination doesn't mean that all the population of a country belongs to one ethnic or national group. It means . . . this country does have a specificity and that specificity is the materialization of the right of a specific

people with a specific culture, with a specific history, to self-determination, to enlisting the power of the state to protect themselves physically, culturally, and, in terms of identity, against the forces of assimilation or liquidation or attack by other groups around them.

This viewpoint, of course, is entirely foreign, indeed offensive, to many American Jews. Over the past seventy-five years, the defining social issue for many American Jews was civil rights for African Americans; many Jews were deeply and personally involved in the struggle, a few were killed in the process, and many Jews identified with the cause.[*] To be involved in American Judaism's social activism was to be antisegregation, for "segregation" meant "evil."

For Israelis to support segregated communities seems a fundamental repudiation of the values that have long been central to American Jews. How could a Jewish state, in which American Jews often take such pride and which has long boasted that it is the only democracy in the Middle East, be open to policies that seem anathema to what has made America such a great country—its open-armed welcome to refugees, which has allowed Jews to succeed so dramatically in their new American home?

None of this makes any sense unless we accept the fundamental premise that Israel and the United States fashioned

---

[*] Many others identified Jews with the cause as well. When Rabbi Abraham Heschel marched with the Reverend Martin Luther King Jr. in Selma, Alabama, in 1965, he was confronted by banners that read: "Koons, Kikes, and Niggers Go Home!" The Jewish embrace of the cause of blacks was at that time a basic fact of American political and cultural life.

very different democracies because they were founded to serve very different purposes. Even committed Americans like Louis Brandeis—who reconfigured his Zionist views to make Zionism and Americanism entirely compatible—imagined a Jewish state as a "legally secured home, where they may live together and lead a Jewish life, where they may expect ultimately to constitute a majority of the population." The great American Jewish justice intuited that Israel could not be a Jeffersonian democracy situated in the Middle East. The Jewish state that emerged decades after Brandeis's work on behalf of Zionism is not a miniature version of America.

Ruth Gavison insists that this difference was both intentional and legitimate. Israel, she says, was never meant to be the sort of democracy that Thomas Jefferson, Alexander Hamilton, and James Madison had in mind for America and largely succeeded in creating.* Israel, unlike the United States of America, is not a "liberal democracy" but an "ethnic democracy"—a democratic system in which all citizens have equal claims on civil and political rights, but in which the majority group (Jews in Israel's case) have some sort of favored cultural, political, and, at times, legal status.

The motivation for this particular kind of democracy in Israel stems neither from racism nor from a desire to do Israel's Arabs ill—it stems from the very purpose of the state, which was, as Balfour put it, to be "a national home for the Jewish people." Even Professor Sammy Smooha, one of Israel's most

---

* It is both obvious and worthy of note that many groups in America have not received their fair share of the country's bounty. That is a critical issue for the future of American democracy, but beyond the scope of this book's discussion.

prolific scholars on the issue of ethnic democracy and a consistent advocate for Israeli Arab rights in Israel, acknowledges that "the democratic framework is real, not a facade."

THERE IS NO DOUBT that laws about separate communities are "edgy." To the extent that they are motivated by racism, they are appalling. But when they are genuinely fashioned to foster the kind of cultural comfort and flourishing that is not possible in most of the Diaspora, many Israelis believe, they may well be legitimate—though citizens and the courts must obviously tread carefully.

Nor is the "edginess" of Israel's focus on protecting the Jewish nature of Israel's cultural ether limited to those laws. It is ubiquitous, appearing virtually everywhere one turns. As noted earlier, Israel's anthem, "Hatikvah," speaks specifically of a "Jewish soul" and Jewish yearning. That clearly makes it difficult, if not impossible, for an Israeli Arab to sing "Hatikvah." Yet Israelis, who are very cognizant of the problem, have so far been willing to live with that tension in order to make Israel's Jewish-purpose central.[*] Similarly, Israel's flag is designed to be in aesthetic conversation with the *tallit*, the traditional Jewish prayer shawl. That, too, undoubtedly complicates citizenship

---

[*] Some have suggested that Israel explore a solution akin to Canada's. Canada has two anthems, one in English and one in French, which are not precise translations one of the other. The French version has distinct Christian references, such as "Il sait porter la croix" (he can carry the cross), that are not found in the English version. In Israel, the suggestion has been made that Israel create an Arabic version that could be sung alongside the Hebrew, but instead of speaking of Jewishness, it would speak of "Israeliness." Thus far, the idea has gotten little traction.

for Israel's non-Jewish citizens, and Israel's founders understood that as well. The same with Israel's national symbol, the Menorah, which is a distinctly Jewish religious symbol.

Even Israel's national language is a way in which the Jewish state communicates the centrality of Jewishness to its very purpose. Israel's State Education Law mandates that the Israeli school system imbue Israeli children with "values of Jewish culture" and "loyalty to the Jewish people," and nothing could be more central to preserving Jewish culture than the Jewish language. Language and culture are intertwined in countless societies (recall the "language wars" in modern Canada and the province of Quebec). *That* was the reason that the 2018 Nation-State Law proclaimed that the state's language is Hebrew and that Arabic would be granted only "special status."[*]

Americans found the law incomprehensible, and therefore objectionable. The *Atlantic* reported that the law "establishes Hebrew as the official language of Israel and downgrades Arabic to a language with 'special status,' even though many people in Israel's sizeable Arab minority primarily speak in Arabic." That was absolutely true. The *Atlantic*, however, was reflecting the discomfort of American Jews, a discomfort that, because Israel is such a different project, most Israelis did not share.

What the American critique missed was that for Israelis, Hebrew is much more than a mere tool of communication; it is symbolic of the rebirth of the Jewish people. That is why, among most Israelis, the primacy given to Hebrew in the Nation-State Law raised very few eyebrows, particularly since Arabic was given

---

[*] Israel is by no means unique in this regard, even among developed democracies. Americans have consistently resisted making Spanish an official language of the United States, even in areas with numerous native Spanish-speakers. Many hoped that President Obama would change that; he did not.

"special" status. Again, the law may have been "edgy," but in its context, it was neither a diminution of democracy nor racially motivated.

THERE IS ANOTHER REASON that Zionists and Israelis were rarely determined to put their faith in American democracy or in the American model—they were less enamored of America than were many American Jews and remained wholly unconvinced that America was the ideal home for the Jews that many American Jews thought it was or could become. Some European Zionists were convinced that the glory days would one day end. America, Bialik was certain, was not as different from Europe as American Jews wanted to believe. "The day will come," Bialik wrote in 1926, when "economic structures in America will shift, and the Jews there will find themselves aside the broken trough. They will be cast out from all the high positions they have achieved, and without doubt, there will come terrible days which no one desires."

Six years later, in 1932, Haim Arlosoroff (a Zionist leader of the Yishuv, whose 1933 assassination case on the beach in Tel Aviv was never solved) explicitly pointed to what he saw as a revival of European anti-Semitism in America. He urged his readers to consider "the obvious fact that we are seeing in our own days, in the United States (which fifty years ago was the very symbol of freedom and inter-ethnic friendship), the rebirth of European anti-Semitism." That anti-Semitism, he said, had taken on distinctly American qualities: social ostracizm, difficulties for Jewish workers and clerks in finding work, and quotas in the major universities. "Add these all together," he said, "and I fear you will see much less cause for optimism."

Then, in the 1950s, as Jacob Blaustein was pushing back at Ben-Gurion, insisting that American Jews needed no home other than their American home, Senator Joseph McCarthy terrorized America with his hunt for Communists and his investigation of "un-American activities." (Tellingly, at the same time that McCarthy was hunting Jews for being Communists, Stalin was persecuting the Jews for being capitalists!) McCarthy's viciousness would stop at virtually nothing. Blaustein himself assailed what McCarthy was doing to America—and by implication, to the security of American Jews. Blaustein worried aloud about "the epidemic of loyalty oaths on university campuses" and a hysteria that fostered "fearful attitudes towards the freedoms to think, to speak, to be ourselves and in fact to be different." Even Blaustein saw some of what worried Bialik and Arlosoroff.

Thankfully, the fears that Bialik and Arlosoroff expressed never reached full fruition, but they were not entirely wrong that America had its underbelly. It was not only McCarthy with whom American Jews had to contend. The *Judenfrage* may never have made its way to America, but other forms of anti-Semitism certainly did. In the nineteenth century, American populists warned that Jewish bankers were undermining the interests of average Americans, and large-nosed Jews often appeared in political cartoons. When, in the early twentieth century, Jews were arriving on American shores in massive numbers, organizations designed to impose immigration limits sprang up.

There were also incidents of anti-Semitic violence, none more iconic in American history than the 1915 case of Leo Frank, who had been falsely accused of murdering a teenage Christian girl. Frank was incarcerated in a Georgia prison, but a mob stormed the prison, seized him, and lynched him. Shortly thereafter, Henry Ford, a titan of American industry, spoke of a "Jewish plan to control the world, not by territorial acquisition, not by military aggression, not by governmental subjugation, but by control of the machinery of commerce and exchange." In Massachusetts in the 1940s, Irish Catholic thugs roamed in gangs in "Jew hunts," assaulting Jews when they found them. Ivy League universities had strict admissions quotas when it came to Jews.

No less problematic was the venomous anti-Semitism of American heroes like Charles Lindbergh and General George Patton. Even after the horrors of the Holocaust, Patton had no compunction about sharing his view that "[others] believe that the Displaced Person is a human being, which he is not, and this applies particularly to the Jews who are lower than animals." Patton recalled seeing a temporary synagogue that had been constructed to allow the Jewish Displaced Persons to commemorate Yom Kippur. "We entered the synagogue, which was packed with the greatest stinking mass of humanity I have ever seen. Of course, I have seen them since the beginning and marveled that beings alleged to be made in the form of God can look the way they do or act the way they act." Those appalling comments did nothing to detract from Patton's status in American lore.

Then there were religious figures like Father Charles Coughlin (who warned of "world Jewish domination"), who, though largely forgotten now, sowed deep fear in American Jews. Decades later, in 2017, when protesters in Charlottesville, Virginia, shouted "Jews will not replace us," American Jews reassured themselves that the offensive chant was just a "blip on the screen." When Bill Clinton willingly sat beside Louis Farrakhan, the notoriously anti-Semitic Nation of Islam leader, at the singer Aretha Franklin's funeral in August 2018 (just weeks after Farrakhan had spoken publicly about "satanic Jews who have infected the whole world with poison and deceit"), Bialik's and

Arlosoroff's warnings might have come to mind if people still read them. The October 2018 murder of eleven Jews in a Pittsburgh synagogue by a man chanting "all Jews must die!" made those prognostications all the more chilling.

Israelis take no satisfaction when such events are reported in the Israeli press. But moments such as these reinforce their sense that there ought to be one place on earth where, whatever the international community might say about its form of democracy, Jews do not have to face such fears. There ought to be one place where events like these do not lead Jews to wonder whether the promise of America for Jews is as limitless as most American Jews have long wished to believe.

COMPETING VISIONS OF THE public square in Israel and America also complicate the relationship between Israel and progressive American Judaism. American Jews are understandably tempted to ascribe Israel's dismissive attitude toward American Jewish religious pluralism, its denigration of Reform and Conservative Judaism, American Jewish openness to changing roles for women, and greater acceptance of the LGBTQ community in Jewish life to the significant political power that the religious right has accrued in recent decades. There is no question that its increased power has enabled Israel's rabbinate to be much less diplomatic about such issues, but here, too, at the heart of this American Jewish disappointment lies a much more fundamental issue.

No one has articulated this better than Einat Wilf, whose comments about American Jews and their impact in Israel figured in the previous chapter. The public religious battles that

are so important to American Jews, so central to their identifica-
tion with all that has made America such a wonderful home to
them, do not speak to Israelis, she says. "Israelis really could care
less how citizens express their religious identity, Jewish or otherwise." Israel's failure to engage with what is such an important
issue to American Jews, she says, is nothing more (or less) than a
massive disconnect.

Why Israelis do not care is another question. The answer,
suggests the scholar Shlomo Fischer (an Israeli sociologist on
whose work Wilf bases much of her own analysis), is that religion in America is seen as a tool for expressing dissent (which
was the very purpose of the United States). Fischer explains:

> The United States is a country whose cultural DNA was
> uniquely formed by dissenting Protestantism, that is by Prot-
> estants who rejected the established Anglican Church and
> formulated religious truth based upon their own religious
> conscience and reading of the Bible. Everyone knows that the
> Pilgrims came to America in search of religious freedom. . . .
> Puritan thinkers who dissented from the ruling notions of
> religious truth in New England . . . worked out the religious
> and civic ideals of the freedom of conscience and religious
> pluralism. What is important to remember is that these were
> religious as well as civic ideals. Hence, religion in America
> goes together with pluralism, civil rights and democracy.

American Jews shared Thomas Jefferson's belief that these
American values—religion as key to dissent among them—
would eventually spread everywhere. In a letter he wrote
two weeks before his death, in what might be characterized

as a deathbed blessing for the United States, Jefferson shared his dream of the legacy of the United States. "May it be to the world," he wrote, "what I believe it will be, (to some parts sooner, to others later, but finally to all,) the signal of arousing men to burst the chains, under which monkish ignorance and superstition had persuaded them to bind themselves, and to assume the blessings [and] security of self-government."

Some of those values have made their way to Israel, but not all. And that, too, has contributed to American Jews' frustration with Israel's "refusal" to embrace America's more liberal religious movements. But that embrace is not likely to happen anytime soon, as Fischer explains:

> Traditional religious Judaism was viewed as an obstacle to the creation of the new Jew who would be self-reliant, rooted in the physical reality of national territory and primary economic production—agriculture and heavy industry, and autonomously creating a new national culture. Hence as Zionism attempted to reconstruct Judaism in a more civil direction—creating a state with a more or less democratic system of government and a new modern national identity, religion was held to be antithetical to this project.

For Americans, religion was a vehicle of dissent, and dissent was key to the American project. In Israel, on the other hand, religion was seen as a barrier to creating the new Jew, when the new Jew was key to Israel's purpose.

Therefore, say both Wilf and Fischer, Israelis did not pin their hopes for a flourishing democratic and civic culture on religion. And that, concludes Wilf, leaves American Jews who seek to effect change in Israel very few good options (other than moving en masse to Israel,* which she does not mention, given how unlikely it is):

> If American Jews are to effect change in Israel to make room for their brand of pluralism, they need numbers. No political change is ever possible without numbers. And there are no numbers in Israel for the kind of Judaism that Americans have in America. To get the big numbers, liberal American Jews have to decide who their actual potential allies are. If they seek Israeli Jews who will have a positive attitude towards religion, then they are likely to be non-liberal Orthodox Jews who reject their form of practice completely. If they seek Israeli Jews who will share their values of pluralism, equality, tolerance, feminism and liberalism, they are, by and large, likely to be the shrimp-eating-Shabbat-driving Jews, whose attitudes to religion range from revulsion to apathy. If Conservative, Reform and generally liberal American Jews seek partners in Israel who share both their liberal values and positive attitude towards religion, they will limit themselves to a pool of citizens that is barely likely to get one seat in the Knesset.

---

* The unlikelihood of American Jews moving to Israel in great numbers is a subject with a long and controversial history. Ironically, it was Joseph Proskauer, of the anti-Zionist camp in the AJC, who said in 1949 after the creation of the state: "We certainly have a right forcefully to discourage Israeli propaganda for immigration from America. We have both a right and a duty to proffer friendly advice regarding the tactics of the Israelis in their international relations. *We do not have the right to try to impose our American concepts on them.*" Many Israelis would say that the American Jewish community has apparently seconded Proskauer's attitude toward immigration but implicitly rejected his stance on "imposing American concepts" on Israel.

THERE IS A PROFOUND irony to the at-homeness that many American Jews feel when they visit Israel. Part of what they fall in love with is that the society is so Jewish in so many ways. The young woman behind the plexiglass window at passport control is Jewish, and so is the man fixing the conveyor belt at baggage claim and the man or woman mopping the floor in the airport terminal. The signs are in Hebrew, and though most tourists can't read or understand them, there is something about the ancient script now being used for everything from directions to advertisements to warnings about which taxis not to take that makes them feel at home in a way they never have before. As Herman Wouk, the American Jewish novelist, put it, "The special feeling that comes to one who has been a member of a minority all his life, and now finds himself in a place where everybody is like him—this extraordinary shift which changes the very nerve signals, as it were—must be a sensation that only a Diaspora Jew who comes to Israel can know. Born Israelis cannot imagine it."

What Wouk was pointing out was this: Israel's "Jewishness," which so many American Jews love, is an outgrowth of its public square being deeply imbued with Jewishness. One cannot have that sort of feeling in the kind of public square that a liberal democracy creates; only an ethnic democracy like Israel can do that. That is the trade-off that Israelis and Americans have each made: Israelis have ceded the option of having a genuine liberal democracy, while American Jews have given up the power of belonging that comes with ethnic democracy.

Wouk was right. Israelis take that sense so for granted that they don't understand it, while for many American Jews it is transformative. Even Isaiah Berlin, much less given to effusive Zionist utterances (he referred to Ben-Gurion as an "efficient demagogue" but to Louis Brandeis as a "saint and a gentleman, a kind of Jewish Lord Balfour"), acknowledged that Israel would provide the sort of comfort that eluded Jews in the Diaspora. "There isn't a Jew in the world known to me," he once remarked, "who somewhere inside him does not have a tiny drop of uneasiness vis-à-vis 'them,' the majority among whom they live."

Part of what exacerbates the complex relationship between American Jews and Israel is the fact that Berlin's observation may no longer be true, especially among a younger generation. The Holocaust seems like ancient history, Israel feels as natural as the rising of the sun and as guaranteed as almost any other human endeavor, and the "uneasiness" (in America) to which Berlin referred is much less on their radar. For them, therefore, the dimensions of Israel's political and cultural life that seem opposed to a Jeffersonian vision of the world loom much more problematic and discomfiting than those issues did for their parents and grandparents.

That there are all these differences between Israeli and American Jews, we need to recall, is not a matter of right or wrong. It is, to return to our couple metaphor, much more akin to two people who, when pressed, have to come to terms with how different they have become. Ultimately, neither can, or should, become like the other: America could not have achieved its greatness were it not a liberal democracy. Israel could not fulfill its intended purpose if it were.

THE FUTURE

7

CHARTING A SHARED FUTURE—AND
WHY THAT MATTERS

So here is where we find ourselves. After decades of marriage, our "couple" finds itself at a crossroads. The relationship is shaky, but not for the reasons we have long assumed. As critically important as are issues such as Israel's incessant conflict with the Palestinians, the rabbinate's intolerance for liberal Judaism, and young Americans' refusal to embrace even the idea of Zionism, none of these are the root cause of the rift. The fundamental issue, as we have seen over the previous four chapters, is that by this point in their respective histories American Judaism and Israeli-ness are fundamentally different. The issues addressed in the previous chapters do not, of course, come close to exhausting the issues that divide these two communities, but they do demonstrate that the real causes of the divide are much more fundamental than the current events that often trigger skirmishes between them. Israeli comportment does matter a

great deal, and Israel (like any country) is surely not beyond
reproach. Still, the crux of the problem between the communities is not what Israel *does*, but what Israel *is*.

The critical question, then, is this: Is there anything that can
be done? Can the relationship be healed? Can it survive? Before
discussing *what* might be done, the more immediate question
to address is *why* the relationship matters in the first place. Why
should we care? How would the Jewish world change were the
relationship to end? What is at stake for each of the parties?

DOES AMERICAN JEWRY REALLY need Israel? While the question itself might once have been considered heretical, that is no
longer the case; in fact, some leading voices are now answering
in the negative. Israel, they say, is a fascinating phenomenon and
in many ways successful beyond what anyone could have imagined at its founding, but at the end of the day American Jews do
not really need it.

That sentiment is by no means limited to the left, to progressives, or to millennials. There are deeply committed Zionist, Orthodox leaders who say the same thing. Few have made
their case more articulately than Rabbi Shmuly Yanklowitz.
Yanklowitz, a modern Orthodox rabbi who defines himself as
a Zionist, has twice been listed by *Newsweek* as one of America's
fifty most influential rabbis. He has this to say:

> Since many of us took our first breaths, we've been taught that
> our priority should be supporting Israel since that is the play-
> ing field for Jewish life; those of us outside of Israel are merely
> on the sidelines. It is as if those who live inside Israel are the
> book and everyone outside the borders are the footnotes.

From my perspective, however, the opposite is true. Israel may become—by reality and necessity—less significant and central to the success of global Jewish life.

Yanklowitz believes that the problem we face is deeper than the fact that Israelis and American Jews are different. Rather, he says, a fundamental part of the problem lies with Israel's short-comings. Those are so very distasteful, he contends, that some Israelis will actually gravitate to American Jewish life:

> Israelis seeking a pluralistic vibrant Jewish life that is au-thentically rooted while also being universalistic, inclusive, feminist, social justice oriented, and innovative will flock more towards American Jewish life. Here, we engage with great respect with other cultures, bring Jewish values into the public marketplace in healthy ways, and have a full spec-trum of pluralistic ways to engage with Jewish life. There is no doubt we have enormous challenges here in American Jewish life: rising anti-Semitism, low affiliation rates, and political challenges (among many others). But, for many, those challenges are far less alienating than state-mandated religious coercion, violent conflict, and sectorial in-fighting (among many others).

What Yanklowitz is essentially saying about the future of the relationship is this: Look, we've grown apart, and we're not going to save this thing. But let's part as more than friends. Let's work toward mutual respect, help each other from time to time, wish for the best for each other, and even from each other. Let's just not pretend that the bond we once had can be saved. It'll be okay.

YET IS THAT REALLY true? There are many reasons to suspect that Yanklowitz's assessment of American Judaism's future *sans* a meaningful relationship with Israel may be wildly optimistic. The first reason is demography: the demographic "balance of power" has been tilting toward Israel ever since the state was created, and the trend is only going to become more pronounced. Once we look at the numbers, the very notion that Israel could become "less central to the success of global Jewish life" seems ever more unlikely.

Since its founding, Israel has been a story of almost miraculous immigration and absorption. In May 1948, there were approximately 650,000 Jews in the newborn state. A mere three years later, that number *had doubled*. By 2018, the number of Jews in Israel had grown to 6,556,000—just under a ninefold growth in a mere seventy years. (The population of the United States in 1948 was approximately 146,000,000. Had the United States grown at the same rate, its population in 2018 would have been 1.3 *billion* people!)

The percentage numbers are equally noteworthy. In 1948, Israeli Jews comprised approximately 5 percent of the Jewish world; by 2018 that number had grown almost tenfold, to just under 50 percent. By 2043, according to Professor Sergio Della Pergola, Israel's leading demographer, the Jewish population of Israel is likely to approximate 10,500,000.

What has transpired in the United States during the same period? In 1948, there were some 5,000,000 American Jews, more than six times as many Jews as there were in Israel by the end of that year. In 2018, there were somewhere around 5,700,000 Jews in America.[*] The number had grown over seven decades,

---

[*] Estimating the number of Jews in America is complicated for many reasons,

but at a snail's pace relative to what had transpired in Israel. Were it not for an American baby boom and Soviet immigration, the numbers might have been even starker. As Charles Krauthammer, the renowned political commentator, once noted, between the 1950s and 1990s "overall U.S. population rose 65 percent. The Jews essentially tread water. In fact, in the last half-century Jews have shrunk from 3 percent to 2 percent of the American population. And now they are headed for not just relative but absolute decline."

Percentages tell an even more dramatic story. In 1948, American Jews comprised approximately 41 percent of the Jewish world, a figure that had dropped slightly, to 39 percent, by 2018. Estimates are that by 2043 there will be 5,300,000 Jews in the United States, at which point, American Jews would represent merely one-third of the world's Jews.

As American Jews' birthrates declined in the late twentieth century, birthrates among most Israeli groups increased, and even among secular Israeli women they held steady (and were higher than birthrates in Europe and in the United States). The demographic seesaw has therefore shifted entirely: in 1948, there were more than six times as many Jews in the United States as there were in Israel (three times as many Jews lived in New York City as lived in the entire Jewish state); by 2043, the situation will be turned on its head—it is predicted that there will be twice as many Jews in Israel as there will be in the United States. The notion that American Jews can afford to shift away

---

including competing definitions of Jewishness. In traditional communities, people are considered Jewish if their mother was Jewish or if they converted. Liberal communities expand that definition to include people whose father (but not mother) was Jewish. Given the high rates of intermarriage in America, the different definitions can lead to wildly disparate numbers.

from serious engagement with Israel seems highly cavalier, according to the numbers if nothing else.

A SECOND REASON THAT American Jews ought not imagine a future without a profound engagement with Israel has to do not with the number of American Jews but with the content of their discourse. There is an irony about discussions of Israel among American Jews. Though many American Jews are deeply frustrated with or even embarrassed by Israel, Israel remains the only subject of Jewish substance that has the capacity to arouse passionate debate across the entire American Jewish political and religious spectrum. Whereas decades ago American Jews were anguished about "Jewish continuity," that subject has virtually disappeared from today's discourse. "Who is a Jew" or "who is a rabbi," issues that were formerly explosive in American Jewish life, have vanished from the communal agenda. Which theological issues still arouse the explosive and divisive debates that Israel does? Conversations about whether democracy is even a Jewish value? Whether Judaism traditionally favors a free market economy or one with guaranteed equality? The LGBTQ community and gay marriage, or standards for conversion, were once lightning-rod issues in the American Jewish community. Today all that debate, too, seems to have ended. Now each subcommunity does what it does, while the others cannot be bothered to care very much. Only when it comes to Israel do the statements and actions of one denomination or segment of the political spectrum immediately arouse passionate reaction from others.

There is a reason for that. The sad reality is that the wealthiest and most politically involved, culturally invested, and secularly educated Diaspora community in the entire history of the

Jewish people is also, by far, the least Jewishly literate community ever created by Jewish people. As a result, too many American Jews, absent Israel, simply do not know enough to have a passionate conversation about almost any other dimension of Judaism. What that means is this: take Israel out of the equation and there will likely be almost nothing left that can arouse the passions of the American Jewish community. But a community devoid of passion is not one that people will find reason to care about.

Even Israel-literacy is exceedingly diminished. According to a 2015 report, for example, over half of Birthright Israel applicants polled do not have "the requisite knowledge to participate in productive conversations about Israel." When asked the question "Amos Oz, David Grossman, A. B. Yehoshua, and Etgar Keret are (a) members of the Israeli Parliament (b) Israeli novelists (c) Israeli soccer stars or (d) founders of the Kibbutz movement" (a question that was deemed the "most difficult" in the survey), a mere 20 percent of respondents (many of them university students) answered correctly. (The people mentioned in the question are among Israel's leading novelists; each is internationally renowned and has had numerous books translated into English.)

Even with a much easier question, "Can you identify the name of the Israeli parliament from among the following: (a) The Bet Din (b) The Kotel (c) The Knesset or (d) The Schwarma," only 60 percent of respondents got the answer right.

American Jewish illiteracy touches all dimensions of Jewish life—religion, culture, history, Israel, and more. "Measuring ourselves by the standard of our tradition," one keen observer commented, "we should note immediately one distinction of the American Jewish community; . . . The distinction that I have in mind is the illiteracy of American Jewry. I mean, its Jewish illiteracy."

This illiteracy, most pronounced among younger generations, yields a widespread tendency to conflate the Jewish with the universal—with ideas that Judaism shares with other traditions—both because those ideas are genuinely important and noble, and because one does not need any particular Jewish knowledge to embrace them with passion and confidence.

In the case of American Judaism, that universalizing conversation almost always morphs into one about *tikkun olam* (to cite the horrendously overused Hebrew phrase now in vogue). Judaism, it is said, is fundamentally about "repairing the world." Yet meaningful Jewish life and community cannot be built *solely* around repairing the world, for there is nothing unique to Jews about wanting to repair the world. Millions of Christians devote their lives and their communities to making the world better. The same is true of Muslims, Buddhists, and devotees of countless other traditions—including many people who have no religious commitments at all.

Some American Jewish intellectuals expressed concern about this universalizing tendency long ago. Cynthia Ozick, one of the great literary voices of American Jewish life, has long argued that universalism will spell the end of meaning in American Jewish life. Jews have to be unique if they hope to make a difference to anyone else, she argues. To make her point, she uses the metaphor of the shofar: "You give your strength to the inch hole, and the splendor spreads wide. . . . If we blow into the narrow end of the shofar, we will be heard far. But if we choose to be mankind, rather than Jewish, and blow into the wider part, we will not be heard at all. For us America will have been in vain." Or, as American-born Israeli author and columnist Hillel Halkin put it pithily, "If ethics are what make a Jew like everyone else, they can't also be what make him a Jew."

Ozick, Halkin, and many others are clearly right. Yet as Dyonna Ginsburg, a leading Israeli social entrepreneur, notes when she observes American Jewish life, there is "a growing sense," particularly among the young, "that *tikkun olam* has emerged as an *alternative*, rather than as a complementary form of Jewish Identity."

Even Peter Beinart, cited earlier for claiming that "young American Jews decided to hold on to their liberalism and to check their Zionism at the door," acknowledges that a critical contributor to young American Jews' feelings about Israel is their lack of basic Jewish literacy. He has called American Judaism an "unprecedented experiment when radical acceptance meets radical illiteracy," noting with irony that we expect young American Jews "to care deeply about something they know nothing about."

Whether this trend toward illiteracy can be reversed is a complex question, and beyond our scope here. For the purpose of our discussion, however, what matters is Israel's contribution to American Jewish discourse. No matter how painful or acerbic at times, it is Israel-centered conversation that has ensured that Jewish conversation in America is *not* entirely like the discourse of other religious traditions. Israel is what gives American Jewish life a sense of difference, of uniqueness, of the particular. Israel is what evokes American Jewish passion.

IF DEMOGRAPHY IS ONE reason that American Jews should not try to craft a Jewish life without an alliance with Israel at its core, and the tepid Jewish discourse that would remain without Israel is another, a third reason has to do with the fact that what Israel affords American Jews is drama, in the very best sense of the word.

Saul Bellow, as we saw earlier, wrote in 1975 that his fictitious character Humboldt believed that "history was a nightmare during which he was trying to get a good night's rest." Given what history had wrought for the Jews of Europe, it was understandable that American Jews would relish that good night's sleep and embrace with gusto the opportunity to sidestep the vagaries and cruelties of history. The question now, however, is whether two generations later, that craving for a good night's sleep has not also robbed American Jews of the profundity that only a life enmeshed in history can provide.

If Bellow was one of the great American Jewish literary voices of the 1960s and 1970s, today one of those voices is Jonathan Safran Foer. Foer's third novel, *Here I Am*, is in some ways an implicit response to Humboldt's worldview, a damning of the comfortable and history-free Jewish life that America has afforded its Jews, and that Foer fears eviscerates meaning.

Here I Am chronicles four generations of one American Jewish family. It explores divorce and the suburban middle class's search for (or loss of) meaning. But it also surprisingly affirms part of Tzipi Hotovely's critique and her implicit claim that American Jewish life might actually need some of the complexity and messiness that Israeli life has to offer.

Early in the novel, a young rabbi delivers a eulogy for the grandfather of Jacob Bloch, the book's television-writer main character. The rabbi, whom Jacob expects to be vacuous, surprises him by addressing the questions that are consuming Jacob. "We've made efforts not to offend or be too noisy," the rabbi says. "To achieve, yes, but not to draw undue attention to ourselves in the process. We've organized our lives around the will to perpetuate our lives."

Yet the rabbi, like Jacob, wonders if that effort to blend in, not to offend, "not to draw undue attention to ourselves," has been good for American Jews. "Has it been good to align ourselves with poignancy over rigor, with hiding over seeking, victimization over will?"

Joining the rabbi in challenging American Jewish comfort and Jacob's vacuous Jewishness is Jacob's secular Israeli cousin, Tamir. As part of his ongoing attempt to persuade Jacob to move to Israel, Tamir says, "If you were capable of standing up and saying, 'This is who I am,' you'd at least be living your own life." So why does Jacob not move to Israel? Because he is the paradigmatic American Jewish wimp, Foer essentially implies. When an earthquake devastates Israel, war erupts, and Israel's destruction seems likely, Jacob tells his wife (even as their marriage is dissolving) that he is going to Israel to fight, and she mocks him. "What, write for the army paper?" Later in their argument, she says, "If we were actually to entertain this utterly ridiculous notion of you in combat for a moment, then we would have to acknowledge that any army that would include you among its fighting ranks is desperate."

It's a fight between a husband and wife on the verge of divorce, but it is also more. It is Foer's indictment of American Judaism, his implicit suggestion that American Jewish life has lost risk, boldness, courage—and therefore drama. (Had Bialik's critique of Kishinev's Jews now come to America?) Foer, too, seems to believe that the wellspring of drama for American Jews is Israel.

That is precisely why Birthright (the idea for which was suggested in the 1990s by Israeli politician Yossi Beilin) actually accomplishes much more than getting young American Jews to Israel. For many participants, the engagement with Israel leads them to begin their Jewish exploration. Len Saxe, an American social psychologist who does much of Birthright's analysis, reported in 2017 that its most recent data suggested that "Birthright's alumni, compared to similar young Jews who did not participate in the program, are more highly connected to Israel, more likely to have a Jewish spouse and raise Jewish children, and more likely to be engaged in Jewish life."[*]

Why are participants in trips to Israel—which are now run by many organizations based both in Israel and in the Diaspora—so deeply affected by that experience? Why do these experiences often impact not only their attitudes to Israel, but their engagement with Jewish life writ large? The reason is that what these young people encounter when they visit Israel is not the homogenized Judaism of their Hebrew schools. Landscapes take on an air of drama and poignancy when they learn that their biblical forebears walked those same hills, now populated once again by the Jewish people. History becomes real when they visit the places of triumph and tragedy, particularly as they are exposed to the selflessness of young people their age who gave their lives to make the state possible. Hebrew is no longer a mind-numbing grammar exercise, but a living, pulsing language spoken only in that one tiny country. The fact that young Israeli soldiers join them on the trip makes all the difference—implicitly, American students cannot help but compare their lives on campus to the lives and challenges of those soldiers and then ask themselves what *they*, the Americans, might do in their own lives to make such a commitment to a cause larger than themselves.

What American Jews come to intuit through their contact

---

[*] The data on Birthright is hotly contested in Jewish professional circles and is beyond the purview of this discussion. Ample anecdotal evidence, however, indicates that the Birthright experience has a life-changing impact on many of its participants.

with Israel and Israelis is that the story of the return of the Jewish people to their ancestral homeland is one of the greatest dramas in the history of humankind. They get a sense of that drama at summer camps or on university campuses, where Israelis are engaged as staff. Thousands of young American Jews have found their encounters with those Israelis the most compelling experience in their Jewish educations. The Israelis, who come from such a different world and live with such different expectations of what life can provide and what they have to give in return, spark a process in these young American Jews that nothing else has previously elicited.

The "magic" of all these encounters with Israelis stems from American Jews being exposed to a version of Jewish life wholly unlike their own lives in the United States. To put matters a bit differently, when it comes to the drama of the Jewish people, there actually *is*, despite Jacob Blaustein's objection to the notion, a new center of the Jewish world. As Charles Krauthammer, not only a uniquely articulate political observer but also a committed American Jew, noted:

> The return to Zion is now the principal drama of Jewish history. What began as an experiment has become the very heart of the Jewish people—its cultural, spiritual, and psychological center, soon to become its demographic center as well. Israel is the hinge. Upon it rest the hopes—the only hope—for Jewish continuity and survival.

Part of the drama emerges from a sense—even among American Jews—that what is at stake in Israel is not merely the Jewish state, but the future of the Jewish people, whom the state was created to save. That is why Krauthammer began by speaking about drama but two sentences later claims that Israel is "the only hope" for Jewish survival. Lest his readers miss his point, he spells it out:

It is my contention that on Israel—on its existence and survival—hangs the very existence and survival of the Jewish people. Or, to put the thesis in the negative, that the end of Israel means the end of the Jewish people. They survived destruction and exile at the hands of Babylon in 586 B.C. They survived destruction and exile at the hands of Rome in 70 A.D., and finally in 132 A.D. They cannot survive another destruction and exile. The Third Commonwealth—modern Israel, born just 50 years ago—is the last.

Jonathan Safran Foer suggests much the same thing in *Here I Am*, this time in the voice not of the rabbi or of Jacob's wife or cousin, but rather of Israel's prime minister. With Israel in crisis, the prime minister calls on American Jews to stand at Israel's side—not out of pity for Israelis, but because they, too, are at stake. "As the prime minister of the State of Israel," Israel's leader says on live television, "I am here to tell you tonight that if we fall down again, the book of Lamentations will not only be given a new chapter, it will be given an end. The story of the Jewish people—our story—will be told alongside the stories of the Vikings and Mayans."

Israel as "the principal drama of Jewish history": the notion was understandably troubling to American Jews decades ago, but at this point it is hard to deny. The idea that a flourishing Jewish community can proceed without Israel as a core part of its identity is simply not realistic. Demography suggests that. American Jewish literacy levels require Israel as a fulcrum for passionate discourse. And if a community needs drama, Krauthammer and Foer—like Philip Roth much earlier—cannot imagine it coming from anywhere but Israel.

AMERICAN JEWS CANNOT FLOURISH without Israel, but the reverse is also true. It is critical that Israeli leaders, who are often far too quick to dismiss the importance of Diaspora Jewry to Israel, understand that Israel, too, desperately needs that relationship.

As far back as the 1990s, Israeli leaders were telling American Jews that the relationship of old was no longer necessary, that Israelis could make do without American Jewish political or economic support. In 1992, at the beginning of his term as prime minister, Yitzhak Rabin (foolishly) told AIPAC that Israel no longer needed its political advocacy. Soon after that, Finance Minister Avraham Shochat annoyed American Jews when he said that Israel Bonds—a program that had probably saved Israel in its early years and was a hallmark of American Jewish support for Israel—were overpriced and that Israel could do better by borrowing money on open markets.

In 1994, when Justice Minister Yossi Beilin addressed the International Conference of the Women's International Zionist Organization (WIZO), he both shocked and infuriated delegates by suggesting that they should stop supporting Israel and instead use those funds to shore up the American Jewish educational system, which he intimated was failing.

More than one Israeli president has told American Jewish audiences that the only thing Israel needs from them is immigration. Ezer Weizman, commander of Israel's air force and later its seventh president, said precisely that to a meeting of the

American Jewish Committee's board of governors, while Moshe Katzav—who followed Weizman as president but was later forced out of office in disgrace—said that Israel had mistakenly "legitimized" the Diaspora and that massive Jewish immigration to Israel was the only solution to "the assimilation that threatens the continuation of the Jewish people."

What has led Israelis to assume such a hostile tone toward a community that helped save the state on more than one occasion? Some of the hostility stems from the attitude of foundational Zionist thinkers toward the Diaspora, as we saw with Bialik and Dinur; "denigration of the Diaspora" is the term for this attitude. Some of it emerged from a false sense of confidence that, with the Oslo Accords, Israel was going to be at peace and its security challenges—and therefore its dependence on others—would lessen dramatically. Some is a legitimate reaction to the too-common paternalism of American Jewish leaders when dealing with Israel. And much has to do with the long-term underlying resentments that we have been examining throughout this book.

In response to this Israeli dismissiveness, American Jews typically argue that the United States is critical to Israel's safety and that American Jews are therefore critical to securing America's support for Israel.

Though that is true, it is not as true as we might assume. We tend to think of the American-Israeli relationship and the military, economic, and diplomatic support that it provides as being as natural as the state of nature. But the United States was not always Israel's chief ally. As Israel was fighting its War of Independence, some of its most critical arms came from Czechoslovakia, which had been instructed to provide them—by Joseph Stalin. Today it can be hard to recall that Israel's stalwart defender in the early years was the Soviet Union, which was both hopeful that Israel's socialist roots would grow even deeper and, no less important, anxious to block American influence in the Middle East.

As the Soviet Union came to understand that Israel was not going to become part of the Communist bloc and recognized that the Arab countries could be better clients, its diplomatic and military support of Israel waned. (As Stalin's horrific murder of some 20 million people became known, socialist and communist elements of Israeli society were repulsed, and whatever pro-Soviet sentiment remained also abated.) France then gradually became a major supplier of arms to the young Jewish state. That relationship lasted for a while, until it collapsed in acrimony for an array of reasons (Europe's dependence on Arab oil not the least among them). Then, beginning most noticeably with the Johnson administration, the United States gradually entered the picture as Israel's ally. That relationship has endured for decades, but those who know Israel's history well understand that every one of these alliances has been ephemeral, and they make no assumption that the current relationship with the United States will last forever.

That is precisely why, as some elements of the Democratic Party began to move away from Israel during the later years of the Obama administration, Prime Minister Benjamin Netanyahu began fostering more intensive Israeli ties to India, China, Russia, other emerging powers, and even Arab countries. Israel has learned over the years not to put all its foreign policy eggs in one basket.

What makes the security argument even less compelling is, again, demography. As approximately 2 percent of America's population, American Jews alone cannot guarantee American support for Israel. There are many congressional districts throughout the country that do not have a single Jewish voter; as Jews continue to drift to the larger urban centers, the number of those districts will grow. However, a congressman from a district with no Jews at all and a congresswoman from New York carry precisely the same weight in a House of Representatives vote. Therefore, strategically savvy organizations like AIPAC have begun reaching out to populations beyond the Jewish community. AIPAC, for example, is building relationships with evangelical Christians (there are more evangelicals in the belt between California and Texas than there are Jews in the entire world!), with veterans (who tend to be conservative on foreign policy issues, to be loyal to America's allies, and to vote at higher rates than others), and with progressives, who represent a growing segment of the Democratic Party.

To be sure, the United States is vitally important to Israel's security, and working to preserve that relationship is one of the most critical objectives of both communities. But for an array of reasons, that role alone will not convince Israelis that they need a relationship with American Jews.

AN EVEN MORE IMPORTANT factor that Israel dare not ignore is the profound cultural, moral, and intellectual contribution that American Jews have always made—and continue to make—to Israel. Yanklowitz was quite right in his assessment of what is great about American life. He spoke about having respect for other cultures, bringing Jewish values into the public marketplace in healthy ways, and being committed to pluralism.

Precisely because American Jews are a small minority in the United States while Israeli Jews are an overwhelming majority in Israel, because the United States is a liberal democracy while Israel is an ethnic one, and because American Jews have honed the art of building relationships with those around them, American Jewish influence in Israel acts as an important corrective to Israel's sometimes narrow, overly ethnocentric instincts.

Many of the most intellectually open and influential institutions in Israel, which enrich its culture and work to deepen its democracy, were founded by and/or are funded by American Jews. Signs of this powerful influence can be seen all over Israel, from the upper Galilee in the north to Eilat in the south. A picture of the depth of the influence can be seen even in a small area of south Jerusalem (where I live). There, a plethora of institutions with uniquely American fingerprints are shaping not only Jerusalem, but Israel. The Israel Democracy Institute, an important think tank, is funded mostly by American Jews. The same is true of the Pardes Institute, which pioneered pluralistic Jewish learning for men and women, a number of whom subsequently moved to Israel. The Shalom Hartman Institute has brought a pluralist conception of Judaism to Israel's public schools; it has launched a unique, theologically pluralist rabbinic ordination program, facilitates discourse between Jews and Muslims, and much more. The influence of American ideas on all these programs is obvious. The three leading women's *yeshivot* in Jerusalem (Nishmat, Matan, and Lindenbaum) have a wide impact on religious Israeli feminism and were all created and funded by North American Jews.

Shalem College was the first (and so far only) institution to import to Israel the American concept of a liberal arts education as a basis for shaping the individuals who will guide Israel in the next decades, much as graduates of America's finest academic institutions have shaped the United States. In the same neighborhood, a new religious community named Zion attracts religious and secular Jews, combines the Ashkenazi and Mizrachi liturgies (very unusual in Israel), and is often attended by Christian and Muslim visitors; it reflects in numerous other ways the pluralism, creativity, and even edginess of American Jewish religious life. Zion, too, is largely funded by American Jews and is led by a rabbi who, while born in Israel to families from France and Morocco, has spent significant time in the United States and Canada. Not far away, the Israel Museum became a truly world-class institution under the leadership of an American director (a graduate of Harvard who had previously served as deputy director of the Museum of Modern Art in New York), and it, too, is funded largely by American Jews. Beit Avi Chai, a cultural center that gives a stage to artists and intellectuals exploring critical political, moral, and creative issues in Israeli society, was founded and is funded by the Avi Chai Foundation, created by an American Jew who left his fortune to enriching Israel's future. The list goes on, almost endlessly, and is replicated in Tel Aviv and—to varying extents— all across the country.

Much more than money is at play here. What these and many other institutions have in common is that they have brought to Israeli society conceptions of education and pluralism, reconceived notions of the roles of men and women in Jewish life, and much more. Israeli religious feminism, today its own potent force, originally derived largely from American Orthodox feminism, which in turn was inspired by American feminism. Many of Israel's most creative and innovative educational institutions, especially high schools and colleges, were first conceived by Americans who imported American views on education.

Israel's founders were almost exclusively educated abroad. That had a profound and broadening impact on their sense of politics, the West, culture, and openness. Today the vast majority of Israeli leaders and many of its leading academics were educated exclusively in Israel. It is not healthy for a tiny country with the population of Los Angeles not to be enriched by a steady stream of cultural innovation and challenge—and if there is any community in the world that provides this to Israel, it is American Jews. Only a very narrow conception of Israeli flourishing could imagine that Israel does not desperately need ongoing substantive interaction with—and learning from—American Jewish life.

ALL OF THIS, HOWEVER, misses what is perhaps the most significant reason that Israelis dare not imagine that a meaningful relationship with American Jews does not matter. For what is really at stake in perpetuating and celebrating that relationship is nothing less than Israel's central reason for being, which is to be not only the state of its citizens but also a state that is fundamentally devoted to the Jewish people.

When American Jews think about Israel being a country devoted to the Jewish people, they think of Israel as a place of potential refuge, a haven to where Jews could flee should their host countries turn on them. Peter Beinart, for example, has said explicitly: "For me, the only aspect of Jewish statehood that is non-negotiable is that Israel must remain a haven for Jews in distress." Israel has already served as a refuge to millions of Jews who fled North Africa, the Soviet Union, and other parts of the world; but Israel-as-refuge alone entirely misses the point of Zionism's radical reimagination of Judaism, which this book has described. American Jews would do well to embrace a much richer conception of Israel's importance to the Jewish world.

Israelis, though, must also appreciate that Israel being a Jewish state must also be richer than the mere fact of its being a state populated mostly by Jews. In an earlier chapter, we saw the controversy over the correct translation of the title of Theodor Herzl's book, *Der Judenstaat*. Herzl, who oversaw the translation of his book into French, wanted it called *L'État Juif*, not *L'État des Juifs*. He meant to say something about the very nature of the state, not the ethnicity of its population. Likewise, Israel's Declaration of Independence says toward its conclusion, "We appeal to the Jewish people throughout the Diaspora to rally round the Jews of Eretz-Israel in the tasks of immigration and upbuilding and to stand by them in the great struggle for the realization of the age-old dream—the redemption of Israel." Zionism's pioneers and Israel's founders always saw a Jewish state as a project of the Jewish people—not of any one subset of Jews who chose to live there.

Israel's being the state of the Jews is a product of much more than any one factor. It is not only that Jews everywhere are citizens-*in-potentia* because the Law of Return guarantees them automatic right to immigrate to Israel. Or that Israeli politicians and American Jewish leaders regularly appear together at important gatherings in both countries. Or that some of American Jews' most powerful Jewish experiences are in Israel, or that many Israelis experience a visit to America as the beginning of their own Jewish search and journey.

What none of those facts capture is the difficult to describe yet critically important fact that the relationship of the Jewish Diaspora to Israel is unlike that of any other Diaspora community to its home country. Consider "Hatikvah," Israel's national anthem. At Jewish gatherings across America (and around the world), "Hatikvah" is sung immediately after "The Star-Spangled Banner" by people who have no intention whatsoever of living in Israel and who understand little or no Hebrew. Singing words that they cannot translate, words of the anthem of a country they have no intention of ever living in, they find themselves deeply moved, sometimes to the point of tears. They may be Democrats or Republicans, religious or secular, young or old— but for generations American Jews have sung that anthem as an expression of some ineffable dimension of their soul. How many people who are not actually French or Canadian citizens sing "La Marseillaise" or "O Canada" with that depth of sentiment?

Interestingly, following Israel's creation, there was some discussion among American Jewish leaders and in American Jewish organizations as to whether American Zionists should cease singing "Hatikvah." After all, some argued, "Hatikvah" was now no longer the anthem of a worldwide movement, but of a foreign sovereign state. Logically, one could have made a very good case for dropping "Hatikvah" in America. Emotionally, however, that could not have worked. And in somehow managing not to decide, American Jews de facto allowed emotion to trump logic. Despite American Judaism's instinctive resistance to "Judaism as peoplehood," in that extraordinary era of devastation and seemingly miraculous rebirth, the sense of Jewish peoplehood that Zionism had provided had become that central to their Jewish sense of self.

It is that sense of peoplehood, rather than mere citizenship, which gives Israel its emotional power. Photographs of Israel's ingathering of Yemenite Jews in the early years of the state remain moving to this day, as do recollections of Israel's rescue of Ethiopian Jews decades later. The one million people who made their way to Israel from the former Soviet Union are also testimony to Israel's magnetic pull, and it is not accidental that there are regular exhibitions about their immigration, successes, and challenges at museums and cultural centers across Israel.

When my wife and I were just married and living in New York, we were sent, like many others, to the Soviet Union to meet with and to help refuseniks: Soviet Jews who asked for permission from the Soviet Union to emigrate but who were harassed and even jailed instead. In preparation, we met only with contacts in New York, but we knew that behind those sending us was the government of Israel, which, because it then had no diplomatic relations with the Soviet Union, was not able to send Israelis. As we made our way from Moscow to Kiev and then to Odessa, mostly (but not always) succeeding in evading the KGB so we could meet with Soviet Jews who wanted desperately to immigrate to Israel, I was moved by the sense of peoplehood that the trip's web of Jewish commitments entailed. The Israeli government was sending young American Jews to support clandestine Jewish Zionists in the Soviet Union. We returned to New York with names and addresses that had been passed to us surreptitiously in crowded gatherings; after passing through New York, the names could then be passed on to Israel, which would issue official "invitations" for those people to exit the Soviet Union.

The outpouring of support for Israel in times of crisis is another demonstration of this deep sense of shared purpose. So, too, was the grief of American Jews for Yitzhak Rabin; they mourned him as if he had been *their* head of state. And in a way, he was. Those are manifestations of what a people do and feel when they are animated by a sense of mutual responsibility. Moments such as those have been repeated hundreds of times in Israel's history, and Israel would do itself irreparable harm were it to imagine that it is a country of only its actual citizens.

I still recall the morning I woke up during the Second Lebanon War in the summer of 2006 and saw in the news that a young American immigrant named Michael Levin had been killed in battle. The brief article mentioned that he'd come to Israel on his own and had no family living in the country. It also gave the time of his funeral, to be held later that day at the military cemetery on Mount Herzl. I told my wife I thought we needed to go to the funeral. It wasn't okay, I said to her, for a young man so far away from home to be killed defending the Jewish state and to have almost no one at his funeral.

She agreed, and a few hours later we headed to Mount Herzl. Long before we got to the entrance, however, traffic stopped and was hopelessly backed up. We eventually got into the site, but nowhere near the proceedings themselves. *Thousands* of people who felt exactly as we did had showed up so that Michael Levin would not be buried alone. Instead, he was buried among a mass of Israelis who had never heard of him until that morning. Moments like that, which those of us who were present that day will never forget, are the times when one most appreciates that peoplehood—not technical citizenship—is what makes Israel what it is.

For me, the most powerful part of every election day in Israel is the time spent on line waiting to vote. We vote at the public school just a few hundred yards from our home. The line is never very long, so the wait is brief. Even in just a few minutes, however, we hear couples talking to each other not just in Hebrew but also in English, French, Russian, and sometimes Yiddish or even Arabic (spoken by Jews from Arab lands).

As I listen to the various languages of the people waiting to vote, I am reminded, just as with the case at Michael Levin's funeral and at similar moments, that Israel is not "just" a state. It is a project of a people, thousands of years old, spread across the globe, united (in differing ways) by a commitment to this enterprise. The sense of purpose that peoplehood lends to Israeli life would end were Israel ever to say that it does not need a relationship with American Jews.* That one foolish step alone could destroy Israel's sense of self and purpose, perhaps beyond repair.

THERE IS YET ANOTHER factor that both communities must recall. Even in the moments during which the relationship is most strained, they need to remember one of the central lessons of Jewish history: the unpredictability of survival.

Most national traditions celebrate great victories, and monuments are created to commemorate triumphs. They range from the glorious (Paris's Arc de Triomphe, for example) to the grand (the Arch of Titus in Rome) to the foolish (such as Cairo's October War Panorama, which portrays the Yom Kippur War as a great Egyptian victory).

Jews have long had a different take on history. The Jewish calendar is replete with dates that mark near-catastrophe or actual destruction. The holiday of Purim marks the close call of the Jews' narrow escape when Haman tried to convince the king to kill all the Jews in his kingdom. There is a fast day to commem-

---

* It is worth noting that there is evidence that a sense of peoplehood is more intact on the Israeli side than it is on the American side. A study conducted by the American Jewish Committee asked Jews in both communities to describe how they felt about their relationship to the other: did they think of the other as siblings, first cousins, extended family, or "not part of my family"? Though responses in the middle categories were rather similar, the sibling and "not part of my family" categories illustrated a wide gap. While 28 percent of Israeli Jews said that American Jews were their siblings, only 12 percent (less than half the Israeli rate) of American Jews said that about Israelis. Conversely, while 31 percent of American Jews said that Israelis were "not part of their family," among Israelis, only 22 percent said that about American Jews. There is work to do on both sides, without doubt. Nonetheless, a sense of peoplehood appears to have eroded much more in the American Jewish community than among Israelis.

orate the beginning of the Babylonian siege of Jerusalem. Another marks the breaching of the city's walls. And a more major fast (the aforementioned Ninth of Av) mourns the destruction of both Temples. In a similar vein, Israel is dotted with thousands of monuments, almost all of them to fallen soldiers in one war or another. Tellingly, there is hardly a single monument to an Israeli victory, of which there have been many.

One of the central points of Israel's culture of memory is to remind Jews that there is no place for complacency in Jewish life. The Jewish tradition focuses not on triumphalism but on the dread of losing all that has been accomplished. An Israel that felt so secure that it came to believe that Jews elsewhere were not critical to the Jewish future would be ignoring the lessons of millennia of Jewish history. Similarly, an American Jewish community that imagined that it, too, was so secure that the Jewish people could live without Israel would be ignoring its own looming existential threats.

Which is the more vulnerable of the world's two largest Jewish communities? Is it American Judaism, with its challenges of assimilation, Jewish illiteracy, intermarriage, and a possibly resurgent American anti-Semitism? Or is it Israel, still at war with the Palestinians, sharing a border with a Hezbollah armed with hundreds of thousands of rockets (many of which are accurate and can hit anywhere in Israel), and situated squarely in the crosshairs of an Iranian regime that boasts of its intent to destroy the Zionist "germ" with nuclear weapons? Can Israel survive economically with a growing Haredi population if they do not become more productive contributors to Israel's economy? What about declining levels of Jewish literacy among Israelis?

If the study of Jewish history teaches us anything, it is that who will survive and who will not has never been in the least bit predictable. When the Second Temple was destroyed in 70 CE, bringing biblical Judaism to an end, who would have surmised that it would be the Pharisees, a small band of scholars teaching in a way that Jews had never known before, who would become the basis of all forms of Judaism—from secular to ultra-Orthodox—to this very day? Could anyone have imagined that a small sect led by a charismatic preacher would become Christianity, one of the world's great religions?

A little-known but chilling Jewish legal opinion issued during the First World War brings this unpredictability into stark, harrowing relief. During World War I, the chief rabbi of Germany was a scholar named Rabbi David Zevi Hoffmann. One of the most important legal arbiters of his time, Hoffmann was asked whether observant Jews ought to evade the German draft so as to avoid the inevitable desecration of the Sabbath that would have been required of them. His fascinating and lengthy response includes the following:

> It is therefore best that you observe the command of the King, and perhaps you will find favor in the eyes of your officers, and they will permit you to observe the Shabbat, and you will [succeed in] doing good for both God and man. For one who comes to purify, the Heavens give him assistance. And if you perform all your actions for the sake of Heaven, all will be at peace with you, and you can abide in the land and remain loyal and peace [will descend] on Israel.

The flowery rabbinic language can be a little difficult to parse, but Hoffmann's extraordinary comment merits note. Here is one of the world's leading Orthodox rabbis telling a young Jew that he should *not* evade the German draft, even though joining the German army will require him to eat nonkosher food, violate the Sabbath, and ignore other holidays. Rather, said Hoffmann, this young man should go into the army so the Jews could prove themselves loyal German citizens; if they did, Hoffmann predicted, they would be able to live out all the promise that Germany then represented.

Hoffmann's era was indeed the golden age of Jewish life in Germany. As Amos Elon, an Israeli historian, noted with sad irony, "Before Hitler rose to power, other Europeans often feared, admired, envied and ridiculed the Germans; only Jews seemed actually to have loved them." No other group of European Jews had made such a valiant attempt to integrate into their host culture. But all those efforts were for naught. Just a few decades after Hoffmann penned that legal opinion, and about fifteen years after he died, Germany initiated an unprecedented genocidal war against the Jews, not only exterminating Germany's own Jews but engineering the murder of 90 percent of Polish Jews (who were then the world's largest Jewish community) and, in all, destroying a third of all the Jews on earth.

The Golden Age of Spain ended with the Inquisition. The glory days of Germany crashed with the Nazis. The Balfour Declaration was followed by a British ban on Jewish immigration to Palestine. In what is thought to be an enlightened era, Jeremy Corbyn has risen to the top of England's Labour Party, and a presidential candidate in the United States pretends not to know who David Duke is. Within just weeks, eleven Jews are murdered in a Pittsburgh synagogue and swastikas appear on the campuses of two Ivy League campuses, Cornell and Columbia. No one can know where this trend is headed.

Jewish history has proven entirely unpredictable. For either of the world's two great communities to imagine with confidence that *they* represent the future of the Jews, and that another enormous community is therefore of no interest to them, would be to have learned nothing at all from millennia of Jewish experience.

"WE ARE A PEOPLE, one people," said Theodor Herzl in *The Jewish State*, the book that launched political Zionism. It was more than a catchy aphorism. Herzl did not know a great deal about Judaism, interestingly, but he had a deep, intuitive understanding of the Jewish people. Without the sense that the Jews were one people, Herzl was certain, neither Zionism nor a Jewish state made any sense. Zionism was always about the redemption of the Jewish people, not the individual Jews who chose to make their way to Palestine or Israel—and it has transformed even the lives of Jews, like those in America, who choose not to make their lives in the Jewish state.

Zionism became the first endeavor on which Jews from the United States and from England, Jews from France and from Iran, and Jews from Russia and from Argentina could collaborate. Centuries earlier, what linked Jews across oceans and continents had been their religious way of life. Once the Enlightenment came to Europe, however, and Jewish secularism became widespread, religiosity could no longer be the glue that bound Jews together. Then Theodor Herzl launched political Zionism, and many Jews were bound once again—across oceans and continents—by the drive to create and then defend a Jewish state.

Zionism has both united and divided the Jewish people in a way that no other cause or movement ever has. And that, as we have seen, is uniquely true of the relationship between American Jews and Israel. The question now is whether the forces of unity can triumph over those of division.

Emma Lazarus, the poet whose "Colossus" is affixed to the base of the Statue of Liberty, wrote another poem, in which she described the Jewish people streaming in two groups, one to their homeland and another to new horizons. "The New Year" says, in part:

> In two divided streams the exiles part,
> One rolling homeward to its ancient source,
> One rushing sunward with fresh will, new heart.
> By each the truth is spread.

"By each the truth is spread." That was an extraordinary insight from a woman who did not live to see either community reach the heights it has. But indeed, there *have* been two sets of truths emerging from these communities—insights and commitments sometimes at odds, yet without which either community would find itself radically impoverished.

To heal the rift that is the subject of this book, the first step that Jews in both communities must take is to acknowledge that Emma Lazarus was right: the "two divided streams" do in fact each spread a truth. Perhaps the beginning of the road back from the precipice is to recognize that each stream needs the truths of the other. Perhaps that is the place to begin, recognizing that neither side can live without the other, that each is a critical contributor to what the Jewish people are today. If that happened, might a dangerously divided people begin imagining a future that bears flickering glimmers of hope and repair?

CONCLUSION

"THAT'S HOW THE LIGHT GETS IN"

In 1880, the combined Jewish population of the United States and Palestine totaled 275,000 people. As the world's Jewish population at that point was approximately 7.8 million, these two communities represented a mere 3 percent of the world's Jews. Today the United States and Israel account for 85 percent of the world's Jews. In other words, almost the entire Jewish world today lives in two communities that for all intents and purposes did not exist 135 years ago. The Jewish people have existed for some 3,500 years; in the last century and a quarter, however, they have essentially had to reinvent themselves.

Much of that reinvention was necessitated by unspeakable and unprecedented tragedy. For centuries, Europe had been the uncontested center and home of Ashkenazi Jewry, but in a paroxysm of genocidal madness, the Nazis and their collaborators exterminated European Jewry. In 1933, before the war, the Jewish population of Europe was about 9.5 million, but by 1950, shortly after the war ended, it was a mere 3.5 million. Two-thirds of Europe's Jews were gone. Some 90 percent of Polish Jews had been slaughtered.

In 1933, approximately 60 percent of all Jews lived in Europe. In 2016, only 10 percent did. European Jewry, the epicenter of the Jewish world, had been wiped out.

Elsewhere, Mizrachi Jewry experienced a tragic end of a different sort. In the years following Israel's creation, North African Arab countries also destroyed their Jewish communities. In 1948, when its Jewish population stood at approximately 75,000, Egypt began arresting Jews and confiscating their property. Cairo's Jewish Quarter was bombed. Jews fled. In 1956, Egypt evicted 25,000 more Jews. Another wave of persecution in 1967 led to more emigration, and Egypt's Jewish population dropped to 2,500. By the 1970s, just a few hundred remained.

Libya was home to some 38,000 Jews in 1948. Then came pogroms and threats, leading many to leave. In 1967, when Jews were subjected to pogroms after the Six-Day War, virtually all the remaining Jews left. Morocco had a Jewish population of 265,000 in 1948. By 1968, only about 50,000 Jews remained. Similar stories unfolded in Algeria, Iraq, Syria, Tunisia, and Yemen. Some Jewish communities in Arab countries essentially ceased to exist; of the Jewish communities of Libya, Iraq, and Yemen, some 90 percent left or were expelled within a decade of Israel's founding. Between 1948 and 1951, a period of merely three years, over 37 percent of Jews from Islamic countries immigrated to Israel.

With Europe's Jews devastated and the Mizrachi Jewish communities of the Levant uprooted and erased shortly thereafter, what had for centuries been the Jewish world's great centers no longer existed. The center of Jewish gravity moved to two places, both of them essentially uncharted territory in the modern era.

Yet while in the twentieth century the center of gravity shifted to the United States and Israel, part of what has complicated the relationship between these two great communities is that the center of gravity is still shifting—this time from a shared role between the United States and Israel to a reality in which the epicenter of the Jewish world will unquestionably be Israel. In the biblical period, virtually all of the world's Jews lived in the Land of Israel. After the Babylonians exiled the Israelites in 586 BCE, however, only a minority remained in the Land of Israel, and never again has a majority of the world's Jews lived in their ancestral homeland. Tellingly, that is apparently about to change. Demographers predict that by 2030, for the first time in some 2,600 years, most of the world's Jews will live in the Land of Israel. Within a generation or two, they believe, approximately two-thirds of the world's Jews will likely live in Israel.

For now, though, the vast majority of the world's Jews are divided between the United States and Israel, and it is thus important that we remind ourselves that both of them are successes beyond what any of their creators imagined. When Jews immigrated to the United States by the millions between 1880 and 1920, hardly anyone imagined Jewish senators and Supreme Court justices. Who could have imagined Jewish universities? Enormous synagogues attended by thousands of people? Jewish presidents of Ivy League colleges? Jewish and Zionist campus organizations by the thousands? Jewish newspapers by the dozens? Jewish writers and artists who would take not only America but the world by storm?

American Jews live in a world that to their great-grandparents would have been unimaginable.

Meanwhile, across the ocean in the Middle East, a fledgling state that appeared to have no natural resources almost collapsed under the weight of mass immigration, yet has more than survived. With determination born of dire necessity, Israel built one of the world's most vaunted military forces. Seemingly without any natural resources, it turned human intellectual capital into a natural resource. It became a "startup nation," a world center for technology and innovation, and a formidable economic machine. A country with the population of Los Angeles wins more Nobel Prizes than most other countries, has numerous universities ranked among the world's finest, produces more books per capita than almost any other country, is ranked among the world's happiest societies—and its future looks no less bright.

Israel's real accomplishment, however, has been the revitalization of Jewish life as it can unfold only in a Jewish state. As Charles Krauthammer put it so beautifully, "Plant a Jewish people in a country that comes to a standstill on Yom Kippur; speaks the language of the Bible; moves to the rhythms of the Hebrew (lunar) calendar; builds cities with the stones of its ancestors; produces Hebrew poetry and literature, Jewish scholarship and learning unmatched anywhere in the world—and you have continuity." Continuity perhaps—or more precisely, the rebirth of the Jewish people of which Zionism's early leaders dreamed.

It seemed only natural that there would exist a strong and permanent bond between these two new communities. Israelis looked to America for political, economic, and diplomatic support, as well as immigration among some communities. They saw much to emulate in America's democratic society. Israel's founders borrowed language from America's Declaration of Independence, admired its forward thinking, and looked with awe on America's belief that anything is possible. American Jews saw in Israel an inspiring combination of idealized socialism, Jewish rebirth, a reimagined Jew, the end of Jewish victimhood, and much cause for pride. They saw some recompense for the Holocaust, a reborn future, and a reason to have hope.

YET THAT MUTUALLY CELEBRATORY relationship is stumbling. On the American side, Israel as a response to the Holocaust is no longer a compelling narrative; researchers often speak of "Holocaust fatigue" among young American Jews. Gone are the days when Israel was seen as the David threatened by a Goliath just across its borders. The magical allure of the quasi-socialist kibbutzim has long since faded. The sense that Israel is in danger of imminent demise and desperate for American Jewish support has passed. Israel has become so successful that its American cousins are not sure it needs them anymore; leading Jewish philanthropists, exposed to the wealth in Israeli society, are increasingly asking why they are sending money abroad to Israel when their own communities need so much support. Israel's conduct of its conflict with the Palestinians upsets, angers, and embarrasses American Jews; what appear to be periodic internal assaults on Israel's democratic values also worry American Jews deeply. American Jews are rightly frustrated that most Israeli Jews know virtually nothing about American Jewish life—its grand history and openness—and the challenges that American Jews have had to face.

On Israel's side, gratitude for American Jewish support is intertwined with a deep sense that American Jews have disappointed Israel, have never lived up to the dreams that Zionism had for them. The world's largest Diaspora community produces only a trickle of immigration, and the few who do immigrate come disproportionately from the Orthodox community. Because the American Jewish educational system essentially decided not to make Hebrew a core component of the American Jewish experience, just as Israelis know very little about American Judaism, American Jews know little about Israeli culture and the internal lives of Israelis, but then (at least as many Israelis see it) hold Israel accountable to standards that to Israelis seem unrealistic given their reality.

When American Jews do demonstrate concern for and about Israel, it is often expressed as either implying or telling Israel how it should act. To Israelis, these insinuations, whether from the right or the left, often feel like an implicit disrespect for Israel as a democracy. It often seems to many Israelis that American Jews assume they understand Israel's best interests better than Israel does and think they know best what risks Israel should take and what sacrifices it must make, even though American Jews themselves have decided not to face or bear them.

As we have seen, however, these are but the surface causes of the rupture. The real issue is that these two new communities developed in response to different fears, were designed to take advantage of radically different opportunities, developed different strategies for survival, and had at their core profoundly different visions of what a renewed Jewish flourishing would look like. If anything, what is surprising is not that the relationship is wounded, but that it has survived intact for as long as it has.

In ways one might not have expected, the early days of the COVID-19 pandemic in 2020 highlighted the growing distance between the world's largest Jewish communities. The coronavirus was not like the crisis faced in 1973, when an endangered Israel desperately needed the support of American Jews. Nor was it like the one in 1976, when Israel was able to send commandos to Entebbe to rescue Jews from harm's way. In 2020, as the world staggered in the face of an unprecedented biological challenge, there was really nothing either community could do to help the other.

But as Israel seemed to fare better than the United States in the early weeks of the pandemic, while Americans were dying by the tens of thousands, American Jews asked, in pain, why Israel was doing nothing to help them. Leaders from both sides began to meet, but even as they did, Israel's deputy foreign minister, Tzipi Hotovely, whom we met in the early pages of this book, said that Israel wanted to help but that Diaspora Jews "are not asking for financial assistance. They want something else. But most people cannot put their finger on what this 'something else' is." It was a metaphor for the larger stress in the relationship. Neither country had ventilators to share with the other; neither could send medical staff to help the other. Israel did not need medical assistance at that point, yet no country of 9 million people could possibly spare the personnel needed to address a crisis in a country of 330 million.

Many expected the rift to deepen in the aftermath of the COVID-19 crisis. With flights suspended and trips to Israel now impossible, the one tool that had been most effective in getting Israel and American Jews to better understand each other had evaporated. Leaders on both sides desperately wanted to do "something." But, as Hotovely pointed out, no one had any idea how to make a real difference.

We can no longer safely assume that the relationship will somehow stumble along. Today many people openly talk about the end of the romance, the demise of the relationship, the fracture of the Jewish people into two largely disconnected communities. Yet, as we saw in the previous chapter, such a rupture would leave both communities profoundly weakened and impoverished. Which leads to the obvious question: is there anything to be done?

"THERE MUST BE SOMETHING concrete we can do," some deeply committed observers say, determined to engineer a solution. Many suggestions have been made, most of them beyond the purview of our discussion. Basing themselves on the once-central World Zionist Organization, some have urged the creation of a Jewish People's Council, a nongovernmental body that they hope would be "part mediating institution, part reconciliation vehicle, part safety valve—for debating and acting together as a people even as not all of us share the same geographical boundaries and many of us have our own responsibilities as citizens in our separate geographic homes." Another suggestion is that the solution might lie in shifting the structure of Israel's government: Israel could have a prime minister who, as is the case today, leads the community of Israel's citizens, while Israel's president could serve as the representative of world Jewry and not just Israel. Israel's president Reuven Rivlin suggested in 2018 that given how successful Birthright had been in creating among American Jews an appreciation for and devotion to Israel, it was time to create a "reverse Birthright" to expose Israelis to the richness of American Jewish life. Some believe that symbolic gestures are critically important: an editor in chief of the *Jerusalem Post* has argued that the millennia-old practice of Israeli and Diaspora Jews having religious calendars that are not entirely aligned needs to end and that Jews worldwide should make a profound statement of unity by synchronizing their religious holidays. Others suggest figuring out which segments of the Jewish world are most responsible for the divide and focusing on shifting *their* world-view. An American-born Haredi former member of Knesset who understands that ultra-Orthodox power and closed-mindedness in Israel are a significant contributor to the rift suggests that, "as long as U.S. Jewry remains engaged and considers a strategy of investing in programs which encourage and facilitate ultra-Orthodox integration into Israeli society, then not too far into the future, the political reality in Israel will allow significant legislative changes to enable U.S. Jewry to feel more welcome and accepted in Israel."

More common than constructive recommendations, however, is a sense of urgency and a call to action with no articulation of what that action might be. "As the communities move farther apart, a new plan for Jewish unity is needed urgently," one well-known American Jewish communal professional wrote, but not surprisingly, he had nothing to say about what anyone should actually do.

On the Israeli side, some are arguing that it is too late, that the best that Israelis and American Jews can do is take the advice of a recent *Ha'aretz* headline: "To Save Their Troubled Marriage, Israel and American Jews Should Consider a Trial Separation." "If it won't help, at least it can't hurt," the columnist wrote. "Their differences are irreconcilable. The end might be nigh. If they were a married couple, they would already be consulting with their lawyers and preparing to file for divorce."

IT IS ACTUALLY NOT surprising that thoughtful people among the longtime leaders of the American Jewish community do not have concrete "engineering" ideas to suggest. The divisions are too deep to pretend otherwise, too foundational for the resolution to be "engineered." When the roots of the discord are so deep, institutional engineering solutions simply cannot do the job. No stopgap measures can create unity of the sort many once dreamed of; that would only paper over the real issue. To go back to our proverbial couple, engineering is akin to making a concerted effort not to leave dishes in the sink or drop socks on the floor. It's a nice gesture that may make things better for a bit, but at the end of the day, unless the key issues are addressed, the next explosion lies around the bend.

Nor is trial separation a good idea, for there is no reason to assume that the communities could walk it back. What is needed is precisely the opposite of a trial separation. Something must be done not to get one side to walk away, but to draw the communities closer. Even in broad strokes, it *is* possible to point to fundamental attitudinal wellsprings from which some progress might be drawn.

The first order of business has to be a fundamental decision not to let the relationship founder, a commitment to the premise that the break must somehow be healed. In 1948, when Israel was just weeks old, American members of Menachem Begin's underground organization, the Irgun, purchased the *Altalena* (the same ship on which David Smith sailed to Israel), loaded it with arms, and sent it to Israel so that the Irgun could have weapons. Though Begin knew nothing about the ship until it approached Israel's territorial waters, David Ben-Gurion was enraged; he assumed that Begin was trying to preserve the independence of his fighting force even after Ben-Gurion had united all the underground operations into one official army under the government's command. After exhaustive negotiations and misunderstandings, Ben-Gurion decided to sink the ship. He ordered his men to prepare to open fire, telling them, "The entire future of this country is in the balance." Yigael Yadin, the IDF's chief of operations, added to the orders, "You might have to kill Jews." The ship *was* sunk, and Jews did die. Ben-Gurion, however, was unrepentant. In fact, he insisted that the cannon that had sunk the *Altalena* was so sacred that it deserved to "stand close to the Temple, if it is built."

Menachem Begin was no less committed to the creation of a Jewish state than was Ben-Gurion, but his worldview was entirely different. Even as his soldiers were being fired upon, and as the Irgun was about to see its cache of arms explode, Begin ordered his men not to return fire. "There must not be a civil war with the enemy at our gates!" he demanded when he addressed his men by radio after the *Altalena* sank. Much later in his life, he wrote, "After my death I hope that I will be remembered, above all as someone who prevented civil war." Today's Jewish world needs another Menachem Begin, a leader whose overriding principle is the prevention of a split in the Jewish people.

Second, no progress will be possible without each side trying to see the other in the best possible light. Institutions cannot bridge the divide if the world's two largest Jewish communities do not begin to appreciate the various differences and tensions that this book has discussed. The beginning of the solution lies in Jews learning about themselves, about the tradition they share, and about each other. There are no institutional shortcuts: each community needs to come to understand what motivates the other, what threatens it, what worries it, and why. We need to understand why we have grown so different, how deeply embedded are our competing worldviews, and how un-likely it is that either of us will change. We need to appreciate that what troubles the relationship is not only what we *do* but who we *are*.

Third, because the two communities are so fundamentally different, both sides need to accept that there will always be di-mensions of their respective behaviors and policies that strike the other as shortsighted, morally questionable, or even dis-loyal. American Jews are clearly correct when they claim that Israel's occupation of the West Bank, and its impact on the lives of Palestinians, is a profound threat to Israel being the moral democracy most Jews want it to be. Millions of Israelis agree with them. Where many American Jews and Israelis differ is regarding what can be done to resolve this conflict. American Jews are convinced that an agreement with the Palestinians and a withdrawal from the West Bank must be possible, while most Israelis who agree with those fundamental moral instincts sim-ply do not believe that the conflict can be settled at present. The argument itself may not be resolvable at present any more than is the tragic conflict.

Perhaps, though, seen through the prism of the differences discussed in this book, American Jews and Israelis who care about their mutual relationship could at least each learn to give the other the benefit of the doubt. Israel is going to take actions for security purposes that will strike many Americans as prob-lematic. American Jews do not need to agree with or condone these actions, but at the very minimum, they ought to recognize that living inside a conflict is very different from observing it from afar. A certain amount of humility ought to color the na-ture and tone of critique. Similarly, Israelis must come to under-stand the instinctive universalism and pluralism that have made

American Jewish life as unprecedented as it is. Israelis may not appreciate American attitudes toward Israel's actions or view sympathetically trends in American Jewish religious life, but if the resentment were tempered by a more profound understanding of what animates these policies and trends, a different sort of discourse could emerge.

Fourth, both sides, if committed to maintaining some sort of a relationship, need to mute the dismissive rhetoric that they too commonly employ. Israeli denigration of Diaspora life—which, as we have seen, is deeply rooted in Zionism—is not helpful. Israeli denigrations of Jews who do not intend to move to Israel (a habit of Ben-Gurion's) or of Reform Jews (much in vogue among today's ultra-Orthodox Israeli leaders) serve no one. By the same token, however, saying that the creation of a Jewish state was a bad idea (recall the comment of J Street founder Daniel Levy), calling Israel a "terrorist state" (as did several delegates to the J Street conference in April 2018), or claiming that in defending its border Israel has "chosen to shoot Palestinians" (the *Forward* headline discussed earlier) serves no purpose. Such reckless and irresponsible statements deplete goodwill and sow bitterness.

That is not to say that the two communities cannot reproach each other. Any ban on honest discourse would also serve no purpose. But in a relationship that matters to both sides, the critical needs to be tempered by the supportive. Sadly, a look at the Facebook pages, Twitter feeds, or Instagram accounts of many American Jewish thought leaders (usually on the left, including some who have been mentioned in this book) reveals a litany of complaints about Israel and scarcely a comment that mentions anything positive. Similarly, American Jews on the right tend to react to any criticism of Israel as treasonous, though they do not think that critique of America (think objection to the Vietnam

War or the civil rights movement) is akin to abandoning America. If, as is also true in human relationships, genuine devotion invariably involves critique, then critique of Israel—or in reverse, critique of steps that American Jews take—is entirely legitimate. The question each side needs to ask itself is whether the manner in which it expresses itself also communicates the care and commitment that lie at the base of the criticism.

One particularly poignant example of doing it right appeared in the pages of the *New York Times*. Convinced that Israel's policy of stopping left-leaning activists at the border and sometimes preventing them from entering the country was foolish and self-destructive, two *Times* columnists, Bret Stephens and Bari Weiss, penned a strong critique but opened it with the following sentences: "In March, the writer Andrew Sullivan described each of us as a 'Zionist fanatic of near-unhinged proportions.' It was a cheap shot. The word 'near' should not have been a part of the sentence. Otherwise, we happily plead guilty as charged. Yet even unhinged Zionists can level criticism at Israeli policies." That kind of language is likely to get Israelis to listen; by the same token, theirs was the kind of rebuke—one clearly predicated on a passionate belief in Israel's importance and right to exist—to which Israelis must learn to listen. The healing, if it is to come, will come from how each side speaks, and from how it listens.

Fifth, there is little value in either side expecting the other to do the impossible. There is something not only intellectually sloppy but fundamentally immoral about American Jewish progressives' insistence that Israel end the occupation but, when asked how, explicitly refusing to offer suggestions. If they have no idea how to end it, why would they assume that Israelis *could* end it but refuse to? Do they imagine that Israeli parents *want* to send their daughters and sons into combat? Just as one can understand why young American Jews want to end the occupation, one should understand just how offensive it is to Israelis when outsiders who have no idea how to end the conflict imply that Israelis are not interested in ending it or insist that Israel's ending the occupation is a prerequisite to their engaging with Israel.

Israelis, in turn, have every right to be convinced that intermarriage is an enormous threat to the future of American Jewish life. Many American Jewish leaders agree, while many others do not. But to rail against intermarriage as if American Judaism has simply decided to commit suicide is foolish and offensive to American Jews. Israeli leaders would foster a much warmer dialogue if, instead of condemning intermarriage, they showed some understanding for the complex blessing inherent in America's welcome of the Jews. The very tolerance that America has shown to its Jewish community is the tolerance that makes intermarriage possible and even likely.

It is true that in American Judaism's most committed corners, Orthodoxy primarily, intermarriage rates remain low. But most American Jews are not Orthodox and are no more likely to become Orthodox than they are to move to Israel. One can bemoan either of those realities, but the expressions of regret, sadness, or even profound disagreement need to emerge from a deep empathy for the challenges that American openness has created for American Jewish survival.

And finally (for now), there are many other steps that would help, including (though certainly not limited to) much more intensive Jewish education among American Jews and a deeper understanding of the values of the West among Israelis. At this moment, however, the sixth dimension of the discourse that needs to emerge is an awareness that a commitment to perfection is the enemy of the possible. Neither American Jews nor Israelis will be the perfect partner the other seeks. That is not possible given the radical divide in their histories, commitments, and values. To insist on perfection is to preclude any partnership; to build a relationship even in the face of imperfection is the only way forward.

Nothing but the muddy messiness of a genuine relationship is going to work. The world's two largest Jewish communities need to recalibrate their expectations of each other. Given how different the two communities have become, neither will ever be the idealized partner each might have once imagined or hoped for. But recognizing the fracture in this relationship, if it leads us to learn what animates the other, may be key to making progress and to beginning a long-overdue process of healing. Sometimes, as Leonard Cohen wrote in his song "Anthem," what is broken is actually key to healing: "There's a crack in everything / That's how the light gets in."

For far too long, neither side has focused on letting the light in. But in darkness, both sides stumble and fall and the damage worsens, perhaps irreparably. As alluring as perfection is, there is also grace to be found in accepting the other for what feels deeply imperfect. The tensions and the divisions in the relationship may be what finally motivate the two sides to try harder to see the world through each other's lenses. Those cracks are real and painful, true, but those cracks, as Cohen suggests, might be what lets the understanding in.

And it is light that the Jewish world needs. Each of its two great communities are wildly successful but face potentially devastating existential threats. If Charles Krauthammer was right that "the return to Zion is now the principal drama of Jewish history" and that on Israel "rest the hopes—the only hope—for

Jewish continuity and survival," then Jews everywhere ought to recognize that no partnership that can strengthen Israel can knowingly be cast away like excess ballast.

Though Israel may seem invulnerable at the moment, those who know Jewish history know how fragile Jewish sovereignty has always been. Just two generations after King David declared Jerusalem his capital, jealousy and resentment between the tribes split their kingdom into two; ultimately, the rivalry and bitterness between them contributed to the fall of each and to the Babylonian Exile.

The second period of sovereignty also came to a crashing end at a moment of infighting. The Hasmonean dynasty ended when the two sons of Queen Salome Alexandra fought over the crown, unwittingly affording the Romans an open opportunity to seize control—thereby ending Jewish sovereignty once again. It would take two thousand years before the Jews got another chance—the chance that came in 1948, with the creation of the State of Israel. Soon, as we have seen, the majority of all the world's Jews will live in Israel. Is anyone in the Jewish world, no matter what their politics, willing to be cavalier about what the loss of Israel—and that population—would mean to the future of the Jewish people?

Jewish life, history has taught, is exceptionally fragile. At times the deadly threats come from the outside. At other times rivalries between the Jews themselves have made communities so vulnerable that they fell. Either way, the lessons of Jewish history ought to be clear.

The light simply must be ushered in. For if history has taught the Jews anything, it is how devastatingly quickly darkness can descend.

ACKNOWLEDGMENTS

I have benefited from the kind support and advice of many people while writing this book, and it is a pleasure to thank them for all they have done to make the volume possible.

Shalem College is not only Israel's first liberal arts college, but it is home to some of Israel's most talented and passionately committed students. That makes it a deeply inspiring place to work, and I have benefited in myriad ways from the insights and questions of my colleagues on the faculty and our stellar students. In particular, my thanks to Daniel Polisar, Seth Goldstein, and Ido Hevroni, for their understanding of the time that writing this book required, even as we were building a college together. Numerous conversations with students have enriched my thinking on the issues discussed in this book, but particular thanks are due to Alissa Symon, with whom I spent dozens of hours as she wrote her senior thesis on issues related to this book, and to Matan Dansker and Matanel Bareli who, once they knew what I was working on, alerted me to some critical original sources.

The Paul E. Singer Foundation funded the research for this volume, as it did my previous book, *Israel: A Concise History of a Nation Reborn*, with generosity and graciousness, and I am deeply indebted to Paul Singer and Terry Kassel for their years of friendship and support. Terry, as usual, had exceedingly important suggestions to make about the tone and shape of the book before I even began writing, and after reading a draft, she offered characteristically invaluable suggestions (many of which are incorporated into the present version). My thanks as well to Daniel Bonner, also of the Singer Foundation, for his ongoing friendship and his support of the project in myriad ways.

I have been honored, for many years now, to serve as the Koret Distinguished Fellow at Shalem College. I am deeply indebted to the Koret Foundation for its ongoing support of Shalem College, and in particular, to Anita Friedman and Jeffrey Farber for all they have done to support my work, for the grand vision they have brought to their partnership with Shalem, and for their many years of warm personal friendship.

I was deeply fortunate to work with two very gifted research assistants while writing this book. Gabriel Faber, a graduate student at Bar Ilan University, was a close partner throughout the entire project. His superb research, careful fact-checking, suggestions of directions to pursue in the argument, and extraordinary recall of everything he has ever read enriched the ideas and text in ways too numerous to list. On many occasions, he suggested creative directions that the narrative might take that would never have otherwise occurred to me. He is also a pleasure to work with, and I am profoundly grateful for his manifold contributions to this book. I am also deeply in the debt of Dorin Erteschik, who joined the project as she was completing her studies at Hebrew University's law school and prior to beginning her clerkship at Israel's Supreme Court. Her research on the writings of Zionism's founders and important intellectuals was stellar—it would have taken a several-volume work to include all the fascinating material she uncovered. This would have been a very different book without Gabe and Dorin, and I am deeply grateful to both.

There comes a rare feeling of deep satisfaction when one's adult son is sufficiently interested in a manuscript to offer to read a rough draft and to then return it with many dozens of insightful suggestions and critiques that dramatically improved the final product. Aviel's interest in the subject persisted, and even until the very last days of writing the book I received from him emails and WhatsApps with sources to check, links to explore, and critical suggestions to consider. Avi is a careful reader and thinker, as well as an able writer and editor, and I will long recall our partnership on this project—and the many hours he devoted to it—with gratitude and with love. That Avi and Dorin decided to get married as this book was nearing completion (I suspect no cause and effect) only added to the joy of our partnership.

Several good friends whose wisdom I deeply appreciate responded graciously to requests that they read a painfully early draft of the book and get back to me with their feedback. Collectively, they invested hundreds of hours in reading and made numerous suggestions that dramatically improved sections of the book. My thanks to Sharon Goldman, Eric Goldstein, Joanna Jacobson, Jonathon Jacobson, Shelly Kassen, Seth Klarman, Adam Koppel, Jay Lefkowitz, David Messer, Daniel Polisar, A. J. Shechtel, Ricky Shechtel, Deborah Swartz, and Andrew Viterbi. Seth Goldstein, my colleague at Shalem College and a devoted friend, read the manuscript several times (and sections of it numerous times), each time making wise and important suggestions. I treasure my friendship with Carolyn Hessel, who for decades has been an inspiration and muse to countless Jewish writers, and thank her, as well, for the wisdom with which she read and commented on several versions of this book.

I am also grateful to a group of friends in Boston who read very early thoughts on the book and offered helpful guidance on the form it should take. I am especially thankful to Rabbi Marc Baker, CEO of Boston's Combined Jewish Philanthropies, for his invaluable suggestions about the tone the book ought to assume.

Several colleagues in the United States and Israel assisted with tracking down sources, making fascinating suggestions for materials to include, wordsmithing, and more. My thanks to Asael Abelman, Lauren Berkun, Richard Block, David Cantor, David Ellenson, Assaf Inbari, Ellie Spitz, Andres Spokoiny, and Gary Zola. Articles by my friends and colleagues Ed Feinstein and Meir Soloveitchik alerted me to fruitful sources on American democracy. Aryeh Halivni, who founded and directs Toldot Yisrael, a project to record video interviews of men and women who helped found the State of Israel, generously directed me to several important interviews, most notably that of David Krakow. David Wolpe, who has been a treasured friend for more than forty years, responded to every email question with alacrity and helped come up with the book's title. My son-in-law Avishay Ben Sasson-Gordis, now a PhD candidate at Harvard University, responded almost immediately to every request for research assistance using Harvard's extraordinary resources, seemingly at all hours of the day and night. Several leading scholars gave unstintingly of their time and wisdom; I am deeply grateful to Professors Shlomo Avineri, Sergio Della Pergola, Ruth Gavison, David Roskies, and Yedidia Stern.

For quiet havens in which to write portions of this book

in various parts of the world, I am grateful to Barbara Duberstein, David Messer, and Sara Crown Star for their warmth and hospitality. My brother and sister-in-law, Elie and Avra Gordis, offered, with unparalleled generosity, a pied-à-terre in New York, as they have done for decades.

Abraham Socher and Allan Arkush, editor and senior contributing editor, respectively, of the *Jewish Review of Books*, invited me to present the ideas that ultimately became this book at the JRB Annual Conference in January 2018. The feedback I received to that presentation encouraged me to write the book and enriched the argument as it unfolded. Abe and Allan have supported my writing in numerous ways over the years, and they have my abiding thanks.

It goes without saying that responsibility for the tone and content of this book, as well as for any errors, is mine alone.

I HAVE HAD THE good fortune to work with Richard Pine, my literary agent, for almost a quarter of a century. I am deeply grateful for his professionalism and friendship, and for the sage counsel he has offered all these years. The Ecco/HarperCollins team are consummate professionals and a delight to work with. To Emma Janaskie, my editor at Ecco/HarperCollins, Dominique Lear, assistant editor, and Miriam Parker, associate publisher, my thanks for all they did to bring this book to life.

FORTY YEARS AGO, JUST after my freshman year of college, I had a chance conversation with a woman at the pool at Camp Ramah in California, and we somehow began speaking about the kinds of lives we wanted to live. I knew in an instant that

I wanted to spend the rest of my life with her, but had no way of knowing then the grandeur of the vision she would bring to our shared journey. Some fifteen years later, when we were still living in Los Angeles, I dedicated my first book to Elisheva. In the years that have transpired, we moved to Israel and built new lives in Jerusalem, raised three children, all now grown, recently mourned the loss of two of our parents, and are now caring for my mother. The vision for the life we built together, where we should live it, and how we should raise our children has been Elisheva's. She was the one who desperately wished to live in Israel and was convinced that we could make a go of it. It is she who still models to our children, in her care for my mother, what selfless devotion is.

Elisheva has also worked tirelessly on this book, as she has on many of my previous books. She painstakingly edited version after version, line by line, on airplanes, at the Cambridge Public Library, at home, and elsewhere. She is a gifted editor, and her manifold suggestions and corrections significantly improved this book.

Our children, and even our granddaughter, are all old enough now to know, each in their own way, what an extraordinary woman their mother and grandmother is. What they cannot begin to fathom is the depth of love, care, and wisdom that Elisheva has brought to my life, for which I am eternally indebted—as a small token of which, I dedicate this book to her with boundless admiration, gratitude, and love.

Jerusalem
February 2019
Adar I, 5779

NOTES

Translations from the Hebrew Bible are typically taken from the *Tanakh: The Holy Scriptures, The New JPS Translation According to the Traditional Hebrew Text*, often with emendations on my part. Selections from the writings of Zionism's early founders were usually found on the Ben-Yehuda Project online, unless otherwise noted; the translations into English are mine.

Introduction: "Why Can't We All Just Get Along?"

3 **"U.S. Jewry just isn't that into you":** Alon Pinkas, "Sorry Israel, U.S. Jewry Just Isn't That into You," *Times of Israel Blogs*, February 2, 2017, http://blog s.timesofisrael.com/sorry-israel-us-jewry-just-isnt-into-you-it-never-was/.

5 **90 percent of American Jews:** The 90 percent figure is based on the data of the Pew Research Center, "A Portrait of American Jews," October 1, 2013, http://www.pewforum.org/2013/10/01/jewish-american-beliefs-attitudes -culture-survey/. The phrase "US Jewry just isn't that into you" was the headline over Pinkas's column; the headline could have been crafted by Pinkas or the editors of *Times of Israel*.

5 **"what Israel is dealing with on a daily basis":** JTA, "U.S. Jews Have It Easy, Don't Send Kids to War, Top Diplomat Hotovely Says," *Times of Israel*, November 23, 2017, https://www.timesofisrael.com/us-jews-have-it-easy-dont -send-kids-to-military-top-diplomat-hotovely-says/.

6   **"What have *you* done in recent years":** Attila Somfalvi, "American Jews, You, Too, Are Responsible for the Rift with Israel" (translated from the Hebrew by the author), YNet, October 22, 2018, https://www.ynet.co.il/article s/0,7340,L-5376687,00.html.

Chapter One: A Mistaken Conventional Wisdom

12   **Only four hostages:** Three hostages were killed in the gun battle, while a fourth was in the hospital and was killed later.

12   **"and freedom and dignity for all":** This was the language of the If Not Now website on March 2, 2018. As is the case with many organizations, the language has been altered numerous times since then. (Screenshots of the website containing this language are on file with the author.)

13   **"Five Ways the American Jewish Establishment":** "Beyond Talk: Five Ways the American Jewish Establishment Supports the Occupation," http://ifnotnowmovement.org/wp-content/uploads/2018/10/INN_2018Report _FINAL.pdf.

15   **"the final victory would be his":** Melvin Urofsky, *We Are One! American Jewry and Israel* (Garden City, NY: Anchor Press, 1978), p. 351.

17   **"destruction of the third Temple":** Daniel Gordis, *Israel: A Concise History of Nation Reborn* (New York: Ecco, 2016), p. 314.

17   **"for every person who appreciates justice and freedom":** Robert P. Wade, "Armory Rally Evokes Emotion, Aid for Israel," *Baltimore Sun*, October 10, 1973, p. A2.

17   **"just 27% of Democrats":** Pew Research Center, "Republicans and Demo -crats Grow Even Further Apart in Views of Israel," January 23, 2018, http://www.people-press.org/2018/01/23/republicans-and-democrats-grow-even -further-apart-in-views-of-israelpalestinians/.

18   **sacred obligation:** The most important discussion of the sanctity of survival as an American Jewish value in the postwar decades is Jonathan Woocher, *Sacred Survival: The Civil Religion of American Jews*, Jewish Political and Social Studies (Bloomington: Indiana University Press, 1986).

19   **"waning love affair":** Steven Rosenthal, *Irreconcilable Differences? The Waning of the American Jewish Love Affair with Israel* (Hanover, NH: Brandeis University Press, 2001).

19   **"support for Israel among American Jews":** Dov Waxman, *Trouble in the Tribe* (Princeton, NJ: Princeton University Press, 2016), p. 20.

19   **"could reach [a] breaking point":** Tamara Zieve, "Ties between U.S. Jews and Israel Could Reach Breaking Point in 2017," *Jerusalem Post*, March 27, 2017, https://www.jpost.com/Diaspora/Ties-between-US-Jews-and-Israel-could -reach-breaking-point-in-2017–485337; Reut Institute, "The Future of the Nation State of the Jewish People: Consolidation or Rupture?," March 2017, https://reutgroup.org/wp-content/uploads/sites/17/2017/04/20170331-Reut -Nation-State-English-FINAL.pdf.

20   **"May Soon Lead to Final Divorce":** Chemi Shalev, "Israel's Irreconcilable Differences with U.S. Jews and the Democratic Party May Soon Lead

to Final Divorce," *Ha'aretz*, September 17, 2018, https://www.haaretz.com /israel-news/.premium-israel-s-differences-with-u-s-jews-and-democrati c-party-may-soon-lead-to-divorce-1.6478913.

20 **"There's a Crisis Between U.S. Jewry and Israel":** "There's a Crisis between U.S. Jewry and Israel, Says Jewish-American Journalist Thomas Friedman," *Ha'aretz*, September 21, 2018, https://www.haaretz.com/israel-news/there-s -a-crisis-between-israel-and-u-s-jewry-says-jewish-american-journalist-thomas -friedman-1.6492435.

20 **"Fracturing of the Jewish People":** William A. Galston, "The Fracturing of the Jewish People," *Wall Street Journal*, June 12, 2018, https://www.wsj.com /articles/the-fracturing-of-the-jewish-people-1528844625.

20 **"American Jews and Israeli Jews Are Headed for a Messy Breakup":** Jonathan Weisman, "American Jews and Israeli Jews Are Headed for a Messy Breakup," *New York Times*, January 4, 2019, https://www.nytime s.com/2019/01/04/opinion/sunday/israeli-jews-american-jews-divide.html.

20 **"The GA's 'We Need to Talk' Slogan":** Chemi Shalev, "The GA's 'We Need to Talk' Slogan Is a Desperate Plea to Save Israel-U.S. Jewish Ties," *Ha'aretz*, October 20, 2018, https://www.haaretz.com/jewish/ga-2018-tel-aviv/.premium -ga-s-we-need-to-talk-slogan-is-a-plea-to-save-israel-u-s-jewish-ties-1.6574721.

21 **"American Jews are from Venus":** Greer Fay Cashman, "Close Encounters," *Jerusalem Post*, June 7, 2018, https://www.jpost.com/Opinion/Clos e-encounters-559440.

21 **"Your first obligation to world Jewry is to survive":** Ibid.

21 **"A Diaspora Divided":** "A Diaspora Divided: Twelve Writers Address the Changing Relationship between American Jews and Israel, 70 Years after the Country's Founding," *New Republic*, September 6, 2018, https:// newrepublic.com/article/150861/diaspora-divided.

22 **"their separate identities":** "It's Time for Israel to Recognize That Diaspora Jews Are Already Home," *The Forward*, April 18, 2018, https://forward.com /opinion/399152/its-time-for-israel-to-recognize-that-diaspora-jews-are -already-home/.

22 **"young Jews have checked their Zionism instead":** Peter Beinart, "The Failure of the American Jewish Establishment," *New York Review of Books*, June 10, 2010, https://www.nybooks.com/articles/2010/06/10/failure-america n-jewish-establishment/.

24 **"unless you're dealing with fanatics":** *Tekumah*, episode 20 (Babel and Jerusalem), at 45:50.

26 **"worse than Holocaust deniers":** "Former Chief Rabbi of Israel Calls Reform Jews Worse Than Holocaust Deniers," *Jewish Telegraphic Agency*, September 6, 2017, https://www.jta.org/2017/09/06/news-opinion/israel-middle-east/for-mer-chief-rabbi-of-israel-calls-reform-jews-worse-than-holocaust-deniers.

26 **"destroying Judaism":** "Haredi Knesset Member: Reform Jews Destroying Judaism, Working Against Israel," *Jewish Telegraphic Agency*, November 11, 2015, https://www.jta.org/2015/11/11/news-opinion/politics/haredi -lawmaker-blasts-reform-jews-accuses-federations-of-corruption.

26   **"Wicked Son":** Haim Lev, "'Reform Jews Are Wicked Son Mentioned in Haggadah,'" *Arutz Sheva*, April 3, 2017, https://www.israelnationalnews.com /News/News.aspx/227676.

26   **While it was David Ben-Gurion:** Quoted in Zvi Ganin, *An Uneasy Relationship: American Jewish Leadership and Israel, 1948–1957* (Syracuse, NY: Syracuse University Press, 2005), p. 99.

28   **The Jewish United Fund of Metropolitan Chicago:** Raphael Ahren: "MKs Backing Conversion Bill Not Welcome in Chicago, Jewish Leader Warns," *Times of Israel*, June 27, 2017, https://www.timesofisrael.com/mks-backing -conversion-bill-not-welcome-in-chicago-jewish-leader-warns/.

28   **Ike Fisher, a leading American Jewish philanthropist:** Aiden Pink, "Jewish Philanthropist May 'Suspend' Aid to Israel over Diaspora Controversies," *The Forward*, July 2, 2017, https://forward.com/fast-forward/376125/jewis h-philanthropist-may-suspend-aid-to-israel-over-diaspora-controversies/. Regarding Rose Halperin's outburst, see Ganin, *An Uneasy Relationship*, p. 226.

29   **relations between the American Jewish press:** Sharett quoted in Ganin, *An Uneasy Relationship*, p. 38.

29   **"Israel's Choice to Shoot Palestinians":** Peter Beinart, "Israel's Choice to Shoot Palestinians Should Horrify—But Not Surprise Us," *The Forward*, May 15, 2018, https://forward.com/opinion/401138/israels-choice-to-shoot-pales tinians-gaza-should-horrify-not-surprise/. In an exchange on Twitter, I was able to confirm with *The Forward*'s opinion editor, Batya Ungar-Sargon, that though the column was written by Peter Beinart, it was she who had composed the headline.

29   **"Natalie Portman Speaks Loudly":** Michael Koplow, "Natalie Portman Speaks Loudly for Young American Jews with Snub of Israel," *The Forward*, April 20, 2018, https://forward.com/opinion/399337/natalie-portman-speaks -loudly-for-young-american-jews-with-snub-of-israel/.

30   **If Not Now occasionally tried accosting Birthright groups:** Jeremy Sharon, "IfNotNow Gatecrash New Birthright Group, Go on East Jerusalem Tour," *Jerusalem Post*, July 15, 2018, https://www.jpost.com/Diaspora/IfNotNow -gatecrash-new-Birthright-group-go-on-east-Jerusalem-tour-562567.

32   **"one has to presume that the 'real' levels of attachment":** Steven M. Cohen and Ari Y. Kelman, "Beyond Distancing: Young Adult American Jews and Their Alienation from Israel," The Jewish Identity Project of Reboot, 2007, p. 7, http://www.acbp.net/pdf/pdfs-research-and-publications/Beyond _Distancing.pdf. Not everyone accepts this reading of the data. Theodore Sasson, in *The New American Zionism* (New York: New York University Press, 2014, p. 7), writes, "it is important to understand that younger Jews have always been less emotionally attached to Israel than their middle-aged and elderly counterparts, and they have tended to become more emotionally attached as they grow older. In other words, the age-related pattern of attachment to Israel observed in so many cross-sectional surveys is not evidence of decreasing attachment across the generations; rather, it is evidence of increasing attachment over the life course." For reasons articulated through-

out this book, however, I believe that Sasson is overly optimistic on this point.

33 **a slight majority of Israeli Jews:** Matti Friedman, "Mizrahi Nation," *Mosaic*, June 1, 2014, https://mosaicmagazine.com/essay/2014/06/mizrahi-nation/.

34 **even Mizrachi feminists:** Pnina Motzafi-Haller, *Concrete Boxes: Mizrahi Women on Israel's Periphery* (Detroit, MI: Wayne State University Press, 2018).

34 **Reverence for religious authority:** Meir Buzaglo, *Safa La-Ne'emanim: Mahshavot 'al ha-masoret [A Language for the Faithful: Reflection on Tradition]* (Tel Aviv and Jerusalem: Keter Publishing and Mandel Foundation, 2009).

35 **"Israel is a Red State and American Jews are a blue country":** The comment is by Steven Cohen, quoted in Jack Wertheimer, "Renewing Spiritual Judaism," in *Twenty-Five Essays About the Current State of Israeli-American Jewish Relations*, American Jewish Committee, n.d., p. 62, https://www.ajc.org/sites/default/files/pdf/2018–06/Twenty-Five%20Essays%20about%20the%20Current%20State%20of%20Israeli-American%20Jewish%20Relations.pdf.

35 **the wolf lying down with the lamb:** Isaiah 11:6 and 2:4.

Chapter Two: A Rift Older Than the State Itself

39 **"I have to inform the Knesset":** Deborah E. Lipstadt, *The Eichmann Trial* (New York: Knopf Doubleday Publishing Group, 2011), p. 3. The technical name of the law to which Ben-Gurion referred is "Nazis and Nazi Collaborators—(Punishment)—Law."

41 **"Jewish catastrophe":** Ganin, *An Uneasy Relationship*, p. 4.

41 **"unspeakable crimes against *humanity*":** Lipstadt, *The Eichmann Trial*, p. 34.

41 **"some *imaginary Jewish ethnic entity*":** "Jungle Law," *Washington Post*, May 27, 1960, p. A16 (emphasis added).

41 **"an act of lawlessness":** Erich Fromm, "Israel and World Jews," *Jewish Newsletter*, June 17, 1960.

42 **"Jewish nationalism tends to confuse":** James L. Moses, *Just and Righteous Causes: Rabbi Ira Sanders and the Fight for Racial and Social Justice in Arkansas, 1926–1963* (Fayetteville: University of Arkansas Press, 2018), p. 97. See also Manuscript Collection No. 17 in the AJC archives, http://collections.american jewisharchives.org/ms/ms0017/ms0017.html.

42 **Berger was more than simply opposed:** For more on Berger, see Ganin, *An Uneasy Relationship*, pp. 13–14. As for the Jewish Voice for Peace, note the description by the Anti-Defamation League, known as a very centrist organization: "Jewish Voice for Peace is a radical anti-Israel activist group that advocates for a complete economic, cultural and academic boycott of the state of Israel." ADL, "Jewish Voice for Peace," https://www.adl.org/resources/backgrounders/jewish-voice-for-peace. As for BDS's true intentions, consider its statement that "peace—or better yet, justice—cannot be achieved without a total decolonization (one can say de-Zionization) of the Israeli state. It is a precondition for the fulfillment of the legitimate rights of the Palestinians." Quoted in Michael Warschawski, *The Case for Sanctions against Israel*, ed. Audrea Lim (New York: Verso, 2012), p. 195.

42   **"a Zionist declaration of war":** Elmer Berger, "The Eichmann Case Judgment," American Council for Judaism, March 28, 1962, p. 20.

43   **"Israel is the only inheritor":** David Ben Gurion, "The Eichmann Case as Seen by Ben Gurion," *New York Times Magazine,* December 18, 1960, p. 7.

43   **suggested that foreign jurists serve:** Hanna Yablonka, *The State of Israel vs. Adolf Eichmann* (New York: Schocken Books, 2004), p. 50.

43   **the American Universities Field Staff:** The American University Field Staff (AUFS) was created by a group of prominent universities in 1951. The plan was for these universities to send their own correspondents and analysts to regions around the world in order "to make this expert knowledge of foreign conditions both more useful and more available." "The American Universities Field Service," http://calteches.library.caltech.edu/133/1/Field.pdf. Edward Bayne himself wrote extensively on Israel and Somalia, as well as on Italy and Iran.

44   **"I thought only an American Jew":** E. A. Bayne, "Israel's Indictment of Adolf Eichmann," *American Universities Field Staff Reports Service: Southwest Asia Series 9,* no. 7 (October 1960), quoted in Lipstadt, *The Eichmann Trial,* p. 35.

44   **"Judaism of the United States . . . is losing all meaning":** "Text of Ben-Gurion's Address Before the World Zionist Congress in Jerusalem," *New York Times,* January 8, 1961, p. 52, https://timesmachine.nytimes.com/timesmachine/1961/01/08/98431205.html?pageNumber=52.

44   **"whoever dwells outside the land of Israel":** BT Ketubbot 10b.

46   **"four corners of the earth":** Isaiah 11:12.

47   **"the dearest man in my life":** Anita Shapira, *Ben Gurion: Father of Modern Israel* (New Haven, CT: Yale University Press, 2014), p. 213.

47   **"Whoever has not had the privilege":** "The London Conference," Summer 1925, https://benyehuda.org/berl/v01_veidat_london.html (translated from the Hebrew by the author).

48   **937,000 Jews in America:** Samson D. Oppenheim, "The Jewish Population of the United States," *American Jewish Year Book,* c. 1918, https://www.census.gov/history/pdf/jewishpop-ajc.pdf, p. 2.

48   **Not all four were even official representatives:** Avi Y. Dechter, "The American Delegate(s) at the First Zionist Congress, Part 2," Jewish Museum of Maryland, posted September 6, 2017, http://jewishmuseummd.org/2017/09/the-american-delegates-at-the-first-zionist-congress-part-2/.

49   **"The followers of a certain religious creed":** Alexander Yakobson and Amnon Rubinstein, *Israel and the Family of Nations: The Jewish Nation-State and Human Rights* (New York: Routledge, 2009), p. 26.

49   **"We are unalterably opposed to political Zionism":** Ganin, *An Uneasy Relationship,* p. 3.

50   **1904 stained-glass window:** Jonathan Sarna, *American Judaism: A History* (New Haven, CT: Yale University Press, 2004), p. 204.

50   **"the Zionist movement has spread":** The Hebrew original appears on the Ben Yehuda Project website, http://benyehuda.org/herzl/herzl_072.html (translated by the author). As it is well known that Herzl did not have a command of Hebrew sufficient to write a letter of this sort, it is not clear whether

he penned it in a different language and had it translated (most likely by his associate Michael Berkowitz, who also translated *The Jewish State* into Hebrew), or whether he communicated the letter's essential ideas and the letter was written in the original in Hebrew (again, probably by Berkowitz). I am grateful to Professor Shlomo Avineri for his consultation on the matter of the letter's origins.

51   **"We are in a serious position and we count on you":** Ganin, *An Uneasy Relationship*, p. 78.

51   **"You cannot dedicate yourself to America":** Robert Murray Thomas, *God in the Classroom: Religion and America's Public Schools* (Westport, CT: Praeger, 2007), p. 40.

52   **"All the men descend from a boat scene":** *Proceedings Americanization Conference: Held under the Auspices of the Americanization Division* (Washington, DC: Bureau of Education, Department of the Interior, May 12–15, 1919), p. 119, https://books.google.com/books?id=uHPziURFhVIC&pg=PA119&dq#v=onepage&q&f=false.

52   **"I recognize the full and complete necessity":** Jon Meacham, *The Soul of America: The Battle for Our Better Angels* (New York: Random House, 2018), p. 177.

53   **"I've spoken of the shining city [on a hill] all my political life":** Ibid., p. 310.

53   **"I cannot for a moment concede":** Yoram Hazony, *The Jewish State: The Struggle for Israel's Soul* (New York: Basic Books, 2000), p. 211.

54   **the titular head of the Zionist movement:** George Berlin, "The Brandeis-Weizmann Dispute," *American Jewish Historical Quarterly* 60, no. 1 (September 1970): 38.

54   **"We should all support the Zionist movement":** Jeffery Rosen, *Louis D. Brandeis: American Prophet* (New Haven, CT: Yale University Press, 2016), p. 151.

54   **"a man is a better citizen of the U.S.":** Louis Brandeis, "The Jewish Problem and How to Solve It" (1915), in Gil Troy, *The Zionist Ideas: Visions for the Jewish Homeland—Then, Now, Tomorrow* (Philadelphia: Jewish Publication Society, 2018), p. 130.

55   **"To be better Americans we must become better Jews":** Pnina Lahav, *Judgment in Jerusalem: Chief Justice Simon Agranat and the Zionist Century* (Berkeley: University of California Press, 1997), p. 18.

56   **"enjoyed by Jews in any other country":** Martin Kramer, "The Forgotten Truth about the Balfour Declaration," *Mosaic*, June 5, 2017, https://mosaicmagazine.com/essay/2017/06/the-forgotten-truth-about-the-balfour-declaration/.

57   **"We raise our voice in warning":** "Protest to Wilson Against Zionist State," *New York Times*, March 5, 1919, p. 7, https://timesmachine.nytimes.com/timesmachine/1919/03/05/97080072.pdf.

58   **"Yankee Doodle Judaism":** Lahav, *Judgment in Jerusalem*, p. 19, quoting Norman Rose, *Chaim Weizmann: A Biography* (New York: Viking Press, 1986), p. 210.

58   **The battles between the American and European Zionists:** The following summary of their conflict is based on the analysis of George Berlin in "The Brandeis-Weizmann Dispute," 38.

58 **"I do not agree with the philosophy of your Zionism"**: Ibid., p. 40.

59 **"a life of natural development"**: Ahad Ha'am, "The Jewish State and the Jewish Problem," https://benyehuda.org/ginzberg/medinat_hayehudim.html (translated from the Hebrew by the author). "Baggage of exile" is a reference to Ezekiel 12:4.

60 **"which history has bequeathed to our people"**: Hayim Nahman Bialik, "On the Destruction of Judaism in the Diaspora and the Rebuilding of the Land of Israel," http://benyehuda.org/bialik/dvarim12.html (translated from the Hebrew by the author).

60 **the Menorah found on Rome's first-century Arch of Titus**: For a brief but fascinating review of the process for selecting Israel's national symbol, see Daniella Gardosh-Santo and Yoram E. Shamir, "The Initial Proposals That Fell Short: How the Israeli National Emblem Was Chosen," on the blog site of the National Library of Israel, https://blog.nli.org.il/en/emblem_of_israel/.

61 **"What is the ideological basis of Zionism?"**: Ben Zion Dinur, "Towards a Clarification of the Foundations of Zionist Education," *Shorashim* (1939): 66–67 (translated from the Hebrew by the author).

62 **"The reconstitution of the Jewish people"**: Quoted in Allan Arkush, "Abba Hillel Silver, Man of the Zionist Hour," *Mosaic*, December 11, 2013, https://mosaicmagazine.com/observation/2013/12/abba-hillel-silver-man-of-the-zionist-hour/.

63 **"and go forward in faith"**: Quoted in ibid.

63 **"the establishment of a Jewish commonwealth"**: Ibid.

63 **almost two decades after Israel's creation**: See Marc Lee Raphael, *The Synagogue in America: A Short History* (New York: New York University Press, 2011), p. 108; "New Jewish Credo Stirs Controversy," *New York Times*, January 3, 1944, p. 9; Roselyn Bell, "Houston," in *The Jewish Traveler: Hadassah Magazine's Guide to the World's Jewish Communities and Sights*, ed. Alan M. Tigay (Northvale, NJ: Jason Aronson, 1994), p. 217; Joshua Trachtenberg, "Review of the Year 5704: Religious Activities," *American Jewish Year Book* 46 (September 18, 1944–September 7, 1945/5705), p. 95; Thomas Kolsky, *Jews against Zionism: The American Council for Judaism, 1942–1948* (Philadelphia: Temple University Press, 1990), p. 80. I am grateful to Rabbi Richard Block, a successor to Abba Hillel Silver at the Temple-Tifferet Israel and for several years the president of the Central Conference of American Rabbis (the national organization of Reform rabbis), for first alerting me to this incident.

64 **Blaustein's family story is a fascinating one**: Ganin, *An Uneasy Relationship*, p. 9.

65 **"American Jews—young and old alike"**: "The Voice of Reason: Address by Jacob Blaustein, President, the American Jewish Committee, at the Meeting of Its Executive Committee," April 29, 1950, available at American Jewish Committee Archives, http://www.ajcarchives.org/AJC_DATA/Files/507.PDF (accessed December 8, 2015), p. 11 (emphasis in original).

65 **"no matter who that spokesman might try to be"**: Ibid., p. 10 (emphasis in original).

65 **"We had cooperated"**: Ibid., p. 9 (emphasis in original).

66 **Ironically, Blaustein's utilitarian take on Israel's purpose:** Quoted in Ganin, *An Uneasy Relationship*, p. 90.

66 **"Jews are in exile where they live in fear"**: Ibid., p. 124.

67 **"No doubt the Jewish people had been in exile"**: Norman Podhoretz, *My Love Affair with America: The Cautionary Tale of a Cheerful Conservative* (New York: Free Press, 2000), 52 (emphasis in original).

67 **"there was no practical difference"**: Sasson, *The New American Zionism*, p. 18.

68 **"the religion of American Jews"**: Sara Yael Hirschorn, *City on a Hilltop* (Cambridge, MA: Harvard University Press, 2017), p. 35.

69 **"Please send them over immediately"**: Ibid., p. 34.

69 **"American Jews of the New Left"**: Ibid., p. 39.

Chapter Three: A Particularist Project in a Universalist World

74 **"faith in the Rock of Israel"**: It is commonly claimed that the phrase "Rock of Israel" was added to the Declaration of Independence as a compromise between religious and secular factions, who were divided over whether God should be mentioned in the text. According to this (incorrect) claim, "Rock of Israel," a classic Hebrew idiom that refers to God, satisfied the religious parties while allowing the secularists to interpret it as referring to the determination of the Jewish people, or to some other nontheistic notion. However, the phrase actually appears in the very first draft (of many that would follow) of a document that mimics the American Declaration of Independence from beginning to end. See Yoram Shachar, "The Early Drafts of the Declaration of Independence" (in Hebrew), *Iyunei Mishpat* (*Tel Aviv University Law Review*) 26 (November 2002): esp. 526–530.

76 **"man, heaven, and the created order"**: Leon Kass, *The Beginning of Wisdom: Reading Genesis* (Chicago: University of Chicago Press, 2006), p. 25.

77 **"scattered them over the face of the whole earth"**: Genesis 11:9.

77 **our first introduction to the Bible's politics:** This reading is, of course, not universally shared. For an objection to this reading, see Michael Walzer, *In God's Shadow: Politics in the Hebrew Bible* (New Haven, CT: Yale University Press, 2012), p. x.

77 **"From these the *maritime* nations"**: Genesis 10:5 (emphasis added). The insertion, quoted in the Jewish Publication Society translation, is based on verses 20 and 31.

77 **But as the Tower of Babel story opens:** I have explored these ideas at much greater length in "The Tower of Babel and the Birth of Nationhood," *Azure* 40 (Spring 5770/2010): 19–36, and "An Inquiry into the Shape and Meaning of Biblical History," *Azure* 45 (Summer 5771/2011): 80–98.

77 **"everyone on earth had the same language"**: Genesis 11:1.

78 **That hope, in a nutshell:** Like any grand idea, even commitments such as this can be used, and sadly have been used, for horrific and immoral purposes. For example, some South African theologians used the Tower of Babel to justify apartheid. As George M. Frederickson writes in *Racism: A Short History* (rev. ed.,

Princeton, NJ: Princeton University Press, 2015, pp. 135–136), "Theologians of the South African Dutch Reformed Church found their scriptural warrant, not in the Curse of Ham that had served some of the slaveholding ancestors, but in the story of the destruction of the Tower of Babel. In their exegesis of this tale, the religious apologists for apartheid identified a God who regarded attempts to unify the human race as manifestations of sinful pride. As a remedy to the evils of universalism, he prescribed a strict division of humanity into separate linguistic and cultural groups, which were commanded, in effect, to keep their distance from each other and to 'develop along their own lines.' If we were to take these ideologues at their word, cultural relativism rather than hierarchical racism would have to be acknowledged as the essence of apartheid." A moral Zionism needs to steer far from such conclusions at all costs.

78   **"Here they first attained to statehood":** Translations of the Declaration are taken, occasionally with minor emendations, from "Declaration of Israel's Independence 1948," Yale University Law School, The Avalon Project, http://avalon.law.yale.edu/20th_century/israel.asp.

79   **"There is neither Jew nor Greek":** Galatians 3:28. Traditional Jews will find this verse interesting because they will immediately recognize the language from three morning blessings found in Jewish liturgy: thanking God for having made "us" Jews and not Gentiles, free people and not slaves, and men and not women. (In traditional Jewish circles, women recite a different third blessing, thanking God for having made them according to divine will, whereas in more liberal circles, the third blessing has been altered altogether.) I am very grateful to Professor Shaye J. D. Cohen of Harvard University for sharing his thoughts on the Galatians passage with me in the summer of 2010, prior to his publishing them. They can now be found in *The Jewish Annotated New Testament: New Revised Standard Version Bible Translation*, ed. Amy-Jill Levine and Marc Zvi Brettler (Oxford: Oxford University Press, 2011), p. 339.

80   **"gave liberty, not alone to the people of this country":** Quoted in Meir Soloveichik, "Saving American Nationalism from the Nationalists," *Commentary*, September 17, 2018, https://www.commentarymagazine.com/articles/saving-american-nationalism-nationalists/ (emphasis added). For further discussion, see also David C. Hendrickson and Robert W. Tucker, "The Freedom Crusade," in *National Interest* 81 (Fall 2005): 14, https://www.jstor.org/stable/42897567.

80   **"who, in the concrete pressure of a struggle":** Quoted in Soloveichik, "Saving American Nationalism from the Nationalists" (emphasis added).

80   **"As long as the Jew denies his nationality":** Troy, *The Zionist Ideas*, p. 38.

82   ***"Universal brotherhood is not even a beautiful dream":*** Quoted in Gregory S. Mahler and Alden R. W. Mahler, *The Arab-Israeli Conflict: An Introduction and Documentary Reader* (Abingdon, UK: Routledge, 2009), p. 45 (emphasis added).

82   **"must necessarily become a Zionist":** Troy, *The Zionist Ideas*, p. 20.

82   **"may be inwrought with affection":** George Eliot, *Daniel Deronda*, introduction by Edmund White, notes by Dr. Hugh Osborne (New York: Modern Library, 2002), p. 15. *Daniel Deronda* was initially published by William Blackwood and Sons in eight parts, from February to September 1876. It was sub-

sequently republished in December 1878 with revisions primarily in those sections dealing with Jewish life and customs.

84 **"Proclaim liberty throughout all the land"**: Leviticus 25:10.

84 **"it is now no more that toleration is spoken of"**: George Washington's Letter to the Hebrew Congregation of Newport, August 21, 1790, https://www.tourosynagogue.org/history-learning/gw-letter.

84 **Taking a page from the biblical prophet**: See Micah 4:4.

86 **"the [American] Jewish radicals improvised"**: Irving Howe, *World of Our Fathers: The Journey of the East European Jews to America and the Life They Found and Made*, anniversary edition (New York: New York University Press, 2005), p. 315.

87 **"the social work Zionism of the Americans"**: Troy, *The Zionist Ideas*, p. 19.

87 **"We are no longer the Jews"**: Walter Isaacson, *Einstein: His Life and Universe* (New York: Simon & Schuster Paperbacks, 2007), p. 520.

87 **"one has to fight it out"**: Ibid.

89 **"we shall never surrender"**: "We Shall Fight on the Beaches," International Churchill Society, https://winstonchurchill.org/resources/speeches/1940-the-finest-hour/we-shall-fight-on-the-beaches/ (emphasis added).

90 **"I am a sectarian and have never been ashamed"**: Marie Luise Knott (ed.) and Anthony David (trans.), *The Correspondence of Hannah Arendt and Gershom Scholem*, ed. Marie Luise Knott, trans. Anthony David (Chicago: Chicago University Press, 2017), p. 43.

92 **"whether or not we are here in Palestine at all"**: Ibid.

92 **"What is dead is the nation"**: Ibid., p. 49.

92 **and practiced the same religion**: Barbara Tuchman, "Israel: Land of Unlimited Impossibilities," in her book of essays, *Practicing History* (New York: Ballantine, 1981), p. 134.

93 **"This principle should be clear"**: Knott and David, *The Correspondence of Hannah Arendt and Gershom Scholem*, p. 49.

93 **"the road not taken"**: Noam Pianko, *Zionism and the Roads Not Taken: Rawidowicz, Kaplan, Kohn* (Bloomington: Indiana University Press, 2010).

94 **"profoundly embarrassing to post-national Europe"**: Mark Lilla, "The End of Politics," *New Republic*, June 23, 2003, https://newrepublic.com/article/67002/the-end-politics.

94 **"*The legitimacy of the nation-state*"**: Ibid. (emphasis added).

95 **"That cause is the crisis in the European idea"**: Ibid.

97 **"one long story of grief, loss and fading away"**: Michael Chabon, "Those People, over There," *Tablet*, May 30, 2018, https://www.tabletmag.com/jewish-arts-and-culture/262965/michael-chabon-commencement (emphasis in original).

97 **"intermarriage also has virtues in its own right"**: David Biale, "Looking Backward and Forward," *Jewish Review of Books*, August 28, 2018, https://jewishreviewofbooks.com/articles/3352/looking-backward-and-forward/.

97 **"Silent Holocaust"**: Lahav Harkov, "'Silent Holocaust' of Assimilation Destroying U.S. Jewry, Haredi Mk Says," *Jerusalem Post*, December 28, 2017, https://www.jpost.com/Israel-News/Silent-Holocaust-of-assimilation-destroying-US-Jewry-haredi-MK-says-520293.

98 **Israel was rated the eleventh happiest:** World Economic Forum, "These Are the Happiest Countries in the World," https://www.weforum.org/agenda/2018/03/these-are-the-happiest-countries-in-the-world/.

99 **"all other sectors of Israeli Jewish society":** Ofir Haivry, "Israel's Demographic Miracle," *Mosaic*, May 7, 2018, https://mosaicmagazine.com/essay/2018/05/israels-demographic-miracle/.

99 **"I want [my children] to marry":** Chabon, "Those People, over There."

99 **"1,008 American respondents":** Ilan Ben Zion and Ricky Ben-David, "Poll: One-State Solution to Conflict Finds Rising Support in U.S.," *Times of Israel*, December 6, 2014, http://www.timesofisrael.com/one-state-solution-finds-rising-support-in-us-poll-shows/.

99 **"political home and voice for pro-Israel":** J Street, "About Us," https://jstreet.org/about-us/#.W6scvhMzZZ0 (accessed September 26, 2018, screenshot on file with author).

100 **"then Israel really ain't a very good idea":** William Kristol, "J Street: Maybe 'Israel Really Ain't a Very Good Idea,'" *Weekly Standard*, March 15, 2011, http://www.weeklystandard.com/william-kristol/j-street-maybe-israel-really-aint-a-very-good-idea.

Chapter Four: Idealized Zion Meets the Messiness of History

105 **"History," he said, "was a nightmare":** Saul Bellow, *Humboldt's Gift* (New York: Viking Press, 1975), p. 4.

105 **The 750,000:** The number of Israelis in America is very hard to calculate. In 2017, Israel's U.S. embassy quoted the figure of 750,000 to 1 million. See Ben Sales, "Why More Israelis Are Moving to the U.S.," *Jewish Telegraphic Agency*, July 31, 2017, https://www.jta.org/2017/07/31/news-opinion/united-states/why-more-israelis-are-moving-to-the-us.

105 **"In my view, Zionism is a movement devoid of messianism":** Gershom Scholem, "Messianism, Zionism, and Linguistic Anarchy," interview on the eve of the appearance of his book *Studies and Sources in the History of Sabbateanism and Its Incarnations [Mekhkarim u-Mekorot le-Toldot ha-Shabta'ut ve Gilguleha]* (Jerusalem: Mossad Bialik, 1974), *Yediot Achronot*, November 22, 1974, http://www.zeevgalili.com/2008/11/837 (translated from the Hebrew by the author).

106 **"We have returned to history":** A. B. Yehoshua, "What Can We Give You and What Can We Receive from You," in *Homeland Grasp [Achizat Moledet]* (Tel Aviv: HaKibbutz HaMe'uchad, 2008), p. 76 (translated from the Hebrew by the author).

106 **"unemployment compensation":** Ibid.

107 **"But this is real and not imaginary":** Tal Kra-Oz, "A. B. Yehoshua Calls American Jews Partial Jews," *Tablet*, February 19, 2013, https://www.tabletmag.com/scroll/124689/a-b-yehoshua-calls-american-jews-partial-jews.

107 **"the Zion that [American Jews] imagined":** Jonathan Sarna, "A Projection of America as It Ought to Be: Zion in the Mind's Eye of American Jews," in *En-*

visioning Israel: The Changing Ideals and Images of North American Jews, ed. Allon Gal (Jerusalem: Magnes Press, Hebrew University, 1996), p. 41.

107 "a land . . . where the material life": Ibid.

108 "America [that] represented modernity's lures": Ibid., p. 44.

108 "developed from—and addressed—the needs": Ibid., p. 42.

108 "a deafening silence": Rafael Medoff, *The Deafening Silence: American Jewish Leaders and the Holocaust* (New York: Steimatzky-Shapolsky, 1987).

110 "You are not the enemy of the system": Philip Roth, *Portnoy's Complaint* (New York: Vintage, 1994) (reprint edition), p. 262.

111 "You should go home": Ibid., p. 269.

112 "The Qibya incident was a tragic": Blaustein quoted in Ganin, *An Uneasy Relationship*, p. 191.

112 they attributed their change of heart: Ibid., p. 192.

113 "What has given us, historically, the strength": David Schipler, "In Israel, Anguish over the Moral Questions," *New York Times*, September 24, 1982, https://www.nytimes.com/1982/09/24/world/news-analysis-in-israel-anguish-over-the-moral-questions.html.

114 "The altar was created to lengthen": Rashi on Exodus 20:21; Rashi based on Mechilta ad loc (translated from the Hebrew and Aramaic by the author).

114 "only blocks dressed at the quarry": I Kings 6:7.

116 they not subjugate the Jews excessively: BT Ketubbot 111a. This translation is based on the Sefaria website, https://www.sefaria.org/Ketubot.111a.4?lang=bi&with=all&lang2=en.

117 "led to the destruction of the temple itself": David Biale, *Power and Powerlessness in Jewish History* (New York: Schocken, 1986), p. 22.

117 "and greater Jewish power": Ibid., p. 23.

117 "had unexpected negative consequences": Ibid., p. 175.

117 It led to utter destruction: Ibid.

118 "'Do not make us cross the Jordan'": Numbers 32:5.

118 "this land will be your possession before the Lord": Numbers 32:20–22.

119 an uncanny resemblance to Joseph Proskauer: Rafael Medoff, "A Controversial Twist on the 'Four Sons,'" David S. Wyman Institute for Holocaust Studies, http://new.wymaninstitute.org/2010/04/a-controversial-twist-on-the-four-sons/.

120 "murder and massacre during the night": Monty Noam Penkower, "The Kishinev Pogrom of 1903," in *Modern Judaism* 24, no. 3 (2004): 187.

120 "directly molded the soul of a generation": Ibid., p. 211.

121 "still seen as the finest": Steven J. Zipperstein, *Pogrom: Kishinev and the Tilt of History* (New York: Liveright, 2018), p. 107.

121 "Revenge for the blood of a small child": Hayim Nahman Bialik, "The City of Slaughter," in Ronen Bergman, *Rise and Kill First: The Secret History of Israel's Targeted Assassination*, trans. Ronnie Hope (New York: Random House, 2018), p. 234. I have substituted my own translation of Bialik from the Hebrew for the translation Bergman uses.

121 **It is likely that the scene as he describes it:** For a superb examination of what we know and do not know about Kishinev, and how the pogrom took on the role that it did in Jewish history and lore, see Zipperstein, *Pogrom: Kishinev and the Tilt of History.*

122 **"Is my wife still permitted to me?":** David G. Roskies, ed., *The Literature of Destruction: Jewish Responses to Catastrophe* (Philadelphia: Jewish Publication Society, 1988), p. 162.

122 **"as unhoused, as wretched as himself":** George Steiner, "Our Homeland, the Text," *Salmagundi* 66 (Winter/Spring 1985): 22, https://www.jstor.org /stable/40547708.

124 **"it wasn't ours at all!":** Haim Hazaz, *The Sermon and Other Stories* (Jerusalem: Toby Press, 2005), p. 237.

125 **"Our Peace-mongers are trying to persuade us":** Quoted in Howard M. Sachar, *A History of Israel: From the Rise of Zionism to Our Time* (New York: Alfred A. Knopf, 1979), p. 186.

126 **"This does not mean that there cannot be":** Vladimir Jabotinsky, "The Iron Wall" (in English), *Jewish Herald* (South Africa), November 26, 1937. The essay was first published in Russian under the title "O Zheleznoi Stene," *Rassvyet*, November 4, 1923. The English version is available at: http://www.daniel pipes.org/3510/the-iron-wall-we-and-the-arabs.

126 **"abandon all idea of seeking an agreement at present":** Ibid.

127 **"greater achievement than Ecclesiastes":** Zipperstein, *Pogrom*, p. 108.

127 **"The Land of Israel has become a refuge":** Joseph Klausner, *Ke-she-Umah Nilchemet al Cherutah* [*When a Nation Fights for Its Freedom*] (Tel Aviv: Medinit Publications, 1936), p. vii (translated from the Hebrew by the author).

128 **a contender for the Nobel Prize:** "Israeli Author Amos Oz Loses Out on Nobel Literature Prize," *Ha'aretz*, October 8, 2009, https://www.haaretz.com /1.5332678.

129 **"we are aliens from outer space who have landed and trespassed on their land":** Amos Oz, *A Tale of Love and Darkness* (Orlando: Harcourt, 2003), pp. 418–419.

130 **"Let us not cast the blame on the murderers":** Aluf Benn, "Doomed to Fight," May 9, 2011, *Ha'aretz*, http://www.haarctz.com/weekend/week-s -end/doomed-to-fight-1.360698 (accessed December 8, 2015).

130 **"Let us not fear to look squarely at the hatred":** Chemi Shalev, "Moshe Dayan's Enduring Gaza Eulogy: This Is the Fate of Our Generation," July 20, 2014, *Ha'aretz*, http://www.haaretz.com/blogs/west-of-eden/.premium-1.606258 (accessed December 8, 2015).

131 **"Ben-Gurion was a transferist":** Ari Shavit, "Survival of the Fittest," *Ha'aretz*, January 8, 2004, https://www.haaretz.com/1.5262454.

131 **"strip Israel's history of its grandeur":** Martin Kramer, address delivered to the Jewish Leadership Conference (JLC) on Jews and Conservatism, New York City, October 26, 2018, "Israel's Founding Fathers," https://www.youtube .com/watch?v=wrdf8MjgUW0&feature=youtu.be.

132 **Decades ago, this ideological purity:** Blaustein quoted in Ganin, *An Uneasy Relationship*, p. 169 (emphasis added).

Chapter Five: People or Religion: Who and What Are the Jews?

135 **"modern facsimile of an Old Testament patriarch":** "A Trumpet for All Israel," *Time*, October 15, 1951, pp. 52–58.

137 **"there isn't one possibility in one hundred":** Ganin, *An Uneasy Relationship*, p. 3.

138 **played "Hatikvah" on the UTS carillon:** Baila Shargel, "The Texture of Seminary Life during the Finkelstein Era," in *Tradition Renewed: A History of the Jewish Theological Seminary of America*, vol. 1, ed. Jack Wertheimer (New York: Jewish Theological Seminary of America, 1997), pp. 534–535.

138 **To the consternation of YU's faculty:** Interview with David Krakow for the Toldot Yisrael Project, http://www.toldotyisrael.org/home/; Aryeh Halivni, interview with David Krakow, November 27, 2017, Teaneck, NJ, https://youtu.be/jlc_rq6ntsw. It is, of course, the nature of oral histories such as these that they are subject to the recollections of those being interviewed. I am grateful to Aryeh Halivni for alerting me to the interview and for his assessment that this interview was reliable. Responsibility for its inclusion is mine alone.

139 **a few men were killed:** For a fuller discussion of the battle surrounding the *Altalena* and Menachem Begin's role in averting civil war, see chapter 7, "A Civil War with the Enemy at Our Gates," in Daniel Gordis, *Menachem Begin: The Battle for Israel's Soul* (New York: Random House/NextBook, 2014), pp. 79–97.

140 **for any academic work he did there:** Interview with Richard Hirsch for the Toldot Yisrael Project, http://www.toldotyisrael.org/home/; Joshua Faudem, interview with Richard Hirsch, October 29. 2018, Boca Raton, FL, https://www.youtube.com/watch?v=l15pQ-KUT20. I am grateful to Aryeh Halivni for alerting me to the interview.

141 **"Why do we celebrate Hanukkah?":** The full picture is more complex and nuanced than can be presented in this space. In traditional Jewish circles, after the lighting of the Hanukkah candles in the evening, those participating recite a brief paragraph—the earliest versions of this little prayer are some two millennia old—called "HaNerot Halalu," or "These Candles." The short recitation is meant to remind the celebrants that the candles cannot be used for any purpose other than commemorating Hanukkah (they cannot be used for reading or for warmth, for example), but it also contains a quick review of the story itself. Why is Hanukkah celebrated? "We kindle these lights on account of the miracles, the wonders, and deliverances and the wars, which You did for our ancestors—in those days, at this season—by the means of Your Holy Priests. For during all the eight days of Chanukah these lights are sacred. We are not permitted to use them, but only to gaze at them, in order that we may give thanks unto Your name for

Your miracles, Your wonders and Your deliverances." There are other traditional versions of the story as well.

142 **"[We thank you also] for the miracles"**: The translation is from Rabbi Jonathan Sacks, *The Koren Siddur* (Jerusalem: Koren Publishers, 2009), p. 130. Reprinted by permission.

144 **"who redeems the nation"**: For the words to Ravina's poem, see https://www.zemereshet.co.il/song.asp?id=395. Translated from the Hebrew by the author.

145 **"To the light—let him come!"**: For the words to Ze'ev's poem, see https://www.zemereshet.co.il/song.asp?id=357&artist=160. Translated from the Hebrew by the author.

147 **not to approach a woman**: Exodus 19:15. It is worth noting, by the way, that this is actually *not* what God tells Moses to say to the people. This gender distinction is Moses's addition, a point explored compellingly by Judith Plaskow in *Standing Again at Sinai: Judaism from a Feminist Perspective* (New York: HarperOne, 1991).

147 **the Israelites are commanded to wash**: Exodus 19:10.

148 **The stained-glass window**: Sarna, *American Judaism*, p. 204.

149 **"Here is the land where milk and honey flow"**: Michael P. Kramer, "Biblical Typology and the Jewish American Imagination," *The Turn Around Religion in America: Literature, Culture, and the Work of Sacvan Bercovitch*, ed. Michael Kramer and Nan Goodman (Abingdon, UK: Routledge, 2011), chap. 10.

149 **"exerted 'a greater influence'"**: Michael Oren, *Power, Faith, and Fantasy: America in the Middle East: 1776 to the Present* (New York: W. W. Norton, 2008), pp. 86–87.

150 **"is expected to change many things"**: Will Herberg, *Protestant Catholic Jew: An Essay in American Religious Sociology* (New York: Doubleday, 1955; reprint, Chicago: University of Chicago Press, 1983), p. 23.

151 **"All the institutions of national Jewish life"**: Chief Rabbi Lord Jonathan Sacks, *The Koren Yom Kippur Mahzor* (Jerusalem: Koren Publishers, 2013), p. xli.

152 **"I will be going to Rome to accept"**: BT Gittin 56b. The transition from Temple-based, sacrificial Judaism to the Jewish life of the rabbis was significantly more complex and nuanced than is described here. The topic has long been, and remains, a focus of much scholarship. Among the dozens of excellent books on the subject, see Shaye J. D. Cohen, *From the Maccabees to the Mishnah*, 3rd ed. (Louisville, KY: Westminster John Knox Press, 2014).

152 **Why did he not beg the Romans**: The Talmudic section puts the question thus: "Rav Yosef read the following verse about him, and some say that it was Rabbi Akiva who applied the verse to Rabban Yohanan ben Zakkai: 'I am the Lord . . . Who turns wise men backward and makes their knowledge foolish' (Isaiah 44:25), *as he should have said to him to leave the Jews alone this time* [emphasis added]."

153 **"Every synagogue became a fragment"**: Sacks, *The Koren Yom Kippur Mahzor*, p. xvi.

154 **This was not always the case:** During the 2017–2018 academic year, I had the pleasure of supervising the research of an outstanding student at Shalem College who was working on issues that overlapped with this book. I learned a great deal from Alissa Symon that year, and I am grateful to her for alerting me to this question about the relationship between the Israeli political left and American progressives. Because she plans to publish her work, I have assiduously avoided using any of the sources she uncovered in her research in this volume.

154 *The War over the Right of Return*: As of this writing, there were plans for Wilf's book to appear in English, but it was not yet out. She summarized her argument in an English interview with Raphael Arhen, "A Self-Declared Leftist Wages War on the Palestinian 'Right of Return,'" *Times of Israel*, July 30, 2018, https://www.timesofisrael.com/a-self-declared-leftist-wages-war-on-the-palestinian-right-of-return/.

156 **There were accusations:** See, for example, Yaniv Kubovich, "Israeli Military Opens Criminal Probe into Border Killings of Two Gaza Teens," *Ha'aretz*, August 21, 2018, https://www.haaretz.com/israel-news/israeli-army-opens-criminal-probe-into-killings-of-two-gaza-teens-1.6407332. As of this writing, those investigations are still ongoing.

156 **sixty Palestinians were killed trying to approach the fence:** "Israel Says at Least 24 of 60 Gazans Reported Killed at Border Were Terrorists," *Times of Israel*, May 15, 2018, https://www.timesofisrael.com/israel-says-at-least-24-of-60-gazans-killed-were-terrorists/.

156 **"Israel's Choice to Shoot Palestinians":** Beinart, "Israel's Choice to Shoot Palestinians Should Horrify—But Not Surprise Us."

157 **A particularly unfortunate instance:** For a discussion of Daniel Solomon's tweet, see Liel Leibovitz, "As an Israeli Hero Dies Saving a Stranger's Life, Five Questions on Moral Clarity," *Tablet*, September 21, 2018, https://www.tabletmag.com/jewish-life-and-religion/271236/ari-fuld-moral-clarity.

157 **"The notion that praying to a god":** Einat Wilf, "Choosing Our Allies," in *Twenty-Five Essays about the Current State of Israeli-American Jewish Relations* (American Jewish Committee, 2018).

158 **those are the issues on which Israelis will always compromise:** This point was actually made by Micha Goodman as part of his discussion with Einat Wilf: "Through Israel's Eyes: Perceptions of the Diaspora," a panel at the American Jewish Committee Global Forum in Jerusalem, June 11, 2018, https://www.youtube.com/watch?time_continue=3&v=8QhP0BelGOY.

158 **"Ever since Israeli Prime Minister Benjamin Netanyahu":** Einat Wilf and Ram Vromen, "Stop Trying to Bring Liberal Judaism to Israel. We Already Have Too Much Religion," *The Forward*, August 8, 2018, https://forward.com/opinion/407701/stop-trying-to-bring-conservative-and-reform-judaism-to-israel-we-already/. For the sake of ease of reading, several of Wilf's separate paragraphs have been combined here. Wording has not been altered.

158 **American progressives are making no progress:** Ibid.; see also her remarks on a panel of the American Jewish Committee Global Forum 2018, "Through

Israel's Eyes: Perceptions of the Diaspora," June 11, 2018, https://www.ajc
.org/news/through-israels-eyes-perceptions-of-the-diaspora.

159 **the decision not to teach Hebrew:** See, for example, Michael Weingrad,
"Can't or Won't Learn Hebrew," Stroum Center for Jewish Studies, University
of Washington, May 13, 2016, https://jewishstudies.washington.edu/hebrew
-humanities/american-jews-hebrew-active-resistance/.

160 **"and did not know how to speak Judean":** Nehemiah 13:23–24.

160 **"I wish to attest to the pain":** Alkalai quoted in Troy, *The Zionist Ideas*, p. 88.

161 **"The Jewish people lacks most of the essential attributes":** Pinsker quoted
in Troy, *The Zionist Ideas*, p. 9.

161 **"We are a people without a country":** Gordon quoted in Troy, *The Zionist
Ideas*, p. 51.

162 **"Klausner went on to enumerate":** Avner Holtzman, *Hayim Nahman Bialik:
Poet of Hebrew* (New Haven, CT: Yale University Press, 2017), p. 169.

162 **"we are not in the mood for becoming artificial cultural irredentists":**
Arthur Hertzberg, "Impasse: A Movement in Search of a Program," *Commentary*, October 1, 1949, in Troy, *The Zionist Ideas*, p. 294.

162 **"Israel and the Diaspora enjoy different advantages":** Robert Gordis,
"Emet V'Emunah: Statement of Principles of Conservative Judaism" (1988),
in Troy, *The Zionist Ideas*, p. 259.

163 **"It is a tragedy to see the language":** Solomon Schechter: "Zionism: A Statement" (1906), cited in Troy, *The Zionist Ideas*, p. 127.

163 **"you tend to translate Zionism":** Ganin, *An Uneasy Relationship*, p. 44.

163 **"Hebrew language the living and cultural language":** Sharett quoted in
Ganin, *An Uneasy Relationship*, p. 63.

164 **"America was the first major Jewish culture":** Leon Wieseltier quoted in
Troy, *The Zionist Ideas*, p. 350.

165 **"ensure the document's eternality":** David Roskies, *Voices from the Warsaw
Ghetto: Writing Our History* (New Haven, CT: Yale University Press, 2019), p. 32.

165 **"an arrogance without precedent in Jewish history":** Leon Wieseltier, "Language, Identity, and the Scandal of American Jewry," in *My Jewish Learning*,
n.d., https://www.myjewishlearning.com/article/language-identity-and-the
-scandal-of-american-jewry/.

Chapter Six: How Naked a Public Square:
A Liberal or Ethnic Democracy?

168 **"A New Law Shifts Israel Away from Democracy":** Ilene Prusher, "A New
Law Shifts Israel Away from Democracy," *Time*, July 24, 2018, http://time.
com/5345963/israel-nation-state-law-democracy/.

168 **"a definitive declaration in favor of a Jewish identity":** Emma Green, "Israel's New Law Inflames the Core Tension in Its Identity," *Atlantic*, July 21,
2018, https://www.theatlantic.com/international/archive/2018/07/israel
-nation-state-law/565712/.

168 **"makes constitutional the second-class status of Arab citizens":** Brent
Sasley, "4 Problems with Israel's 'Jewish Nation-State' Law," *The Forward*, No-

vember 24, 2014, https://forward.com/opinion/israel/209785/4-problems-with-israel-s-jewish-nation-state/.

168 **"Why all the commotion over a law"**: Yohanan Plesner, "Israel's Nation-State Bill Would Undermine Jewish Democracy," *The Forward*, July 17, 2018, https://forward.com/scribe/405784/israels-nation-state-bill-would-undermine-jewish-democracy/.

169 **"mentors of American pluralism"**: Cited in Steven Bayme, "Foreword" to Jonathan D. Sarna, "American Jews and Church-State Relations: The Search for 'Equal Footing,'" 1989, https://www.brandeis.edu/hornstein/sarna/christian jewishrelations/Archive/AmericanJewsandChurchStateRelationsEqualFooting .pdfhttps://www.brandeis.edu/hornstein/sarna/christianjewishrelations /Archive/AmericanJewsandChurchStateRelationsEqualFooting.pdf.

169 **as old as the First Amendment**: Even older is the "separation" term, which was borrowed from Roger Williams, the founder of the first Baptist church in America and a passionate advocate of religious freedom, who in 1644 spoke of a "hedge or wall of separation between the garden of the church and the wilderness of the world." See Harold Berman, "Religion and Law: The First Amendment in Historical Perspective," in *Emory Law Journal* 35, no. 4 (1986): 777–794.

170 **"the naked public square"**: Richard John Neuhaus, *The Naked Public Square: Religion and Democracy in America* (Grand Rapids, MI: W. B. Eerdmans, 1984).

171 **had to be based on tradition of some sort**: Ibid., pp. 21, 47.

171 **"politics becomes civil war carried on by other means"**: Ibid., p. 21.

172 **"Herzl entitled his famous booklet"**: This and the following examples are taken from Yoram Hazony, "Did Herzl Want a 'Jewish' State?," *Azure* (Spring 5760/2000): 37 ff.

174 **"In my view, this prohibition is part of the substantive question"**: Ethan Bronner, "On the Eve of Passover, Bread Stirs Deep Thoughts in Israel," *New York Times*, April 18, 2008, https://www.nytimes.com/2008/04/18/world /middleeast/18israel.html.

174 **"Bones recovered from the excavations of the small early Israelite villages"**: Israel Finkelstein and Neil Asher Silberman, *The Bible Unearthed: Archaeology's New Vision of Ancient Israel and the Origin of Its Sacred Texts* (New York: Simon & Schuster, 2001), p. 119.

175 **Pigs being perhaps the paradigmatic symbol**: For a fascinating discussion of the law and its cultural roots and implications, see Daphne Barak-Erez, *Outlawed Pigs: Law, Religion, and Culture in Israel* (Madison: University of Wisconsin Press, 2007).

175 **an illegitimate limitation on citizens' autonomy**: HCJ 953/01, *Solodkin v. Beit Shemesh Municipality* (2004), IsrSC 58(5) 595, available in English at: https://supremedecisions.court.gov.il/Home/Download?path=English Verdicts01\530\009\A19&fileName=01009530_a19.txt&type=4.

176 **"she'll try again and again"**: Yehuda Amichai, "The Suicide Attempts of Jerusalem," in *The Poetry of Yehudah Amichai*, ed. Robert Alter (New York: Farrar, Straus & Giroux, 2015), p. 178 (translation by Benjamin and Barbara Harshav).

178 **"Lucy, it's nothing personal":** "Jewish 'Fauda' Star's Marriage to Muslim News-woman Gets Condemnations from Right," *Times of Israel*, October 11, 2018, https://www.timesofisrael.com/jewish-fauda-stars-marriage-to-muslim-newswoman-gets-condemnations-from-right/.

178 **"admissions review boards":** HCJ 2311/11, *Sabach v. Knesset* (September 17, 2014, unpublished); HCJ 6698/95, *Keadan v. Israel Land Administration* (2000), IsrSC 54(1) 258.

179 **was motivated by racist instincts:** Israel Democracy Institute, "Generations Will Weep," July 11, 2018, https://www.idi.org.il/ministerial-committee/24192 (translated from the Hebrew by the author).

179 **"Just as I oppose discrimination":** David Ben-Gurion, from a debate with Brit Shalom, 1924, http://benyehuda.org/ben_gurion/anaxnu30.html (translated from the Hebrew by the author).

180 **"In other words, everyone wants separation":** Shmuel Rosner and Camil Fuchs, *#Israeli Judaism: A Cultural Revolution* (Hevel Modi'in: Kinneret, Zmora-Bitan Dvir, 2018), p. 144. (Translated from the Hebrew by the author.)

181 **plans to evict some forty thousand Sudanese and Eritrean:** A good summary of the issues can be found in Emma Green, "African Deportations Are Creating a Religious Controversy in Israel," *The Atlantic*, January 30, 2018, https://www.theatlantic.com/international/archive/2018/01/african-migrants-israel/551747/.

182 **"freedom for the majority to chart the country's course":** Ruth Gavison, "The Jewish State: A Justification," in *New Essays on Zionism*, ed. David Hazony, Yoram Hazony, and Michael Oren (Jerusalem and New York: Shalem Press, 2006), p. 24.

183 **"Koons, Kikes, and Niggers Go Home!":** Julian E. Zelizer, "Trump Needs to De-militarize His Rhetoric," *The Atlantic*, October 29, 2018, https://www.theatlantic.com/ideas/archive/2018/10/americas-long-history-anti-semitism/574234/.

184 **"legally secured home":** Quoted in Troy, *The Zionist Ideas*, p. 129.

185 **"the democratic framework is real, not a facade":** Sammy Smooha, "The Model of Ethnic Democracy," European Centre for Minority Issues Working Paper 13, October 13, 2001, p. 24.

186 **"loyalty to the Jewish people":** State Education Law of 1953.

186 **Israel is by no means unique in this regard:** See the petition at Change.org, "President Obama: Make Spanish the Second Official Language of United States!," https://www.change.org/p/president-obama-make-spanish-the-second-official-language-of-united-states.

186 **"establishes Hebrew as the official language of Israel":** Green, "Israel's New Law Inflames the Core Tension in Its Identity."

187 **"there will come terrible days which no one desires":** Hayim Nahman Bialik, "On America," http://benyehuda.org/bialik/dvarim_shebeal_peh23.html (translated from the Hebrew by the author).

187 **"I fear you will see much less cause for optimism":** Haim Arlosoroff, "Letters," December 20, 1914, http://benyehuda.org/arlosoroff/047.html (translated from the Hebrew by the author).

188 **"to be ourselves and in fact to be different":** Ganin, *An Uneasy Relationship*, p. 132.

189 **Irish Catholic thugs roamed in gangs:** These incidents, and more, are discussed in Zelizer, "Trump Needs to Demilitarize His Rhetoric," on which these paragraphs are based.

189 **"who are lower than animals":** Eric Lichtblau, "Surviving the Nazis, Only to Be Jailed by America" (February 7, 2015), *New York Times*, http://www.ny times.com/2015/02/08/sunday-review/surviving-the-nazis-only-to-be-jailed-by-america.html (last viewed December 7, 2015).

191 **"The United States is a country whose cultural DNA":** Shlomo Fischer, "American Jews Are Protestants, Israeli Jews Are Catholics," *Times of Israel Blogs*, December 13, 2013, http://blogs.timesofisrael.com/american-jews-are-protestants-israeli-jews-are-catholics/.

192 **"May it be to the world":** Cited in William Kristol, "The Choice They Made," *New York Times*, June 30, 2008, http://www.nytimes.com/2008/06/30/opinion/30kristol.html?_r=1&hp&oref=slogin.

193 **"We certainly have a right forcefully":** Proskauer quoted in Ganin, *An Uneasy Relationship*, p. 34 (emphasis added).

193 **"barely likely to get one seat in the Knesset":** Wilf and Vromen, "Stop Trying to Bring Liberal Judaism to Israel."

194 **"Born Israelis cannot imagine it":** Quoted in Troy, *The Zionist Ideas*, p. 314.

195 **the sort of comfort that eluded Jews in the Diaspora:** Evan Goldstein, "Sir Isaiah's Modest Zionism," *Ha'aretz*, June 5, 2009, https://www.haaretz.com/1.5061019.

195 **"the majority among whom they live":** Quoted in Troy, *The Zionist Ideas*, p. 154.

Chapter Seven: Charting a Shared Future—and Why That Matters

200 **"Since many of us took our first breaths":** Shmuly Yanklowitz, "Alienated from Israeli Policies: The Diaspora as the New Jewish Center?," *Jewish Journal*, April 4, 2018, http://jewishjournal.com/uncategorized/232673/alienated-israel-diaspora-new-jewish-center/.

202 **the Jewish population of Israel is likely to approach:** Private email exchange with the author (copy on file with the author).

203 **"overall U.S. population rose 65 percent":** Charles Krauthammer, "At Last, Zion," *Weekly Standard*, May 11, 1998, https://www.weeklystandard.com/charles-krauthammer/at-last-zion. Krauthammer notes that it was the postwar baby boom and then the influx of 400,000 Jews, mostly from the Soviet Union, that enabled American Judaism's numbers to hold steady for a while. Once the baby boom and Soviet Jewish immigration ended, the decline could no longer be masked.

203 **there will be 5,300,000 Jews:** Professor Sergio Della Pergola predicts 5,300,000 Jews in the US in 2043, a slight dip from his estimates of the numbers at present. For an alternative prediction, see Edieal Pinker, "The Future Is Now," *Jewish Review of Books*, August 29, 2018, https://jewishreviewofbooks.com

/articles/3354/the-future-is-now/. The two estimates differ, but agree that there will be a slight decrease in the number of American Jews.

203 **birthrates among most Israeli groups increased:** Dafna Maor, "With Fertility Rising, Israel Is Spared a Demographic Time Bomb," *Ha'aretz*, May 29, 2018, https://www.haaretz.com/israel-news/with-fertility-rising-israel -is-spared-a-demographic-time-bomb-1.6131135.

203 **twice as many Jews in Israel:** In a private correspondence with the author, Professor Sergio Della Pergola of the Hebrew University, Israel's leading demographer, predicts approximately 5,300,000 million Jews in the United States and 10,500,000 in Israel.

205 **"the requisite knowledge to participate":** Amanda Borschel-Dan, "Most Birthright Applicants Functionally Illiterate about Israel," *Times of Israel*, November 2, 2015, https://www.timesofisrael.com/most-birthright-applicants -functionally-illiterate-about-israel/.

205 **"Can you identify the name":** Ibid.

205 **"Measuring ourselves by the standard of our tradition":** Wieseltier, "Language, Identity, and the Scandal of American Jewry."

206 **"For us America will have been in vain":** Cynthia Ozick, "America: Toward Yavneh," *Judaism* 19 (Summer 1970): 280, 282.

206 **"If ethics are what make a Jew":** Hillel Halkin, "Letters to an American Jewish Friend: The Case for Life in Israel," *Mosaic*, November 3, 2013, https:// mosaicmagazine.com/essay/2013/11/letters-to-an-american-jewish-friend/.

207 **"a complementary form of Jewish Identity":** Dyonna Ginsburg, "Re-Anchoring Universalism to Particularism: The Potential Contribution of Orthodoxy to the Pursuit of *Tikkun Olam*," in *The Next Generation of Modern Orthodoxy*, ed. Shmuel Haim (New York: Yeshiva University Press, 2012), p. 14 (emphasis added).

207 **"when radical acceptance meets radical illiteracy":** Video of debate between Peter Beinart and Daniel Gordis, Congregation Beth Israel, Tustin, California, September 11, 2016, https://www.youtube.com/watch?v=9lFvWz_hu50 at 57:00—59:30.

208 **"We've made efforts not to offend":** Jonathan Safran Foer, *Here I Am* (New York: Farrar, Straus & Giroux, 2016), p. 349.

209 **"If you were capable of standing up":** Ibid., p. 399.

209 **"If we were actually to entertain":** Ibid., p. 423.

210 **"more likely to be engaged in Jewish life":** Leonard Saxe, "Has Birthright Been Successful?," *Ha'aretz*, December 21, 2017, https://forward.com /scribe/390553/has-birthright-been-successful/.

211 **"the principal drama of Jewish history":** Krauthammer, "At Last, Zion."

212 **"alongside the stories of the Vikings and Mayans":** Foer, *Here I Am*, p. 447.

213 **Israel no longer needed its political advocacy:** David Hoffman, "Rabin Criticizes Congressional Lobby for Israel," *Washington Post*, August 17, 1992, https://www.washingtonpost.com/archive/politics/1992/08/17/rabin -criticizes-congressional-lobby-for-israel/92093719–54ce-4582-bc0f-066613bf2 480/?utm_term=.f2c102487452.

213 **by borrowing money on open markets:** Steven Bayme, "Israel and American Jewry: Oslo and Beyond," Jerusalem Center for Public Affairs Article 28, January 6, 2008, http://jcpa.org/article/israel-and-american-jewry -oslo-and-beyond/.

213 **they should stop supporting Israel:** "Beilin's Remarks on Jews' 'Charity' Raise Hackles in Israel and Diaspora," *Jewish Telegraphic Agency*, January 8, 1994, https://www.jta.org/1994/01/18/archive/beilins-remarks-on-jews-charity -raise-hackles-in-israel-and-diaspora.

214 **"the assimilation that threatens the continuation of the Jewish people":** Michael Arnold, "'Don't Legitimize Diaspora,' Israel's New President Warns," Jewish Agency for Israel, September 15, 2000, http://www1.jafi.org.il /papers/2000/sep/forsep15.htm.

216 **building relationships with evangelical Christians:** See AIPAC, "AIPAC's Christian Community," https://www.aipac.org/connect/communities/your -church.

216 **with veterans:** "U.S. Veterans Experience Israel," *AIPAC in Action*, August 2016, http://www.aipacinaction.org/region/southwest/u-s-veterans-experience -israel/.

219 **"the only aspect of Jewish statehood that is non-negotiable":** Peter Beinart, "Young Anti-Zionists: Be Uncomfortable, Like I Am with My Zionism," *The Forward* (December 26, 2018), https://forward.com/opinion/416306/young -anti-zionists-be-uncomfortable-like-i-am-with-my-zionism/.

220 **Herzl, who oversaw the translation:** Hazony, "Did Herzl Want a 'Jewish' State?"

221 **"Hatikvah" was now no longer the anthem:** Ganin, *An Uneasy Relationship*, p. 18. Interestingly, some resistance in Diaspora communities to singing "Hatikvah" has emerged of late, precisely because it is the anthem of a different sovereign state. See, for example, the discussion of an incident in Cape Town, South Africa, in November 2018, in "Two Herzlia Pupils Facing Disciplinary Action for Taking a Knee during Israeli National Anthem," *News24*, November 14, 2018, https://www.news24.com/SouthAfrica/News/two -herzlia-pupils-facing-disciplinary-action-for-taking-a-knee-during-israeli -national-anthem-20181114.

221 **at museums and cultural centers across Israel:** See, for example, Hagay Hacohen, "Scenes from Lives of Russian-Jewish Immigrants Star at Israel Museum," *Jerusalem Post*, December 10, 2017, https://www.jpost.com/Israel -News/Culture/Scenes-from-Russian-Jewish-immigrants-lives-to-star-at -the-Israel-Museum-517580. In June 2018, Jerusalem's First Station, a popular outdoor food and cultural center, staged an exhibition about Russian Jews, with photographs of what they looked like when they were refuseniks and how they appeared as contemporary Israelis. Other examples abound.

224 **A study conducted by the American Jewish Committee:** "AJC 2018 Survey of American and Israeli Jewish Opinion," https://www.ajc.org/news/ajc -comparative-surveys-of-israeli-us-jews-show-some-serious-divisions.

226 **"It is therefore best that you observe the command of the King":** David
Zevi Hoffmann, *Melamed Le-ho'il* 1:42. Hoffmann's response is not dated, so it
is impossible to know with certainty whether this opinion was written during
the First World War. Hoffmann addresses this question twice, in 1:42 and 1:43.
The two responses are very similar, but 1:42 is somewhat more elaborate. For
a discussion of a similar issue faced by the French Jewish community, see Leo
Landman, *Jewish Law in the Diaspora: Confrontation and Accommodation* (New
York: Shulsinger Bros., 1968), pp. 135ff.

227 **"only Jews seemed actually to have loved them":** Amos Elon, *The Pity of It
All: A Portrait of the German-Jewish Epoch, 1743–1933* (New York: Metropolitan
Books, 2013), p. 10.

227 **No other group of European Jews:** This point is made by Eva Figes in a review
of Elon's book, "A Love Gone Sour," *Guardian*, May 10, 2003, https://www
.theguardian.com/books/2003/may/10/featuresreviews.guardianreview19.

228 **"We are a people, one people":** Theodor Herzl, *The Jewish State* (New York:
Herzl Press, 1970), p. 33.

229 **"In two divided streams the exiles part":** Emma Lazarus, "The New Year,"
in *Emma Lazarus: Selected Poems and Other Writings*, ed. Gregory Eiselein (New
York: Broadview Press, 2002), available at: https://www.poetryfoundation.
org/poems/46788/the-new-year-56d226cd558be.

Conclusion: "That's How the Light Gets In"

232 **Libya was home to some 38,000 Jews in 1948:** The source for all these examples is "Displacement of Jews from Arab Countries 1948–2012," Justice for
Jews from Arab Countries, http://www.justiceforjews.com/main_facts.html.

232 **over 37 percent of Jews from Islamic countries immigrated to Israel:** Colin
Shindler, *A History of Modern Israel*, 2nd ed. (New York: Cambridge University
Press, 2013), p. 64.

233 **Demographers predict that by 2030:** Amotz Asa-El, *The March of Jewish Folly*
[in Hebrew] (Rishon LeZion: Yediot Ahronot Books and Chemed Books,
2019), pp. 356–357.

234 **"Plant a Jewish people in a country":** Krauthammer, "At Last, Zion."

237 **"are not asking for financial assistance":** Raphael Ahren, "Minister: Israel
ready to help world Jewry fight virus, but not exactly sure how," *Times of Israel*,
May 1, 2020, https://www.timesofisrael.com/minister-israel-ready-to-help
-world-jewry-fight-virus-but-not-exactly-sure-how/.

238 **"part mediating institution":** Natan Sharansky and Gil Troy, "Can American
and Israeli Jews Stay Together as One People?," *Mosaic*, July 9, 2018, https://
mosaicmagazine.com/essay/2018/07/can-american-and-israeli-jews-stay
-together-as-one-people/.

238 **the representative of world Jewry and not just Israel:** Tal Keinan, *God Is in
the Crowd: Twenty-First-Century Judaism* (New York: Spiegel and Grau, 2018).

238 **Israel's president Reuven Rivlin suggested:** Michael Bachner, "Rivlin
Calls for 'Reverse Birthright' Trips to Better Israel-Diaspora Ties," *Times of
Israel*, October 22, 2018, https://www.timesofisrael.com/rivlin-calls-for

-reverse-birthright-trips-to-better-israel-diaspora-ties/.

238 **an editor in chief of the *Jerusalem Post*:** Yaakov Katz, "Defining a Nation," *Jerusalem Post*, October 5, 2018, https://www.jpost.com/Opinion/Editors -Notes-Defining-a-nation-568715.

239 **"as long as U.S. Jewry remains engaged":** Dov Lipman, "How to Strengthen the Israeli-Diaspora Relationship," *Times of Israel Blogs*, June 13, 2018, https:// blogs.timesofisrael.com/strenghtening-the-israeli-diaspora-relationship/.

239 **"As the communities move farther apart":** There are, of course, myriad ex- amples of such claims. This language is taken from Steven Bayme, "Bridging Gaps, Building Peoplehood," *Times of Israel Blogs*, June 11, 2018, https://blogs .timesofisrael.com/bridging-gaps-building-peoplehood/.

239 **"Israel and American Jews Should Consider a Trial Separation":** Chemi Shalev, "To Save Their Troubled Marriage, Israel and American Jews Should Consider a Trial Separation," *Ha'aretz*, November 26, 2018, https://www .haaretz.com/opinion/.premium-to-save-their-marriage-israel-and-american -jews-should-consider-a-trial-separation-1.6687067.

241 **"You might have to kill Jews":** Jerold S. Auerbach, *Brothers at War: Israel and the Tragedy of the Altalena* (New Orleans: Quid Pro Books, 2011), p. 67.

241 **"stand close to the Temple, if it is built":** Avi Shilon, *Menachem Begin: A Life*, trans. Danielle Zilberberg and Yoram Sharett (New Haven, CT: Yale Univer- sity Press, 2007), p. 130.

243 **calling Israel a "terrorist state":** The nature of the exchange was shared with me over social media by Alissa Schramm, a Shalem College student, in real time as she attended the conference and confirmed once again upon her return to Israel.

244 **"Yet even unhinged Zionists can level criticism at Israeli policies":** Bret Stephens and Bari Weiss, "Why Is Israel Scared of This Young American?," *New York Times*, October 10, 2018, https://www.nytimes.com/2018/10/10 /opinion/israel-lara-alqasem-bds.html.

244 **explicitly refusing to offer suggestions:** The classic example of this is If Not Now. See Abraham Riesman, "The Jewish Revolt," *New York* (July 2018), http://nymag.com/intelligencer/2018/07/ifnotnow-birthright-ramah-bds -israel.html.

INDEX